FINGAL COUNTY LIB

MA

MA
PH

Items
may
acces
To rer
online
posta
to th

CultureShock!

A Survival Guide to Customs and Etiquette

bangkok

Dan Waites

D1627829

mc Marshall Cavendish
Editions

© 2014 James Daniel Waites & Marshall Cavendish International (Asia) Pte Ltd

Published by Marshall Cavendish Editions
An imprint of Marshall Cavendish International
1 New Industrial Road, Singapore 536196

All rights reserved

No part of this publication may be reproduced, stored in a retrieval system or transmitted, in any form or by any means, electronic, mechanical, photocopying, recording or otherwise, without the prior permission of the copyright owner. Request for permission should be addressed to the Publisher, Marshall Cavendish International (Asia) Private Limited, 1 New Industrial Road, Singapore 536196. Tel: (65) 6213 9300, fax: (65) 6285 4871. E-mail: genref@sg.marshallcavendish.com

The publisher makes no representation or warranties with respect to the contents of this book, and specifically disclaims any implied warranties or merchantability or fitness for any particular purpose, and shall in no events be liable for any loss of profit or any other commercial damage, including but not limited to special, incidental, consequential, or other damages.

Other Marshall Cavendish Offices:
Marshall Cavendish Corporation. 99 White Plains Road, Tarrytown NY 10591-9001, USA ■ Marshall Cavendish International (Thailand) Co Ltd. 253 Asoke, 12th Flr, Sukhumvit 21 Road, Klongtoey Nua, Wattana, Bangkok 10110, Thailand ■ Marshall Cavendish (Malaysia) Sdn Bhd, Times Subang, Lot 46, Subang Hi-Tech Industrial Park, Batu Tiga, 40000 Shah Alam, Selangor Darul Ehsan, Malaysia

Marshall Cavendish is a trademark of Times Publishing Limited

National Library Board, Singapore Cataloguing-in-Publication Data:

Waites, James Daniel, 1980- author.
Culture shock! Bangkok : a survival guide to customs and etiquette / Dan Waites. – Singapore : Marshall Cavendish Editions, [2014]
pages cm
Includes bibliographical references and index.

ISBN : 978-981-4408-59-2 (paperback)

1. Bangkok (Thailand) - Social life and customs. 2. Etiquette - Thailand - Bangkok. I. Title. II. Series: Culture shock!
DS589.B2
959.3 -- dc23   OCN864372730

Cover photo: The Phra Sri Ratana Chedi in the Grand Palace

All photos by Francis Wade

Illustrations by TRIGG

Printed in Singapore

ABOUT THE SERIES

Culture shock is a state of disorientation that can come over anyone who has been thrust into unknown surroundings, away from one's comfort zone. *CultureShock!* is a series of trusted and reputed guides which has, for decades, been helping expatriates and long-term visitors to cushion the impact of culture shock whenever they move to a new country.

Written by people who have lived in the country and experienced culture shock themselves, the books provide all the information necessary for anyone to cope with these feelings of disorientation more effectively. The guides are written in a style that is easy to read and cover a range of topics that will arm readers with enough advice, hints and tips to make their lives as normal as possible again.

Each book is structured in the same manner. It begins with the first impressions that visitors will have of that city or country. To understand a culture, one must first understand the people—where they came from, who they are, the values and traditions they live by, as well as their customs and etiquette. This is covered in the first half of the book.

Then on with the practical aspects—how to settle in with the greatest of ease. Authors walk readers through topics such as how to find accommodation, get the utilities and telecommunications up and running, enrol the children in school and keep in the pink of health. But that's not all. Once the essentials are out of the way, venture out and try the food, enjoy more of the culture and travel to other areas. Then be immersed in the language of the country before discovering more about the business side of things.

To round off, snippets of basic information are offered before readers are 'tested' on the customs and etiquette of the country. Useful words and phrases, a comprehensive resource guide and list of books for further research are also included for easy reference.

CONTENTS

Acknowledgements	vii
Some Notes on Language	viii
Map of Bangkok	x

Chapter 1
First Impressions — 1

Culture Shock!	5
Changing Times	7

Chapter 2
Overview of the City and its History — 10

BANGKOK: A SELECTED HISTORY	11
Timeline of Events	12
Taksin and Thonburi	17
The Founding of Bangkok	19
King Mongkut	19
King Chulalongkorn	21
The End of Absolute Monarchy	24
Phibun's Nation	25
The Death of Rama VIII	27
Sarit's Despotic Paternalism	28
King Bhumibol Adulyadej	29
1973 and 1976	31
Premocracy	34
Black May	34
The Asian Financial Crisis	36
Thaksin Shinawatra and the Thai Political Crisis	37
CITY OVERVIEW	57
Climate	57
Planning #fail	59
Linear Development	62
Rattanakosin and Dusit	62
Banglamphu	65
Thonburi	67
Yaowarat and Pahurat	68
Charoen Krung	69
Silom and Sathorn	71
Pathum Wan	71
Ratchathewi	74
Sukhumvit	75
Khlong Toei	78
North Bangkok	79

Chapter 3
People — 81

Minorities	85
Chinese	86
Indians	88
Other Foreigners	90
Values and Beliefs	92
Family	92
Hierarchy	93
Hi-so	96
What's In a Name	98
On the Surface	100
'Don't Think Too Much'	101
Hot Hearts and Cool Hearts	102
Martial Flavour	103
Fashion and Fads	104
Techno Joy	107
White is Beautiful	108
Sanuk	109
Money and Luck	111
Spiritual Beliefs	113
Buddhists and More	113
Buddhist Precepts	115
Making Merit	118
In Decline?	120
Spirits and Power	122
Evil Spirits	124
Amulets and Tattoos	126

Chapter 4
Fitting In — 129

High and Low	131
Dress and Modesty	133
Why *Wai*	134
The 'F' Word	137
Keeping Your Cool	138
Speaking and Listening	140
Visiting Someone's Home	145

Friendliness	146
Making Thai Friends	146
Class	147
Thai-*Farang* Relationships	148
Dating	151
The Sex Divide	152
Public Affection and Keeping Up Appearances	154
Staying Clean and the Sniff Kiss	155
Mia Noi and Mistresses	156
Just For *Kiks*	156
Prostitution	158
LGBT	161

Chapter 5
Practicalities 164

What to Bring	165
Visas	166
Work Permits	169
Accommodation	170
Money	178
Toilets	180
Getting Around	182
Buying a Vehicle	193
Health and Hospitals	195
Food Shopping	196
Staying Informed	196
Schools	199
Births, Marriages and Deaths	200

Chapter 6
Food 203

Eating with Thai People	207
Typical Dishes	208
Thai Service	213
Tipping	215
Finding Places to Eat	215
Splashing Out, Thai-Style	218
Street Food	223
A Guide to Bangkok Street Stalls	227
Food Courts	234

Foreign Cuisine	234
Vegan/Vegetarian	239

Chapter 7
Having Fun 240

Nightlife	241
Music	251
Cinema and Film	254
Green Spaces	256
Festivals	258
The Weekend Getaway	263
Literature and Illiterature	266
More Ideas	267

Chapter 8
Learning the Language 269

Characteristics of Thai	272
The *Farang* Speaks Thai!	277
To Write or Not to Write	278
How to Learn Thai	280

Chapter 9
Doing Business 285

Thai Working Culture	286
Managing Thai Staff	288
Finding and Working with a Thai Business Partner	290
Corruption	291

Chapter 10
Fast Facts 295

Local Politics and Government	298
Famous Bangkokians	299
Culture Quiz	308
Do's and Don'ts	312
Words and Phrases	314
Resource Guide	318
Further Reading	327
About the Author	331
Index	332

DEDICATION

To Mum, Dad and Matt

FINGAL COUNTY LIBRARIES	
FCL00000450486	
Bertrams	08/04/2014
915.93	£12.99
MA	

ACKNOWLEDGEMENTS

Thanks go first to my agent Greg Lowe, without whom this would never have happened at all. Thanks also to Francis Wade for his excellent photography, feedback and friendship. And thanks to Justin Lau for his great editing job. Then, in no particular order, a big thank you to Naphalai Areesorn, Barnabé Réaud, Catherine Wentworth, Gaby Doman, Crystal Wilde, Charlie Campbell, Chamaiporn Siangyen, Jirawadee Sangrayab, Eric Haeg, Shane Danaher, Tim Footman, Lawrence Osborne, Benjamas Chantiwas and Kris, all of whom generously gave feedback or allowed me to pick their brains in the process of writing this thing. A final thanks go to Byron Perry, Nicholas Altstadt, Andrew Scott, Danielle Hannon-Burt, Jordan Katz, Leslie Gildea and Dominic Earnshaw for patiently listening to me going on about this project for months on end, and not completely derailing my motivation to finish it.

SOME NOTES ON LANGUAGE

The Thai word '*farang*' is used liberally in this book. Technically, it means a 'white' or, to use the old-fashioned term, 'Caucasian' person. The author realises the reader of this book could be of any race or nationality, and so may not identify with the term '*farang*'. But the word is so common in expat usage that to avoid it completely seemed excessively cautious. What's more, many non-white people from the West have told me that they relate to the term when used in the Thai context, and have not been offended when described as such themselves. I apologise in advance for any offence caused.

I've also used the word 'ladyboy', which is what male-to-female transsexuals are referred to as in Bangkok. Some gender rights activists object to this term, saying its continued use serves as a constant reminder to transsexuals of the lives they've tried so hard to leave behind. While this argument is motivated by admirable compassion, the reality is that in the main Thai transsexuals still use the term 'ladyboy' themselves, and that Western-style political correctness has shown little sign of taking hold in Thailand in this area. Perhaps some Thai transsexuals do take offence at the term, but in the course of research for this book I've been unable to find evidence of that. I've therefore used the term 'ladyboy' in these pages. If the term does come to be deemed 'offensive' in coming years, I apologise to future readers.

As we'll see in Chapter 8 of this book, there's little agreement in Thai language studies on a standard system for romanising the Thai script. The Royal Thai General System of Transcription (RTGS) isn't up to the task, since it doesn't give the reader enough information about the words to know how to pronounce them properly. For example, it doesn't tell you what the tone of a word is, even though the tone is crucial to determining its meaning, and it doesn't distinguish between long and short vowels.

Having said that, this book isn't intended to teach you Thai. And systems that are better suited to the task tend to involve the use of symbols that intimidate the casual reader, with strange accents and extra letters to represent sounds that don't exist in English. As a result, in this book, I've gone with the RTGS, though with one small modification: the use of the letter 'j' to distinguish the sound of 'จ' from that of 'ฌ'. In the standard RTGS, both letters are curiously represented as 'ch', despite the former sounding like the English 'j'.

In the case of proper nouns, including the names of people and neighbourhoods, I've used the standard spellings, even where they deviate from the RTGS. So in this book, it's 'Patpong', not 'Phatphong'. That has the added benefit of ensuring you don't ask any taxi drivers to take you to 'Fatfong', which wouldn't – as you probably know – get you very far.

MAP OF BANGKOK

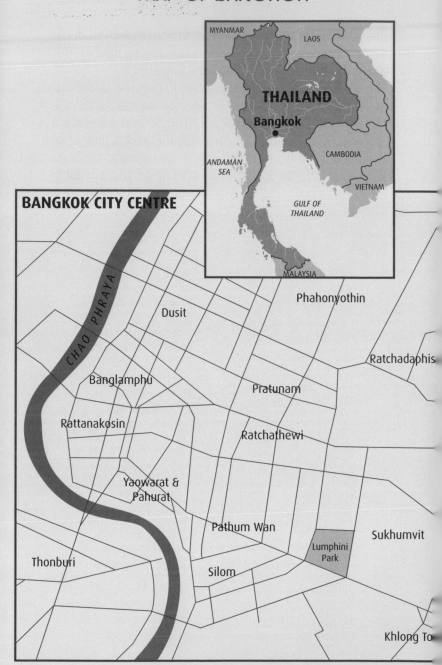

MYANMAR

LAOS

THAILAND

Bangkok

CAMBODIA

*ANDAMAN
SEA*

VIETNAM

*GULF OF
THAILAND*

MALAYSIA

BANGKOK CITY CENTRE

CHAO PHRAYA

Phahonyothin

Dusit

Ratchadaphis

Banglamphu

Pratunam

Rattanakosin

Ratchathewi

Yaowarat &
Pahurat

Pathum Wan

Sukhumvit

Lumphini
Park

Thonburi

Silom

Khlong To

MALAHIDE LIBRARY
PH: 8704430

FIRST IMPRESSIONS

CHAPTER 1

CROWNING BANGKOK THE WORLD'S BEST CITY IN 2012, *Travel + Leisure* turned to the hoariest travel-writing cliché of them all. 'It's no surprise that this city of contrasts, 10 million strong, has captured the No. 1 spot overall for three years and counting. Gilded Buddhist temples are juxtaposed with slick skyscrapers; long-tail boats ply the peaceful river. The sweet and spicy food – served on the street or from the top of high-rise towers – is addicting, and so is the affordable shopping.'

Ah, 'city of contrasts'. No one would deny that the sacred, profane Thai capital is home to some jarring juxtapositions. At Ratchaprasong intersection, in the roaring heart of the city's shopping district, the Erawan Shrine stands amid clouds of incense smoke. Its railings are festooned with marigold garlands offered by devotees who come to the site to petition the four-headed Hindu god Brahma for better fortune. On the frosted glass windows behind the shrine is a name, neither 'Erawan', nor even that of Brahma himself, but another kind of deity: 'Alexander McQueen', the designer behind the frighteningly expensive boutique to the rear.

But 'contrasts' doesn't quite capture it. Show me a city without contrasts and I'll show you a gleaming, imagined utopia, not an Earth-bound metropolis. Even Singapore has its slums; Geneva, its sex district. But Bangkok: what to make of this jumbled mess of ersatz European boulevards, International-style skyscrapers, Vegas-esque 'entertainment' strips, fascistic monuments, palaces, temples, soaring neoclassical high-rises, ramshackle *khlong* communities and row upon row of shophouses? Spare us your 'city of contrasts' – this is a city of chaos.

That must be part of the appeal. The Thai capital is one of the most popular tourist destinations on the planet. When *Travel + Leisure*'s readers voted Bangkok the world's best city in 2012, it was the third consecutive year they'd done so. They did it again in 2013. A visitor can hardly fail to be taken by the freewheeling atmosphere of the Thai capital: vibrant, loud, surprising; often crass, sometimes sublime, and just a little bit dangerous.

The city's inhabitants can make a very different first impression. Newcomers to Thailand rarely fail to be charmed by the *wai*, the graceful prayer-like gesture that Thais use as a greeting. A *wai* says a lot more than just 'hello'. When a Thai initiates a *wai* with another person, he or she is

acknowledging that person's superior social standing. The *wai* speaks of an intensely hierarchical society, one in which every citizen has their place. It's the tip of an iceberg – a shibboleth of status and belonging.

Of course, your first encounter with Thai people may be less endearing than this travel-brochure 'welcome to Bangkok'. You may be greeted by a stony-faced immigration cop at the beginning of a long shift, in no mood for chatter, let alone smiles or *wais*. You might then run into a gruff taxi driver at the airport rank, who barely glances at you as he shoves your baggage into the boot of his green-yellow cab. It takes all sorts to make a city.

The Thai, in general, have a certain ambivalence about foreigners. Although their country was never formally colonised, it was shaped profoundly by its relations with the West. The country escaped colonisation partly because of its rulers' shrewd assessments of the way foreigners think. In the colonial era, the Thai kings reformed Siam to present it as *siwilai* ('civilised') and thus avoided getting 'civilised' by the French and British themselves.

To this day, Thais remain shrewd judges of what visitors want. There are many reasons for the popularity of Thailand as a tourism destination. But one, surely, must be the skill with which the Thai have gauged what visitors want out of the country, and served it to them, whether it's Ye Olde Siam – the Thailand of the floating market and silk *jongkraben* – or the Day-glo hard-rock raunch of Patpong, Nana and Soi Cowboy.

While we're here, we might as well address a certain gently swaying, bored-looking elephant in the room. Bangkok has a reputation – one which the Thai people are understandably sensitive about. To many it hardly seems fair that the city is singled out as a sex-tourism destination when the vast majority of cities around the world include red-light districts. Nevertheless, the 'industry' in Bangkok is significant, and it's been used as a lure for tourists ever since the Vietnam days. Whatever your feelings about it, foreigners who live in Bangkok are likely to encounter it, however superficially, so this book won't brush it under the carpet.

I think it's fair to say Bangkok's appeal tends to the visceral over the cerebral. 'When a man is tired of London, he is tired of life,' said Samuel Johnson. 'When a man is tired of Bangkok, he is tired of food,' might serve the Thai capital better. The city may not have the sheer range of cuisines in cities like New York and London, nor as many opportunities to indulge in cutting-edge, paycheck-guzzling gastronomy. But so what. I submit that there is no better place on Earth to eat well on a budget than Bangkok. And with apartments renting for a quarter of the price they might go for in the pricier cities of Europe and North America, many expats get to enjoy the kind of lifestyle here that they'd never achieve back home.

CULTURE SHOCK!
But I'm not here to sell Bangkok to you. If you've bought this book, you already have an interest in the city. You may even be in the middle of the 'honeymoon phase' of cultural

adaptation. During this early stage of living in an alien culture, everything about your new surroundings seems exciting, interesting, attractive, or whatever other gushy adjective you'd care to insert here. Bangkok can be a thrilling place to be when you're under this mentality. As with a new lover, the place's flaws are ignored or even seem endearing: the endless noise is stimulating, your inability to communicate a challenge, your body's intolerance of the spicy food an opportunity to lose some flab.

After the honeymoon comes the hangover. Learning to live with people with a culture very different from your own is difficult. Communication problems can become infuriating. The different way things are done can stop seeming quaint, intriguing or funny, and become annoying, perverse or irrational. Those who spent their honeymoon phase asking themselves why they never came to Thailand sooner may suddenly find themselves eating their words.

This is the 'crisis phase', the stage of adaptation people often refer to as 'culture shock'. Many people respond to these feelings by withdrawing from the local people and associating only with other foreigners. It's an easy thing to do in a large city like Bangkok, with a big expat population. Some resort to constant griping and complaining about the hosts and the country. Some yearn for home, and some can't overcome that yearning and leave: the 'one-year wonders'.

Others have reasons for staying – a family or business, for example – and never seem to escape this phase. Many of the Internet forums used by Thailand expatriates are inhabited by people like this: men – it's usually men – who seem to hate almost everything about Thailand and its people, yet for whatever reason can't leave. Perhaps they came here with high hopes; now they have only disillusionment. It's hard not to think of the phrase, 'Be careful what you wish for'.

For most people who stay here in the long term, this phase, too, passes. It's now that the real process of adjusting and adapting to the host culture can begin. Those who are naturally curious will make the quickest progress. Once you understand why things are the way they are, they often cease to be so threatening.

Some people reach a stage of complete comfort with their new host culture, so that it starts to feel like home. Some even start to feel like one of the locals. In Thailand, that's relatively rare, and we'll look at the reasons why later. To head down this road, there's no substitute for throwing yourself into the culture, learning the language and getting involved with the local people. But I hope this book will help you in its own way.

CHANGING TIMES

Here's the advice of Kukrit Pramoj, 13th prime minister of Thailand, writer and scholar: 'There are certain institutions which a Thai respects... They are his religion, which is mostly Buddhist, his king and his parents. If you say to a Thai that his politicians are rotten he will kiss you on both cheeks. If you tell him that he is a crook, he will deny it with great good humour and will not take offence. If you call his wife a bitch he will agree with you completely and ask you to have a drink to that. But as for those three institutions which I have already mentioned, I would advise you to leave well alone... since according to police statistics, the percentage of premeditated murders in this country is very low; most murders are committed in sudden passion.'

Kukrit never lacked wit, but as with everything in life, the truth isn't so simple. Committing 'Thai values' to print is a perilous business, and there are disclaimers that need to be made here – if only for this writer's peace of mind. First, and most obviously, to say that 'all Thais believe such and such' is absurd. For every supposed belief or rule that can be identified in a culture, you'll find people who believe or do the opposite. There are Thais who don't believe in ghosts or eat spicy food. There are Thais who tend to say exactly what they think, and aren't afraid to be confrontational. Even a statement like 'all Thais love the king' can be challenged – as anyone who's taken a few taxi rides will know – though lèse-majesté laws make doing so daunting for a resident of the country.

Thai culture is, like all cultures, a work in progress. Values, customs and etiquette are changing in 21st-century Bangkok. Most cultural guides to Thailand will tell you it's taboo for men

and women to touch in public. These days it's not remotely unusual to see couples walking hand in hand, or standing in each other's arms on the Skytrain. Has touching in public become acceptable to Bangkok's residents? Or is it more that the anonymity of the big city means people – particularly the young – can get away with breaking the rules? Asking Thai people this question will land you with a bunch of different answers. In times of rapid social change, it will always be thus.

In this globalised, hyper-connected age, the pace of that change is rising. The trends affecting most human societies today – urbanisation, increasing materialism and technological dependence, declining focus on the spiritual – are at work here, and more advanced than in other parts of Thailand. What's more, the millions of tourists who pass through the city each year, the large expatriate community and the presence of so many international organisations and companies mean Bangkokians – with the possible exception of those in tourist towns like Pattaya and Phuket – are much more likely to be influenced by foreigners and their ideas than other Thais.

You might even question the idea that Bangkok was ever a Thai city in the first place. Waves of Chinese immigration and commercial domination have made it Sino-Thai, and given it a different ethos from the rural hinterland. Here, the Confucian values of the Chinese – respect for ancestors, thrift, diligence – mingle with those of the Tai, an agricultural people with values deriving from village life, informed by Buddhism and, more fundamentally, animism.

The gamut of Thai beliefs and values is vast, and the idea that they can be codified anywhere, least of all in a book of this scope, is absurd. Instead, I hope to have picked out some of the more interesting facets of Thai society that you'll come across in Bangkok. It will be up to you to fill in the gaps – but that's half the fun of living here.

OVERVIEW OF THE CITY AND ITS HISTORY

CHAPTER 2

BANGKOK: A SELECTED HISTORY

The word 'sprawling' may be overused in writing on cities, but in the case of the Thai capital, it's entirely deserved. Climb the Baiyoke Tower II, the tallest building in the metropolis, and the scale becomes apparent: there's nothing but city in every direction, save south, where Bangkok is thwarted by the ocean.

This is the quintessential primate city – one that dwarfs all others in its country or region. Thailand's next largest cities of Hat Yai, Nakhon Ratchasima (Korat) and Chiang Mai are little more than towns in comparison. Primate cities tend to grow in dictatorships, where power is concentrated and proximity to the ruling clique is the only route to riches. Thailand's long history of rule by absolute monarchs and military strongmen is writ large in the vast girth of its capital.

In the mid-18th century, you'd have little reason to suspect that the small riverside trading settlement of Bangkok had great things ahead of it. Ayutthaya was then the capital of the Siamese empire, having served as the seat of Thai kings since 1350. It had a population roughly equal to London or Paris. Bangkok, whose name is believed to derive from the Thai words 'bang', meaning 'place', and 'makok', a type of tree with olive-like fruit, was little more than a colony of Chinese traders on the banks of the Chao Phraya River.

But things would soon change. The Siamese had already been warring with the neighbouring Burmese for hundreds of years. In 1767, a Burmese army reached Ayutthaya and sacked the city. The invaders engaged in an orgy of looting and burning that has never to this day been forgotten – or entirely forgiven – by the Thai. During the attack, the Siamese ruler, King Suriyamarin, fled the city and later died of starvation. He was to be the last king of Ayutthaya.

Timeline of events

1767:   The Burmese sack Ayutthaya. Taksin establishes capital of new kingdom at Thonburi.

1782:   Buddha Yodfa Chulaloke (Rama I) crowned king, beginning the Chakri dynasty. Taksin executed. Bangkok city pillar erected.

1785–6: The Nine-Armies Wars. Burmese invade Siam. Siamese forces defeat the Burmese.

1809:   Rama I dies. His son, Prince Itsarasunthon inherits throne as Rama II.

1824:   Mongkut ordained as a monk. Rama II dies. His eldest son, Prince Chetsadabodin becomes King Rama III. First Anglo-Burmese War begins.

1826:   British defeat Burmese, bringing their empire to the border of Siam. British and Siamese sign Burney Treaty, agreeing to define boundaries and terms of trade.

1828–9: Lao rebellion. Vientiane destroyed by Siamese forces.

1851:   Death of Rama III. Mongkut becomes Rama IV.

1855:   Signing of the Bowring Treaty between Siam and the United Kingdom.

1862:   Mongkut builds Charoen Krung ('New Road'), Bangkok's first paved road.

1868:   Mongkut dies of malaria. Chulalongkorn crowned for the first time. Chaophraya Suriyawong becomes regent.

1873:   Chulalongkorn crowned for the second time as Rama V.

1893:   Franco-Siam Crisis. France sails gunboat up Chao Phraya, training weapons on the Grand Palace. Siam cedes Laos to France.

1897:   Chulalongkorn makes his first visit to Europe. He
        returns and orders the construction of European-
        style Dusit Palace and Ratchadamnoen Avenue.

1903:   Ratchadamnoen Avenue completed.

1904:   Britain and France sign Entente Cordiale, ending
        rivalry in Southeast Asia.

1907:   Siam cedes Battambang, Siem Reap and
        Sisophon in Cambodia to France.

1909:   Siam cedes Malay states of Kelantan, Trengganu,
        Kedah and Perlis to British.

1910:   Chulalongkorn dies. His son, Vajiravudh, becomes
        King Rama VI.

1912:   Hualamphong Railway Station completed.

1925:   Construction of Lumphini Park. Vajiravudh dies
        without a male heir. His brother, Prajadhipok,
        becomes King Rama VII.

1932:   Military coup topples Prajadhipok, ending
        absolute monarchy. First constitution comes into
        force.

1933:   Fresh coup installs Phahonyothin as prime
        minister. Royalist Boworadet rebellion fails.

1934:   Pridi Phanomyong founds Thammasat University.

The Chakri Maha Prasart Throne Hall of the Grand Palace, sometimes
referred to as a *'farang* wearing a Thai hat'.

1935: King Prajadhipok abdicates. Ten-year-old Ananda Mahidol becomes King Rama VIII. Regency appointed.

1938: Luang Phibunsongkhram becomes prime minister.

1939: Name of Siam changed to Thailand. Second World War begins. Phibun has Democracy Monument built in celebration of the 1932 move to constitutional monarchy.

1940: France falls to Germany. Thailand invades Laos and Cambodia. Japanese-brokered agreement sees France cede parts of Laos and Cambodia to Thailand.

1941: Japan invades Thailand. Thailand gives Japanese passage rights on its territory. Phibun erects Victory Monument to celebrate Thai victory over France the previous year.

1942: Thailand declares war on the United States and Great Britain.

1944: National Assembly forces Phibun to resign. Khuang Aphaiwong becomes PM for the first time.

1945: Japan surrenders. Pridi declares war null and void. Khuang resigns.

1946: Khuang elected premier as leader of newly formed Democrat Party. Resigns after two months. Pridi elected. Ananda shot dead. Pridi forced to flee abroad after Democrats claim he is responsible.

1947: Army coup overthrows civilian government, installs Khuang as premier again. Thailand restores provinces in Laos and Cambodia to France in exchange for French promise not to veto Thai admission to United Nations.

1948: Coup group threaten to seize again, forcing Khuang to resign. Luang Phibunsongkhram becomes prime minister.

1950: Construction and naming of Sukhumvit Road.

1957: Field Marshall Sarit Thanarat launches coup,

ousts Phibun. Goes to United States for urgent medical treatment.

1958:   Sarit returns, declares martial law, arresting more than 100 government critics.

1963:   Sarit dies. Thanom Kittikhachorn becomes leader, beginning another decade of military rule with deputy Praphas Charusathian.

1964:   The United States begins moving its air fleet to bases in Thailand.

1971:   Thanom stages coup against his own government, dissolving parliament.

1973:   Massive student protests against the 'Three Tyrants' – Thanom, Praphas and Thanom's son Narong – lead to violence and bring down the Thanom government. Siam Centre, one of Bangkok's first shopping malls, opens.

1976:   Thanom returns from exile. Massive protests end with a massacre at Thammasat University, in which at least 46 die. Thanin Kraivichien's hardline regime takes power. Many student activists flee to the jungle to fight with the Communist Party of Thailand.

1977:   Thanin ousted. General Kriangsak Chomanand takes power.

1980:   General Prem Tinsulanonda takes power.

1988:   Chatichai Choonhavan becomes prime minister.

1991:   Chatichai deposed in coup. Anand Panyarachun becomes prime minister.

1992:   Elections held. Coalition appoints General Suchinda Kraprayoon as prime minister. Massive protests result in massacre in Bangkok. Chuan Leekpai elected prime minister.

1995:   Banharn Silpa-archa becomes prime minister.

1996:   Chavalit Yongchaiyudh becomes prime minister.

1997:   Asian financial crisis. Collapse of the baht. Chuan returns as prime minister. Thailand secures massive bailout from International Monetary Fund.

1999:   BTS Skytrain opens.

2001:   Thaksin Shinawatra's Thai Rak Thai Party wins election and forms coalition government.

2003:   Thaksin's War on Drugs policy results in as many as 2,500 extra-judicial killings of drug dealers.

2004:   Insurgency in Deep South begins. MRT system opens in Bangkok.

2006:   Military coup ousts Thaksin. Council for National Security, a military junta, takes power. Thai Rak Thai dissolved.

2007:   People's Power Party, Thaksin's new proxy party led by Samak Sundaravej, wins general election. Anti-coup groups united as United Front for Democracy Against Dictatorship (UDD), now better known as the 'red shirts'.

2008:   People's Alliance for Democracy (PAD) protests begin. Protesters occupy Government House. Constitution Court disqualifies Samak as PM. Somchai Wongsawat becomes premier. PAD seize Suvarnabhumi and Don Muang airports. PPP dissolved. Abhisit Vejjajiva becomes prime minister.

2009:   Anti-government protests by red shirts in Bangkok. Protesters storm Royal Cliff Beach Resort in Pattaya, forcing cancellation of ASEAN summit.

2010:   Massive red-shirt protests in Bangkok. More than 90 people killed in army crackdown. Central World shopping mall, stock exchange and around 30 other buildings set on fire.

2011:   Thaksin's Pheu Thai Party wins general election in a landslide victory. Yingluck Shinawatra becomes prime minister. Massive floods affect 66 of Thailand's 77 provinces.

2013:   Pheu Thai ram an Amnesty Bill through parliament that result in charges being dropped against Thaksin and other leaders involved in the political crisis. Massive protests begin, led by the Democrat Party's Suthep Thaugsuban, aiming to bring down the Yingluck government.

Taksin and Thonburi

It was the man who later became known as King Taksin the Great who was to change Thai fortunes. Born in 1734 to a Chinese tax collector from Guangdong and his Thai wife, Taksin started life known only as 'Sin'. After entering the service of the Ayutthayan king, he eventually became governor of Tak, today one of Thailand's 77 provinces, and took the title 'Phraya Tak' or 'Taksin'.

Having escaped Ayutthaya before it was destroyed, Taksin fled to Chantaburi. From there he was able to muster a force of his own, and in November 1767, he sailed up the Chao Phraya river with 5,000 men and seized the settlement of Thonburi, on the opposite bank of the river to Bangkok. Realising that Ayutthaya would always be difficult to defend from the Burmese, Taksin founded a new dynasty with Thonburi as its capital. He was to be its only king.

Taksin and Thaksin

There's an obvious resemblance between Taksin's name and that of Thaksin Shinawatra, the controversial ex-prime minister of Thailand. Although the two names are pronounced differently in Thai, this similarity hasn't gone unnoticed. Both men were of Chinese stock and neither were related to the major ruling cliques of their time. Some people have gone as far as to claim that Thaksin is the reincarnation of King Taksin, returned to Earth to take revenge on the Chakri kings.

In his 15 years on the throne, the charismatic Taksin's accomplishments were impressive. He managed to retake all the land formerly controlled by Ayutthaya, soon ruling over territory that includes today's Thailand, Laos and Cambodia and even parts of Burma and Malaysia. In 1778, his childhood friend Chao Phraya Chakri, the highest-ranked noble in the kingdom, led a siege on Vientiane, eventually taking the city and carrying the sacred Emerald Buddha – today the pride of Bangkok's Grand Palace – back to Thonburi.

As well as expanding his empire, Taksin patronised the arts and fervently promoted the teachings of Buddhism. But his obsession with religion was to become his undoing. As his reign went on, Taksin apparently grew increasingly erratic. He became obsessed with religious practice and fasting in the belief it would give him the ability to fly. He became paranoid and tyrannical. He flogged monks who refused to recognise him as a god and executed many of his own officials, even imprisoning and torturing his own wife and children.

Eventually, so the story goes, his officials could take no more. Taksin was overthrown in a coup d'etat, and the coupmakers demanded that Chao Phraya Chakri be crowned king. Chakri returned to Thonburi from Cambodia, where he had been waging war on Taksin's behalf. He restored peace in the capital and was crowned king on April 6, 1782. He was later given the title King Buddha Yotfa Chulaloke, or Rama I. The Chakri dynasty had begun.

Soon after, Rama I put the 'mad' King Taksin to death. According to popular legend Taksin was killed in the fashion traditionally reserved for kings. The Siamese believed that a drop of royal blood could not be spilled on the ground.

White Elephant Diplomacy

'It began with a quarrel about white elephants; at least that is what they believe on the banks of the Menam River.' With these words, Alec Waugh – Evelyn's less famous older brother – opens his account of the history of the Thai capital, *Bangkok: The Story of a City*. In the middle of the 15th century, Waugh explains, the King of Burma, Tabishwethi, asked the King of Ayutthaya to give him one of his white elephants. When the Siamese King Chakkraphat refused him, Tabishwethi used it as a pretext to invade Siam, ushering in three hundred years of war between the two kingdoms that culminated in the Burmese sacking of Ayutthaya in 1767.

White elephants have traditionally been considered sacred in Southeast Asia. In Thailand, even to this day, they automatically become the property of the king – at least in a symbolic sense. In feudal times, only the very rich could afford to keep a white elephant; the beasts could not be put to work, and were thus a huge drain on resources. It's said that Siamese kings would give them as gifts to lesser nobles with whom they were displeased. The noble would have no choice but to look after the animal – and be ruined in the process.

White elephants are also seen as sacred in neighbouring Myanmar. Even though the country no longer has a monarchy, Burmese rulers still see the beasts as symbolic of their own legitimacy. It was considered something of a diplomatic faux pas when, in June 2013, Thai Foreign Minister Surapong Tovichakchaikul requested that Myanmar lend Thailand one of its white elephants for display in Chiang Mai Zoo. Unsurprisingly, given the historical connotations, Naypyidaw refused the request, diplomatically telling the Thai side that it would be 'too difficult' to transport one to Chiang Mai.

Taksin was sealed in a velvet bag and beaten to death with a sandalwood club.

The founding of Bangkok

Soon after becoming king, Rama I decided to move the capital of his empire across the river from Thonburi to Bangkok. The location was better protected from attacks by the meander of the river. He also saw the potential for rice cultivation on the wetlands to the east of the Chao Phraya.

The Chinese traders who were already living in the area were forced east to Sampheng, still the centre of Bangkok's Chinatown today. Rama I named his new capital Rattanakosin, meaning 'keeping place of the Emerald Buddha', after its most valuable relic – the green statue he himself had taken from Vientiane only four years earlier.

Unlike Taksin, who had hoped to break with the Ayutthaya Empire, Rama I built his new city in the image of the old capital. Boatloads of bricks from Ayutthaya were ferried down the Chao Phraya River and used to construct the buildings and city walls. In its earliest days, Bangkok had no roads, and most of its population lived on the river. Canals were the city's thoroughfares, earning it the nickname 'Venice of the East'.

King Mongkut

King Mongkut, who took the throne in 1851, might be the best-known Siamese monarch in the West, due entirely to the writings of Anna Leonowens, the Anglo-Indian governess to his children in the 1860s.

A grand mouthful

Bangkok has the longest official name of any city in the world: *Krungthepmahanakhon Amonrattanakosin Mahintharayutthaya Mahadilokphop Noppharatratchathaniburlrom Udomratchaniwetmahasathan Amonphimanawatansathit Sakkathattiyawitsanukamprasit.* This translates as: 'City of angels, great city of immortals, magnificent city of the nine gems, seat of the king, city of royal palaces, home of gods incarnate, erected by Visvakarman at Indra's behest.'

Most Thais can still recite the whole thing, generally because of a song, the lyrics of which consist of the name repeated over and over again. The name went through several iterations during the reigns of different kings. This full ceremonial name was given to the city by King Mongkut, who became king in 1851. Today, Thais simply refer to it as 'Krung Thep' – 'City of Angels'. To foreigners, the city has always been 'Bangkok'. It's easier that way.

Leonowens's memoirs inspired a 1944 novel, *Anna and the King of Siam*, and the cheery Yul Brynner musical of 1956, 'The King and I'. Neither are held in much esteem for their historical accuracy, and the latter was banned in Thailand due to its 'disrespectful' portrayal of the monarch as a capricious Oriental despot, albeit with a soft centre.

In Thailand, the real Mongkut is known for his pioneering interest in science and technology, particularly astronomy and geography. He had an ambivalent relationship with the West. Despite admiring Western learning – and giving his children, including the future King Chulalongkorn, a European-style education – Mongkut was the first Siamese monarch to come under serious pressure from Western imperialism.

During the reign of Mongkut's predecessor, Rama III, the British empire had arrived at the frontiers of Siam after their defeat of the Burmese in the First Anglo-Burmese War. In 1855, Sir John Bowring, the British governor of Hong Kong, arrived in Siam to negotiate a treaty. Having seen the treatment the Burmese had received at the hands of the British in the Second Anglo-Burmese War of 1852, Mongkut knew he was dealing with a formidable enemy, and he was forced to agree to unequal terms.

The main outcome of the Bowring Treaty was the abolishment of the Royal Storage, the mechanism through which the king maintained a monopoly on foreign trade. Import taxes were slashed to 3 per cent and ordinary people were allowed to trade with foreigners, previously a crime punishable by death. British subjects were also allowed to own land in Siam and became subject to British law, rather than Siamese justice, a status known as 'extraterritoriality'.

The Bowring Treaty was the pivotal moment in 19th-century Siam's dealings with the West. It effectively brought Bangkok and the rest of Siam into the system of global trade. Soon after, Siam concluded similar agreements with the United States, France and other powers in an effort to counterbalance the British. The unequal nature of the treaty was a humiliation for Siam in many ways, and it was not to be the only one during Mongkut's rule. In 1863, King Norodom of Cambodia, a Siamese vassal, placed his country under French protection.

During King Mongkut's time, Siam remained at its heart a feudal monarchy, as it had been for hundreds of years. But he did introduce some tentative reforms. Although the ministries of government remained in the hands of a small number of aristocratic families, he employed foreign technical advisors in certain areas. He built Charoen Krung, Bangkok's first road, in 1855. He tried to improve the condition of slaves and women, allowed his subjects to gaze on his face when he appeared in public, and started the practice of printing laws in a government gazette.

Mongkut's love of science and technology was to be his undoing. In 1868, he set out on an expedition to the village of Wakor in Prachuap Khiri Khan province in order to witness a total solar eclipse. Using modern Western techniques, Mongkut had predicted the exact place and time of the eclipse. On the way back to Bangkok, both Mongkut and his son Chulalongkorn caught malaria. Six weeks later, Mongkut was dead. Today, three technology institutes in and around Bangkok are named after him.

King Chulalongkorn

With the possible exception of King Bhumibol, Chulalongkorn (Rama V) is Thailand's most revered monarch. He brought Siam into the 20th century and managed to preserve its sovereignty against the very real threat of European colonial ambitions. His role as 'the great moderniser' has made him a kind of patron saint of the Thai middle class, and his photograph continues to grace walls in homes, offices and businesses across Bangkok.

Chulalongkorn was crowned at the age of 15 on November 11, 1868. A regent ruled until 1873, when Chulalongkorn was crowned a second time, this time as king in his own right. Having used the intervening years to travel widely and observe the colonial administrations of the British and Dutch in Singapore, India and Java, the young king was full of ideas on how to modernise Siam.

Like his father, Chulalongkorn understood the threat

the European empires in Southeast Asia posed to Siam. He realised that if his country was to remain independent, he would need to convince the Europeans that it was 'civilised' – '*siwilai*', in the Thai rendering. And so his reign was characterised by reform. He centralised power and introduced Western-style bureaucratic practices. He reduced the influence of the aristocratic families that traditionally ran Siam's ministries and installed his brothers in positions of power. And he curbed many of the cultural practices most frowned on by the West, including slavery and corvée labour.

The king was able to justify many of these reforms in terms of Buddhist ethics, and so defend himself against

The mandala system

You can translate the words 'city', 'town', 'land' and 'country' using a single Thai word: '*muang*'. There's a good historical reason for this. Until the 19th century, the political organisation of Siam and its neighbours was very different from what was common in Europe. A 'state' like Siam didn't have clearly defined territorial boundaries. Instead, Siam was a network of *muang* – city states of varying sizes.

Each *muang* had a sphere of influence. The smaller *muang* paid tribute – generally sending goods and slaves – to more powerful ones. For example, the king of Chiang Mai might pay tribute to the king of Siam a certain number of times per year. States could also pay tribute to more than one ruler. In the 19th century, Cambodia often paid tribute to both the Vietnamese and Siamese courts.

A client *muang* could expect protection from its patron – including from attacks by the patron himself. The client would also have to supply troops if the more powerful state requested them for other military adventures. Other than that, clients were generally allowed to run their fiefdoms as they saw fit. There are similarities between this kind of relationship and the patron-client arrangement still common in Thai society. Indeed, it was essentially the same thing, with the more powerful ruler being the patron of the lesser one.

Things changed in the 19th century, when the British and French empires arrived at Siam's borders. As historian Thongchai Winichakul shows in *Siam Mapped*, after the British conquered southern Burma the British envoy to the court of Rama III, Captain Henry Burney, asked the Siamese where their border with Burma lay. The Siamese were confused by the question. They replied that if the British wanted to know, they should ask the local inhabitants themselves. The idea of a border, in the modern sense, didn't make much sense to the Siamese at the time. The process of drawing up Siam's borders was an integral part in the making of the country as a modern nation state.

charges that he was 'Westernising' the country. There were setbacks and resistance from vested interests, but Chulalongkorn eventually succeeded in turning Siam from a feudal monarchy, in which the monarch had little control over the feudal lords who ruled the various *muang*, to an absolute monarchy, in which the king ruled the whole kingdom.

He faced serious challenges along the way. In the 19th century, France had taken control of Vietnam and Cambodia, and in 1887 formally established the colony of French Indochina. In the early 90s France turned its attentions to Laos, long a vassal of Siam. The French claim on Laos rested on the dubious claim that Vietnam had held suzerainty over the country. In March 1893, the French consul in Luang Prabang, Auguste Pavie, demanded the Siamese evacuate troops east of the Mekong.

When the Siamese refused, the French sent troops into Laos. Siamese resistance led to the killing a French officer, giving the French an excuse for war. In July 1893 they sent two gunboats up the Chao Phraya, coming under fire but forcing their way to Rattanakosin. With guns trained on the Grand Palace, the Siamese were forced to cede Laos to France and submit to various other humiliating conditions.

More losses were to come. In the first decade of the 20th century Siam lost the remaining parts of Laos it still held as well as Battambang, Siem Reap and Sisophon in western Cambodia. Then it was the turn of the British. In March 1909, Siam yielded rights to the Malays states of Kelantan, Trengganu, Kedah and Perlis in exchange for a British promise to end extraterritoriality. Overall, Siam was forced to cede almost half the territory under its control to the French and British.

In 1897 and 1907, Chulalongkorn embarked on two grand European tours. The first Siamese king to visit Europe, he was treated as an equal by the monarchs who received him. He not only saw the grand architecture of cities like London, Paris and Berlin, but also witnessed the poverty of the West. The visits filled him with the confidence that Siam could take what it needed from the West, without necessarily compromising its own values. Having seen the appearance of 'civilisation' with his own eyes, he embarked on a grand building programme in Bangkok, resulting in the Dusit Palace complex, Ratchadamnoen Avenue and the fine Renaissance-style buildings of Rattanakosin.

Chulalongkorn died of kidney disease in 1910 after spending 42 years on the throne. He has a national holiday dedicated to him, Chulalongkorn Day, which falls on his birthday, October 23.

The end of absolute monarchy

During the reigns of the next two kings, Vajiravudh (Rama VI) and Prajadhipok (Rama VII), the process of modernisation started by Mongkut and Chulalongkorn continued. A growing cohort of the brightest Siamese, both aristocrats and commoners, were receiving European educations and gaining exposure to ideologies like democracy, socialism and nationalism. This led to a growing awareness among the elite that the logic of modernisation led away from absolute rule by the king.

In February 1927, a group of seven Siamese students, including military men like Plaek Khittasangkha and leftist intellectuals like Pridi Banomyong, met in Paris and began to plot an end to absolute monarchy. Calling themselves the 'Promoters', they formed a new political party, the Khana Ratsadorn (People's Party). They returned to Siam and quietly built support for their goal.

On 24 June, 1932, the group acted, seizing control of the country in a coup d'etat. The king, who was playing golf when he heard the news, decided against fighting the coup. 'I could not sit on a throne besmirched by blood,' he later wrote. The king told the People's Party that he was willing to remain the country's constitutional monarch, and that he had always favoured granting the people a constitution.

In October 1933, a royalist counter-coup, the Boworadet Rebellion, failed to retake power from the People's Party. King Prajadhipok's strained relations with the People's Party deteriorated. On March 2, 1935, he abdicated while in England. 'I am willing to surrender the powers I formerly exercised to the people as a whole, but I am not willing to turn them over to any individual or any group to use in an autocratic manner without heeding the voice of the people,' he wrote. He never returned to Siam and died from heart failure in England on May 30, 1941.

Phibun's nation

Plaek Phibunsongkhram, often referred to simply as Phibun, had a profound effect on Thai society. Phibun was prime minister and military dictator of the country for two periods in its history: 1938–44 and 1948–57. Many of the things today recognised as 'Thai culture' were invented during Phibun's long, autocratic rule.

Often referred to as a 'revolution', what happened in 1932 was something less than that word implies. The Promoters realised that the uneducated population of their country weren't yet ready for democracy. Once the first Constitution was promulgated in late 1932, the military and civilian factions quickly fell out. With the civilians lacking support from a still-uneducated public, the military faction took control.

By 1938, Phibunsongkhram had become prime minister, ahead of his leftist rival Pridi. Phibun was born Plaek Khittasangkha to a humble family in Nonthaburi in 1897. He entered military service and rose through the ranks quickly, eventually receiving the rank and title Luang Phibunsongkhram from King Prajadhipok. Phibun was an admirer of European fascism. Believing the country needed strong leadership at a time of crisis – he was prime minister for most of the Second World War – he had written admiring articles about Mussolini and Hitler before coming to power.

His rule was characterised by authoritarianism and fervent nationalism. Much of this nationalist sentiment was directed against the Chinese. This was partly due to a belief that the Chinese were profiteering at the expense of ordinary Thai, much in the way the Jews were viewed in Germany. The government also had legitimate concerns about growing Chinese nationalism in Thailand, as well as the large amount of money Chinese immigrants were remitting out of the country.

Phibun hiked taxes on the commercial class – which meant the Chinese – shut down most Chinese newspapers and restricted the study of Chinese in schools. In 1939, he changed the name of the country to Thailand. This was partly meant to emphasise that the country belonged to the Thai, as opposed to the Chinese. It was also meant to suggest some kinship with other Tai peoples in the region.

Between 1939 and 1942, Phibun issued a series of 12 'Cultural Mandates' aimed at modernising the Thai nation. These dictats required Thais to know the national anthem, use Central Thai (as opposed to local dialects), eat with a spoon and fork (as opposed to hands), buy Thai products and dress in 'modern' (meaning 'Western') fashion: men in jackets, trousers, shirt and tie; women in blouses, skirts, hats and gloves. Everyone had to wear shoes.

People were forbidden from eating more than four meals a day and from chewing betel nut. A later decree dictated that husbands should treat their wives with respect, refrain from beating them, and kiss them on leaving for work or coming home. Many of these decrees were resented by the people, including one dictating that no Thai could receive service at a government office unless he or she was wearing a hat.

Until 1932, the Siamese national anthem had been the Sansoen Phra Barami, or Royal Anthem, which still accompanies the films about the king that play before movies in Thai cinemas. Following the 1932 coup, it had been replaced with a new, more martial-sounding tune, the Phleng Chat Thai. After Phibun changed the country's name, he launched a competition to create new lyrics. He ordered that the anthem be played in public at 8am and 6pm every day and for the public to stand at attention while it was on. The practice continues to this day. Notably, the song does not mention the monarchy.

Phibun also promoted the greeting 'sawatdi', which had been coined in the mid-1930s by Phraya Uppakit Silpasan, a Thai language expert and Chulalongkorn University professor. Thais had previously hailed each other by asking each other 'Where are you going?' or 'Have you eaten?'. And he made the decidedly non-Thai phad Thai the country's national dish, hoping to reduce the population's dependency on rice. Some sources believe the dish may even have been invented in Phibun's household *(see page 209)*.

Phibun built a personality cult around himself as the *phunam* ('leader') of the country. Much like King Bhumibol today, his picture was everywhere. In part, what Phibun was doing was continuing the process of refashioning Thailand's image begun by Mongkut and Chulalongkorn. He played an undeniably important role in building the Thai nation. In 1957 he was ousted by another military dictator: Sarit Thanarat.

The death of Rama VIII

Following the abdication of King Prajadhipok, Ananda Mahidol became King Rama VIII of Thailand at the tender age of nine. At the time, he was at school in Switzerland with his younger brother, Bhumibol. A regency was appointed to rule in his place.

In 1938, Ananda visited Siam for the first time as its king, for a two-month visit in which he was received by rapturous crowds. During the Second World War, Pridi served as regent for Ananda, while secretly running the Free Thai resistance against the Japanese occupation. The young king wasn't to return until after the end of the war.

In December 1945, Ananda returned for another visit to Thailand, as the country had become known. A one-month trip was extended to six months. But just a few days before Ananda was due to leave Thailand, tragedy struck. On June 9, 1946, the young king was found dead in his bedroom in the Grand Palace. He had been shot in the head.

The real story of what happened to Ananda remains a mystery. All the principal players are now dead, except King Bhumibol, the last person to report seeing Ananda alive. A radio announcement after the death said Ananda had accidentally shot himself while toying with his pistol, though most historians believe this to be unlikely, given the pressure required to discharge the type of gun that killed him.

In 1955, after a lengthy trial, Ananda's secretary Chaleo Patoomros and two royal pages, Butr and Chit, were executed on charges of conspiracy to kill the king. But even at the time, few believed the three were actually guilty of the crime.

Sarit's despotic paternalism

Sarit Thanarat, who ruled Thailand from 1957 until his death in 1963, was to take a very different approach to nationhood from Phibun. He was every bit as authoritarian, cracking down heavily on 'leftists', abrogating the constitution, dissolving parliament and banning all parties save his own Revolutionary Party. But where Phibun had denigrated the monarchy, Sarit revived it.

Sarit saw that the young king could become a unifying figure for the country – and that the military could be strengthened by styling itself as his defenders. He encouraged Bhumibol to make more public appearances and publicly pledged allegiance to him. During this period, many old royal ceremonies were revived, as well as the practice of prostration, which had been abolished by Chulalongkorn. The king began to personally give out all university degrees and toured the country, starting many of the Royal Projects that were to make him hugely popular with the Thai people.

Unlike Phibun and the People's Party founders, Sarit and his clique had been educated entirely in Thailand, and they had a more inward-looking vision of what the country should become. His slogan 'Nation, Religion, King' summed up the ideology he had in mind. He promoted 'traditional' Thai values of hierarchy and paternalistic rule. As foreign imports, ideas like egalitarianism and 'human rights' went out the window.

Despite Sarit's authoritarianism, he was a popular leader. With support from Thailand's chief Cold War ally, the United States, the country grew twice as quickly as it had under Phibun. He directed investment to parts of the country that had been neglected, including the Northeast, where he himself had come from.

Sarit's authoritarian government kept strict control of the media. After his death in 1963, the truth about his corrupt regime came out. His family fought for control over his estate, which turned out to amount to some US$150 million – an absolutely colossal sum then. He had also owned countless properties and businesses and been a serial womaniser, with more than fifty mistresses.

King Bhumibol Adulyadej

At the time of writing, several people are serving sentences in Thai prisons for lèse-majesté – insulting the monarchy, which is criminalised in Article 112 of the Thai Criminal Code. As this book is intended to be distributed in Thailand, it needs to be understood from the outset that a rounded picture of the status and history of the monarchy cannot be painted in these pages. There are things which simply cannot be said. With that caveat out the way, let's first note that many Thais have a deep love for King Bhumibol Adulyadej (Rama IX), who is the longest-serving head of state in the world. Bhumibol is the only monarch most Thais have ever known. Over his long reign, the king has transformed from a callow, ceremonial monarch with little real power to the widely revered 'father of the nation' he is today.

Following his brother's death, Bhumibol returned to Switzerland to complete his studies. His uncle, Prince Rangsit, became regent. On October 4, 1948, the young king was in a car accident that cost him the sight in his right eye. While recuperating in Lausanne, he was visited often by MR Sirikit Kitiyakara, the vivacious blue-blooded daughter of the Thai ambassador in Paris. After returning to Thailand, the couple were married on April 29, 1950. A week later, on May 5, Bhumibol was crowned king. The anniversary is celebrated as a national holiday, Coronation Day.

King Bhumibol and Queen Sirikit have four children: Princess Ubol Ratana (born 1951), HRH The Crown Prince Maha Vaijralongkorn (born 1952), HRH The Princess Maha Chakri Sirindhorn (born 1955) and HRH The Princess Chulabhorn Walailak (born 1957). Princess Ubol Ratana relinquished her title in 1972 to marry an American, Peter Jensen. (They later divorced and she returned from the United States in 2001.)

Of the various iconic images of the monarch that hang from walls across the kingdom, some of the most striking are those of the bespectacled monarch on his many working visits to subjects in rural Thailand, camera around his neck, notebook in hand. From the Sarit era onwards, Bhumibol was styled as a kind of 'development king', avatar of the nation's progress from agricultural backwater to modern industrial state. To this end he initiated thousands of 'Royal Projects', including irrigation systems, land reform and the introduction of new crops.

Today, Bhumibol is one of the world's richest rulers, due mostly to the royal family's vast land holdings in Bangkok. These are managed by the Crown Property Bureau, a tax-exempt entity that also has stakes in some of Thailand's biggest companies. In 2011, *Forbes* magazine estimated Bhumibol's net wealth at more than US$30 billion, making him the world's richest monarch. The palace disputes the figure.

Bhumibol is famous for his wide range of hobbies. A jazz lover, the king was an accomplished saxophone player and has jammed with several jazz legends, including Benny Goodman, Stan Getz and Lionel Hampton. He was a skilled sailor and boat designer. He also holds a number of patents, including several related to rainmaking.

The monarchy is supposed to be 'above politics'. Nevertheless, the king has been known to make a number of dramatic interventions in Thai history, most notably in 1973 and 1992 (*see pages 31–35*). In contrast with some of the pork-fed 'money politicians' who sit in Thailand's House of Representatives, the king might seem an almost Messianic figure. To some he is a bodhisattva: a being destined for enlightenment, a future Buddha.

But some observers point out that it could only be thus. The current constitution of Thailand states that the King 'shall be enthroned in a position of revered worship and shall not be violated'. Article 112 mandates sentences of three to 15 years in prison for anyone who 'defames, insults or threatens the King, the Queen, the Heir-apparent or the Regent'. The institution is not subject to public scrutiny, and only positive coverage of the monarchy sees the light of day in the Thai media. A programme devoted entirely to news about the royal family airs on terrestrial channels each evening.

It should be noted that Bhumibol has spoken out in favour of criticising his own record. In his famous 2005 birthday address, the king said: 'Actually, I must also be criticised. I am not afraid if the criticism concerns what I do wrong, because then I know. Because if you say the king cannot be criticised, it means that the king is not human.' He also added: 'If the king can do no wrong, it is akin to looking down upon him because the king is not being treated as a human being. The king can do wrong.'

Nevertheless, the king's words seemed to have little effect on his people. Prosecutions for lèse-majesté actually increased in the years following the speech. There were an estimated 400 trials between January 2006 and May 2011. The use of Article 112 is undoubtedly linked to the Thai political crisis of recent years.

In recent years, Bhumibol's health has declined. In 2009, he moved to Siriraj Hospital, where he stayed for several years. In July 2012, he was joined there by Queen Sirikit, who had suffered a stroke. In August 2013, the royal couple moved to Klai Kangwon Palace in Hua Hin. Discussion of the inevitable royal succession is taboo, and there has been almost no public debate about it in Thailand.

1973 and 1976

The years 1973 and 1976 are forever ingrained as milestones in the history of Bangkok and Thailand as a whole. The period saw the first mass revolts against military rule, as student activism became an important driver of social change in the country. Both years saw mass protests that ended in massacres in Bangkok – a pattern that continues almost to this day.

By 1973, Thailand had been under continuous military rule for a quarter of a century. The country had developed rapidly during the Sarit era, and a growing middle class was beginning to tire of the generals' authoritarianism. It was the height of the Cold War and Thailand was an important ally of the United States. Other countries in the region were falling to communism and support for the Communist Party of Thailand (CPT), which was fighting an insurgency in the North and Northeast, was growing.

Sarit had been succeeded by another military dictator, Thanom Kittikhachorn. Thanom, his deputy Praphas Charusathien and son Narong (who was also Praphas's son-in-law) had become known as the 'Three Tyrants'. Many students, disappointed at Thailand's lack of progress towards democracy, wanted rid of the Thanom regime and a constitution put in place. In October 1973, several student activists, including the leader of the National Student Centre of Thailand, Thirayuth Boonmee, were arrested for distributing anti-government leaflets. The arrests sparked massive demonstrations in Bangkok.

By the morning of October 13, around 400,000 protesters had gathered around Democracy Monument and Parliament. It was at this point that King Bhumibol stepped in. The government, probably at Bhumibol's request, agreed to release the arrested students. Bhumibol summoned Thanom and Praphas to Chitrlada Palace and had them agree to draft a new constitution. He then received a delegation of students. What was said in the meeting isn't entirely clear, but the students emerged elated and claiming victory – they had, after all, been met by the king himself, just like the generals.

Nevertheless, that wasn't the end of the protests. The Thanom government was still in power. The next day, October 14, the protests turned violent and several students were beaten by police. Troops were brought in and the authorities opened fire on the protesters. Soldiers fired machine guns at the crowds from helicopters. At least 77 people were killed and hundreds wounded. Amid the carnage, Bhumibol ordered the gates of his palace to be opened to allow students to take shelter. That night Bhumibol appeared on television to announce that the Thanom government had resigned. The protests didn't completely end until October 16, when it was announced that the 'Three Tyrants' had fled the country.

These events were incredibly important in the shaping of the country's perception of the king. He was seen to have taken the people's side against a tyrannical government. It was also the first time that ordinary people had gathered in their masses to force a change of leadership in the ruling elite. For the next three years, Thailand experimented with parliamentary democracy. The Pramoj brothers, Seni and Kukrit, alternated as prime minister, but no party was able to achieve a stable majority. The oil crisis led to recession and communists took power in Laos, Cambodia and South Vietnam. In 1975, the Pathet Lao communist group had overthrown the Laotian monarchy and sent the king, queen, crown prince and the king's brothers to 're-education camps', where they later died.

The royal family and military establishment were worried. The students were becoming increasingly radical and the CPT's insurgency continued. The right responded with communist witch hunts – a kind of Thai McCarthyism. Right-wing paramilitary organisations such as the Red Gaurs and Village Scouts were established. Another, Nawaphon, had 50,000 members by 1975, many of whom were trained in advanced military techniques, including assassination.

In 1976, things came to a head. Thanom, the former dictator, returned from exile to Thailand. In protest, students staged a sit-in at Thammasat University. In reference to an incident a week earlier in which some workers had been found hanged after protesting against a factory owner, the students staged a mock-hanging. The next day, photos of the event appeared in several newspapers. It was alleged that the students had hanged an effigy of Crown Prince Vajiralongkorn.

That was all the encouragement the rightists needed. On October 6, with radio stations urging them to 'kill the communists', a mob of 10,000 gathered at the gates of Thammasat, armed with rifles, swords and clubs. The police and Red Gaurs attacked the campus with rocket launchers and assault weapons. Students who tried to escape the campus were set upon by the crowds. Some were burned alive or hanged, others raped or beaten to death. Many of the bodies were burned, strung up and mutilated. By the end of the day, the military had moved in and suspended the constitution.

The official death toll was 46, though some estimate more than 100 people were killed. None of the perpetrators were ever brought to justice. Many prominent student leaders were forced to flee to the jungles of Northeastern Thailand, into the security of CPT-controlled areas.

Following the coup, a civilian, former high court judge Tanin Kraivixien, was installed as prime minister. He turned out to be even more authoritarian than many of his military predecessors, engaging in a ruthless campaign to suppress leftists and making membership of a communist organisation punishable by death. Blanching at Tanin's extremism, the military deposed him in 1977 – in yet another coup.

Premocracy

Now in his nineties, General Prem Tinsulanonda isn't seen often these days, though he remains highly influential. Born in 1920 in Songkhla province, Prem had a distinguished military career. In February 1980, as army chief, he forced the resignation of then-premier General Kriangsak Chomanand and became prime minister himself. He was to remain in the post until August 1988.

In contrast to the 1970s, the 1980s under Prem were a prosperous and stable time for Thailand. The economy boomed. Although Prem had led anti-insurgency operations in Thailand in the 1970s, as prime minister he famously offered amnesty to these so-called 'communist terrorists'. As a result, many of the former student activists who had fled the city during Thanin's regime returned.

As a military ruler, he employed a more consensual approach than had his strong-man predecessors. He also enjoyed the firm support of the king. Today Prem is the head of the Privy Council, the King's advisory group, all of whose members are personally appointed by the monarch.

Since the coup that ousted Thaksin Shinawatra in 2006, Prem has become a controversial figure. Thaksin has accused Prem of being behind his overthrow, making him unpopular with the Pheu Thai and red-shirt faithful who back the exiled leader. Prem and the coup leaders have denied he had any involvement in the ouster.

Black May

The events of May 1992 are known in Thailand as 'Black May'. As in 1973, people rose up against military rule – and died for the cause on the streets of Bangkok. And once again, King Bhumibol was seen to have made a decisive intervention in politics that confirmed his reputation as the moral arbiter of the nation.

On February 23, 1991, the army commander-in-chief, General Suchinda Kraprayoon, overthrew the elected government of Chatichai Choonhavan. The coupmakers, who called themselves the National Peace-Keeping Council (NPKC), imprisoned Chatichai and appointed Anand Panyarachun as prime minister. A new constitution was promulgated and elections scheduled for March 22, 1992.

After the elections, a government coalition was formed which appointed General Suchinda as prime minister. Massive public protests followed. Suchinda announced that he would support a constitutional amendment banning officials who had not been elected from serving as premier. But the two main coalition parties later announced that they favoured transitional clauses that would allow Suchinda to serve as prime minister for the remainder of the parliamentary term

On May 17, more huge protests against Suchinda began, led by former Bangkok governor Chamlong Srimuang. Some 200,000 people filled Sanam Luang, and the protests turned violent. At 12.30am, Suchinda announced a state of emergency. Troops were called in and the violence spiralled out of control. Chamlong was arrested. The protests then shifted to Ramkhamhaeng University in the east of the city. By the evening of May 19, 50,000 had gathered there.

On the morning of May 20, Princess Sirindhorn made a plea on television for an end to the violence. Later the same day, Crown Prince Vajiralongkorn did the same. At 9.30pm, there was a final, extraordinary broadcast. The camera showed King Bhumibol sitting on a chair before Suchinda and Chamlong, who were sitting on the floor. The king reprimanded the two leaders, calling on them to end the conflict and find a solution through parliamentary procedure. Afterwards, Suchinda released Chamlong and, on May 24, resigned.

More than 52 people had died, with many more disappearances and injuries. At least 3,500 people were arrested, some of whom said they had been tortured. The army's reputation was severely damaged, and it was to stay out of politics for almost a decade and a half. As in 1973, the events had confirmed Bhumibol's reputation as a unifying force before a new generation of Thais.

The Asian financial crisis

The 1997 Asian Financial Crisis, often referred to as the Tom Yam Kung Crisis because it began in Thailand, had a devastating effect on the Thai economy and brought a long period of growth to an end. The legacy of the crisis is still visible in the Bangkok cityscape. Hundreds of unfinished buildings were abandoned as finance dried up in the wake of the crisis. Many remain unfinished to this day.

The Thai economy grew at a lightning pace in the late 1980s and early 90s. Many Bangkokians were getting rich through property development, and a significant portion of the city's high-rises were built during this period. But by the mid-90s it became clear that a bubble was developing. There was a huge property oversupply, rents began to fall and liquidity began to dry up. The prime minister of the time, Chavalit Yongchaiyudh, saw the crisis coming, but political pressures meant he was unable to push through the economic reforms that might have prevented it.

In May 1997, the Thai baht, which had been pegged at 25 to the US dollar, was hit by massive speculative attacks. The Thai government ran out of foreign reserves to support the currency and was forced to float it on July 2. The baht began to collapse, investors pulled out their money and developers and financiers went bankrupt. The baht lost half its value and the Stock Exchange of Thailand fell 75 per cent.

In November, Chavalit resigned and was succeeded by Democrat Party MP Chuan Leekpai, who became premier for a second time. Chuan's government was forced to negotiate a US$17 billion rescue package with the International Monetary Fund (IMF) to restore confidence in the Thai economy. The deal forced the bankruptcy of many of the country's biggest financial institutions. It also forced the country to accept stringent new regulation frameworks designed to increase transparency and accountability.

It was to take years for the Thai economy to recover from the economic shock, and many of Thailand's richest people were ruined by the crisis. Hundreds of building projects were abandoned and remain unfinished today. Among the most prominent are Sathorn Unique, a crumbling, half-built neoclassical skyscraper close to the intersection between Charoen Krung and Sathorn Road by Rangsan Torsuwan (*see page 59 and 61*).

Even more dramatic is SV Garden, not one but four decaying high-rises that haunt the riverside beside Rama III Road in Yannawa. The developers had aimed to transform the area into a new CBD. When one of its 11 lenders failed, the project ground to a halt, and four of the towers were never finished.

Less imposing – but no less poignant – is the Hopewell Project, named after the Hong Kong company that signed up in 1990 to build a 60km multi-level road and rail system called the Bangkok Elevated Road and Train System (BERTS). The first line, from Hualamphong Train Station to Don Muang Airport, was originally meant to open in 1995. But costs soared and the crisis killed the project before it could be finished. Still standing along the route, like a kind of post-industrial Stonehenge, are more than 1,500 blackened concrete stanchions. Many are collapsing. The Bangkok Metropolitan Administration has promised to demolish most of them to make way for a new railway project.

Thaksin Shinawatra and the Thai political crisis

The mercurial figure of Thaksin Shinawatra has dominated Thai politics for more than a decade now. At the time of writing, he likely remains Thailand's most talked-about politician – despite living in self-imposed exile in Dubai. His name evokes strong feelings in almost all politically engaged Thais. To some, he is the saviour of the nation; to others, its ruin personified.

The story of Thailand's political crisis of the last few years is a difficult one for a writer based in the country to tell. Not only does it concern its most visible players – politicians, generals, media moguls, businessmen, activists and voters – it's also inextricably linked with palace politics. Thaksin is the focus of the ire of his highly vocal enemies, but their animus does not end with him. Books and series of books have been written on the subject. Some cannot be bought in Thailand.

It's nevertheless worth at least attempting to tackle the subject here. It's one that has had very real consequences for people living in Bangkok. It led to the complete shutdown of Bangkok's two major airports in 2008 and has turned parts of the city into virtual war zones three times since then. In April and May 2010, it led to the violent deaths of more than 90 people in the centre of the city. At the time of writing, protestors led by former deputy prime minister Suthep Thaugsuban were attempting to destroy the government of Thaksin's sister Yingluck. Ominously, they were also vowing to 'cleanse' Thailand of the influence of the Shinawatra family.

Predicting the future of Thai politics is a quixotic endeavour. By the time this book is in the stores, Yingluck may still be prime minister. Or Suthep may have succeeded in his bid to remove her from government. In such a case, more violence would be all but inevitable.

Thaksin's rise

Thaksin Shinawatra was born into one of the richest and most influential families in Chiang Mai in 1949. His great-grandfather had been an immigrant from Guangdong, China. A former policeman with a doctorate in criminal justice from Houston State University, Thaksin built a telecommunications empire in the 1980s and 90s. By the time he entered politics in 1994, he was already one of the richest people in Thailand and his company, Shin Corp, was worth billions.

In 2001, Thaksin was swept to power in an election as leader of his own political party, Thai Rak Thai ('Thais Love Thais'). Initially enjoying broad support even among the Bangkok establishment, Thaksin launched a raft of policies aimed at benefiting his political base in Thailand's poor North and Northeast. Among them was the country's first universal healthcare programme, the '30-baht Health Scheme'. He directed infrastructure investment into rural Thailand, building roads in places that had been more or less ignored by Bangkok governments over the previous century.

Thaksin's economic programme became known as 'Thaksinomics'. He ordered state-run banks to loan to villagers, farmers and SMEs at low interest rates. He signed free-trade agreements and pushed for privatisation of state-owned enterprises, most notably EGAT, the national electricity company. He poured money into 'mega-projects', the largest being Suvarnabhumi International Airport. Thaksin's policies were denounced by his critics as 'populism' – superficial moves aimed at pleasing 'uneducated' voters. Regardless, during the Thaksin years the Thai economy boomed.

Thaksin also had an authoritarian streak. His interior minister, Purachai Piumsombun, led a crackdown on Bangkok's famously freewheeling nightlife, forcing nightclubs and bars to close at 2am on the dot. Purachai's 'social order' campaign made him popular with the public, but less so with venue owners, the police and the foreigners who had been drawn to the city for its racy nightlife.

Thaksin's most notorious policy was his brutal 'war on drugs'. By the time he came to power, methamphetamine use had become a serious problem to Thai society. Newspapers carried daily stories about brutal crimes carried out by young people high on 'ya ba' ('crazy drug'), the Thai nickname for meth. In 2003 Thaksin launched a violent crackdown on drug dealers. Between 1,000 and 2,500 alleged dealers were murdered in extra-judicial killings. Little effort was made to hide the fact that the murders were state policy. Human rights activists were aghast, but the campaign was hugely popular with the public and couldn't have happened without the broad support of the Thai establishment. Though Westerners tend to cite this policy as evidence of the man's tyranny, even his worst critics within Thailand hardly mention it.

Thaksin was also accused of badly mishandling the insurgency that began in 2004 in Thailand's Muslim-majority Deep South provinces of Pattani, Yala and Narathiwat. Massacres took place on his watch, most notably at the Krue Se Mosque in Pattani and at Tak Bai in Narathiwat. In the latter incident, the army detained some 1,300 Muslim protesters at a police station and forced them into trucks, stacking them on top of each other like cargo. They were driven to an army camp five hours away in Pattani. By the time they arrived, 78 had died of suffocation or organ collapse. Thaksin, often careless with his words, claimed the victims had died because they were weak from fasting for Ramadan.

Despite his popularity at the ballot box, Thaksin was no

democrat. He talked of 'rewarding' districts that voted for Thai Rak Thai with funds and punishing those that didn't. He suppressed the media, using his influence to remove critical programmes from the TV airwaves. He had government agencies pull lucrative advertising from newspapers who adopted an anti-government line and attacked academics who questioned his policies. Despite – or perhaps because of – all this, Thaksin's popularity only rose. In 2005, Thai Rak Thai won a landslide victory, taking 377 of 500 seats in parliament, a majority of 254. Thaksin had become the first prime minister in Thai history to serve a full electoral term.

Thaksin's fall

Thaksin made some powerful enemies during his premiership. Much of Bangkok's bureaucratic, aristocratic and political elite were disenfranchised by his election victories. The army, its reputation in tatters ever since the events of 1992, had seen its budgets fall every year since the financial crisis of 1997. A powerful coalition of forces began to coalesce that wanted to see the back of this electorally popular demagogue.

A protest movement against Thaksin's rule began to take shape. It was led by Sondhi Limthongkul, a media mogul and former friend of Thaksin who had fallen out with the premier. He founded an organisation called the People's Alliance for Democracy, who distinguished themselves by wearing yellow shirts. Yellow is the colour of King Bhumibol.

Most of the PAD's supporters were upper- and middle-class Bangkokians, Southerners and state enterprise employees who opposed Thaksin's privatisation proposals. Sondhi used his media empire, including his TV station ASTV and *Manager* newspaper, to build opposition to his erstwhile friend. Chamlong Srimuang, who had led the 1992 protests against military rule, also became a PAD leader, bringing with him members of Santi Asoke, the ultra-conservative Buddhist sect with which he was involved.

The fervently royalist PAD began to claim that Thaksin was taking on a presidential bearing and showing a lack of deference to King Bhumibol. He was allegedly attempting to meddle in palace politics. In April 2005, Thaksin presided over a merit-making ceremony at Wat Phra Kaeo, Thailand's most sacred temple and home of the Emerald Buddha, an old symbol of the Chakri dynasty's legitimacy. The prime minister was pictured sitting in the chair usually reserved for the king. Thaksin's office claimed King Bhumibol had granted permission for the ceremony to take place, but the damage was done.

The PAD also accused Thaksin of rampant corruption. Thaksin's graft, it was claimed, took a different form from the usual kickbacks associated with Thai politicians. He was accused of 'policy corruption' – implementing policies that unfairly benefited his telecoms businesses.

Things came to a head in January 2006, when the Shinawatra family sold its 49.6 per cent stake in Shin Corp to Thailand-based nominees of a Singaporean company, Temasek. The family netted around THB73 billion without having to pay any capital gains tax. Thaksin's critics claimed the Shinawatra clan was selling out the country to foreign capitalists.

To shore up his legitimacy after this barrage of criticism, Thaksin announced fresh elections. Opposition parties, including the Democrats, boycotted the poll, which nevertheless took place in April 2006. Pheu Thai's candidates ran unopposed in many constituencies and the election's validity came into serious question.

On April 4, Thaksin had an audience with the king, from which he emerged looking shaken and announced he would be 'stepping back' from politics. The PAD asked the king to appoint a new prime minister but Bhumibol refused, instead telling the courts that they must find a way out of the impasse. In May, the Constitution Court ruled to invalidate the election. Thailand's parliamentary democracy appeared to have ground to a halt.

On September 19, 2006, the army made its move. While Thaksin was in New York, army chief General Sonthi Boonyaratglin sent his tanks into Bangkok and took control of the government. No shots were fired. The coupmakers issued a pronunciamento that night citing Thaksin's alleged corruption, abuse of power, creation of division and disrespect to the king as reasons for his removal. The coup was initially welcomed by many residents of the capital. Some came out to congratulate the soldiers and give them food and flowers.

The junta called itself the Council for Democratic Reform Under Constitutional Monarchy. It quickly changed its name to the Council for National Security (CNS), apparently concerned that the previous name implied it had royal support. Nevertheless, a member of the Privy Council, General Surayuth Chulanont, was appointed prime minister.

The CNS promised to hold elections within one year. In the meantime it attempted to destroy Thaksin's influence. Thai Rak Thai was dissolved and 111 of its executives, including Thaksin, were banned from politics for five years. The junta also set up an Assets Examination Committee (AEC) to investigate accusations of corruption against the ousted premier. In June 2007, the AEC ordered a freeze on all of Thaksin's bank accounts, denying him and his family access to a THB77 billion (US$2.3 billion) fortune.

The junta abrogated the 1997 Constitution and began a process to draft a new one that was more to the army's taste. The new charter reduced the powers of the prime minister, mandated a half-appointed senate and gave the judiciary sweeping powers to dissolve political parties who committed electoral malfeasance. It also reduced the influence of the government over the army promotions process. The CNS used its year in power to hike the military's budget. By July 2007 it had leapt 24 per cent to US$4.6 billion.

Not everyone was happy with these developments. In late 2006, several pro-democracy and pro-Thaksin groups held small rallies in Bangkok to protest against the coup. In March the next year, they demonstrated outside the house of General Prem, accusing him of being behind Thaksin's removal. In June, the groups announced that they were uniting as one organisation: the United Front for Democracy against Dictatorship (UDD). The UDD began to wear red shirts at its protests, red representing the people in the Thai tricolour of nation, religion and king.

The CNS made it illegal to criticise the new draft charter and spent millions on a massive advertising campaign promoting it. It threatened to cling on to power if the people didn't vote in the constitution's favour. In August 2007, while the country was still under martial law, a referendum took place; 59.3 per cent voted for the charter and it was adopted as the Thai Constitution. It is still in force today.

Yellow turmoil

Destroying Thaksin was to prove more difficult than the generals had hoped. The Thai Rak Thai party took over the smaller People's Power Party and altered its logo to resemble its own. Thaksin selected veteran right-winger Samak Sundaravej, who had played an ignominious role in the 1976 Thammasat Massacre, to lead the party, presumably hoping he could serve as a bridge with the army and royalist elite.

A general election was eventually held on December 23, 2007. The PPP won 233 of 480 seats, just shy of a majority. To the army's dismay, the PPP was able to patch together a coalition and form the government with Samak as premier. The cabinet was stuffed with Thaksin loyalists. On February 28, Thaksin returned to Thailand, touching his forehead to the tarmac in a typically showy display for the cameras. The PPP set about challenging the AEC's legitimacy in a bid to save Thaksin's assets and reputation.

The coup had seriously knocked Thailand's international credibility. Staging another was out of the question. Thus Thaksin's enemies channeled their energies into the PAD, which resumed its rallies. In August 2008, the yellow shirts broke into and occupied Government House. They were to stay there for several weeks. The army chief, Anupong Paochinda, and national police chief, Patcharawat Wongsuwan, refused to listen to Samak's demands to remove the protesters. It was clear which side they were on.

Over the course of 2008, Thaksin's side came under a judicial barrage. Several of his deputies were convicted of malfeasance and other crimes. In August, Thaksin and his wife Potjaman fled to England as the AEC investigation went on. In October, Thaksin was sentenced in absentia to two years in jail for a conflict of interest related to his wife's purchase of a plot of land on Bangkok's Ratchadaphisek Road.

Then came the 'judicial coup'. In September, the Constitutional Court removed Samak from office. His crime was to have received payment for continuing to host his cooking show, *Cooking and Grumbling*, while serving as prime minister. He was replaced as PPP leader – and prime minister – by Somchai Wongsawat, Thaksin's brother-in-law by his marriage to Yaowapha Shinawatra.

In November the PAD announced a 'final battle' to drive the Thaksinite government from power. By now, clashes between the UDD and PAD were common. On November 24, the PAD launched what it called 'Operation Hiroshima'. Thousands of its protesters flooded both of Bangkok's airports, Don Muang and Suvarnabhumi. The airports were shut down. Hundreds of thousands of tourists were left stranded in Thailand. The damage to the economy – and Thailand's reputation – was piling up.

General Anupong appeared on a TV chat show and said Somchai should resign. In the event, Somchai didn't have to. For a second time, the Constitutional Court stepped in to bring down a Thaksin-aligned government. It found the PPP, as well as two other parties, guilty of electoral fraud in the 2007 election. All three parties were dissolved. The next day, Somchai stepped down.

On December 5, the Democrat Party announced it had enough support to form a coalition government. Among its partners were the so-called 'Friends of Newin' faction of the PPP. Newin Chidchob, the godfather of Buriram province, had long been one of Thaksin's most trusted lieutenants. Newin, who had himself been 'banned' from politics when Thai Rak Thai was dissolved, had apparently been talked into defecting by Democrat Party 'troubleshooter' Suthep Thaugsuban. There were also rumours that he had been coerced by Anupong.

On December 15, Abhisit Vejjajiva, the leader of the Democrat Party, was voted prime minister in parliament. Despite not having won the most seats in an election since 1992, the Democrats had taken power. Newin's newly minted Bhumjai Thai Party was given the interior ministry and the lucrative transport portfolio. The PPP denounced its demise as another 'judicial coup'.

Red turmoil

It was in these troubled circumstances that Abhisit Vejjajiva began his term as prime minister of Thailand. Born in Newcastle and educated at Eton and Oxford, Abhisit was exactly the kind of polished leader many middle-class Bangkokians yearned for. But he wasn't destined to accomplish much. The genie of the disruptive street protest was out of the bottle: if the yellow shirts could bring down a government, the red shirts could too.

The UDD had learned much from the PAD's successes. A TV station, D-Station, had been set up in 2009 to broadcast anti-government propaganda in the manner of ASTV. The UDD began staging rallies in Bangkok. The movement's leaders, a mixture of Thaksin loyalists and activists, took it in turns to make fiery speeches denouncing the 'undemocratic' government. Their core leaders were long-time Thaksin loyalist Jatuporn Prompan, the talented speechmaker Nattawut Saikua, and veteran politician Veera Musikapong. They attacked the Bangkok establishment as the *'amaat'*, an old term meaning the 'elite'. The red shirts – their leaders included – were meanwhile styled as the downtrodden *'phrai'* ('serfs') of the old *sakdina* feudal system (*see page 95*).

The greatest *phrai* of them all, Thaksin, regularly appeared at these events in digital form, phoning in from his home in Dubai to whip up the crowd. He accused a powerful figure 'outside the constitution' – General Prem – of conspiring to destroy him, and promised his own triumphant return. To the international media, Thaksin played the wronged democrat. When asked what his aims were, he told *Le Figaro:* 'Democracy, symbol of liberty, equality and fraternity, like you, the French!... And then it is also necessary that I manage to recover my frozen assets.'

In March 2009, the UDD set up a protest camp outside Government House. In April, taxi drivers blockaded Victory Monument for 30 hours, bringing the city to gridlock. In Pattaya, a mob of red shirts invaded the hotel in which an ASEAN summit was due to take place. International leaders had to be flown to safety by helicopter, dealing a humiliating blow to Thailand's image. On his way back to Bangkok,

Abhisit's car was attacked by red shirts, who smashed the windows and injured his driver.

On April 13, the first day of Songkran, the army moved 10,000 troops into the city to end the protests. They used tear gas and fired live rounds into the air to scare off the protesters. Some red shirts clashed with the troops and government supporters. By 10am the next morning, the remaining 4,000 protesters at Government House surrendered and 13 red-shirt leaders were arrested. The government claimed only two people died, both shot by red shirts while trying to defend their neighbourhoods. The UDD claimed six people had been shot by troops and their bodies secretly hauled away.

Thaksin and the UDD had made an almighty push to unseat Abhisit – and failed. Commentators piled in to pronounce the demise of Thaksin as a force in politics. They were to be proved very wrong. The next year, as a ruling on Thaksin's frozen assets approached, the UDD threatened fresh protests. In February 2010, the Supreme Court ruled that Thaksin had used his power as prime minister to favour Shin Corp and seized THB46 billion of his frozen assets. Thaksin had been left THB30 billion in what could be seen as a compromise decision.

The UDD announced it would be holding a new mega-protest to demand that Abhisit dissolve parliament and call new elections. In the middle of March 2010, red shirts started to arrive in the capital in droves. Many had come to openly support Thaksin. For others, the fight was about fairness and democracy. Some of them had undoubtedly been paid to attend, which critics claimed rendered the UDD little more than a rented mob. But the same argument could have been applied to the PAD.

Official estimates put the protesters' initial numbers at 50,000–100,000. They first settled in the area of Phan Fah bridge on Ratchadamnoen Avenue. The protests began peacefully, but with a gory flourish that augured ill for what was to come. Nurses collected 1,000 litres of blood from red-shirt donors. It was then poured onto the ground in front of Government House, the Democrat Party headquarters and Abhisit's house.

On April 3, the protest spread to Ratchaprasong intersection, the very heart of Bangkok's shopping district. On April 7, red shirts stormed Parliament, forcing ministers and MPs to flee the building. The next day the government declared a state of emergency, establishing an ad hoc body tasked with dealing with the crisis called the Centre for the Resolution of the Emergency Situation (CRES). It was initially led by Suthep, Abhisit's deputy, who was to play a key role in dealing with the protest.

What made the 2010 protest different from those that had gone before was the presence of the so-called 'men in black' – mysterious black-dressed fighters who clashed with security forces at night before melting away into the city. The UDD denied any connection with the group. The Truth for Reconciliation Commission, a fact-finding body later set up to investigate the events, found that they were connected to Major-General Khattiya Sawasdipol, a rogue army specialist and red-shirt leader who went by the nom de guerre 'Seh Daeng'. Others claimed they were a rogue faction of the army, which was itself split between 'yellow' loyalists and 'watermelons' – apparently green, but red on the inside.

On April 10, the CRES deployed thousands of soldiers to clear the Phan Fah Bridge site of protesters. At night, the troops were ambushed by the men in black, who attacked them with grenades and rifles. In panic, soldiers returned fire. By the end of the night, 26 people, including Reuters cameraman Hiro Muramoto and five soldiers, were dead. At least 860 were wounded.

On May 3, Abhisit offered a five-point 'road map' to reconciliation, which would include the holding of fresh elections in November that year. Some of the red-shirt leaders wanted to take the deal, though hardliners – reportedly including Seh Daeng and Thaksin himself – prevailed. The protests continued with the goal of forcing an immediate dissolution of parliament.

On May 12, the government announced that it was going to clear the protesters, who by then had occupied Bangkok's central shopping district for more than a month. The next day, Seh Daeng was shot by an unidentified sniper while being interviewed by Thomas Fuller of the *The New York Times*. He died four days later. On May 14, the CRES declared 'live-fire zones' around the protest site in which soldiers were authorised to use live rounds against 'terrorists', a term they failed to define clearly. Red-shirt guards and the 'men in black' clashed with soldiers. Unarmed protesters were killed. The death toll rose steadily.

The protest finally ended on May 19. Around noon, the leaders surrendered and declared the end of the demonstration as the army closed in on the site. Many protesters took shelter in the grounds of Wat Pathum Wanaram, between the Central World and Paragon shopping malls. Unknown gunmen, alleged to be soldiers, opened fire on people in the temple, killing six including a volunteer nurse.

As the protest dispersed, several buildings in Bangkok were set on fire, including Central World and the Thai Stock Exchange. Mobs also set fire to government buildings in other provinces, including Khon Kaen, Udon Thani, Ubon Ratchathani and Mukdahan. By the end of the protest, at least 92 people were dead and 2,000 had been injured. To many, it had felt as if the country had teetered on the brink of civil war.

In the aftermath a large but undisclosed number of arrests were made in Bangkok and around the country. Red shirts were rounded up for alleged involvement in the arson attacks. Others were arrested merely for violating the 'emergency decree', which had banned continued participation in the protest once it was imposed.

Yingluck Shinawatra and Suthep's return

The red shirts – not to mention Thaksin – were to get their election in July 2011. Thaksin had installed his youngest sister Yingluck as the top candidate of his newest proxy party, Pheu Thai ('For Thais'). Yingluck was an experienced businesswoman, having worked in many of Thaksin's companies and served as CEO of Advanced Info Service. She was also a complete political novice.

The move turned out to be a masterstroke. The photogenic 44-year-old stuck carefully to her talking points and endeared herself to the public with her easygoing charm. The party promoted a raft of policies aimed squarely at its aspirational base: a 300-baht daily minimum wage, free tablet PCs for all schoolchildren, credit cards for farmers. The party made it clear that its ultimate boss hadn't changed with the slogan 'Thaksin thinks, Pheu Thai does'. The Democrats tried to portray the party as representing those who had 'burned down the country', but failed to convince voters with a lacklustre campaign.

Once again, Pheu Thai won by a landslide, taking 265 of 500 seats against just 159 for the Democrat Party. Despite achieving a majority, Pheu Thai opted to form a coalition government with five smaller parties. Yingluck had become Thailand's first female prime minister. Thaksin, written off by many as a political force just two years previously, had once again put a proxy party into government.

Yingluck's victory heralded two years of apparent stability. The Democrats had been comprehensively defeated and there was little they or their allies could do about a government still flush with democratic legitimacy.

In late 2011, Thailand faced some of the worst floods in its modern history. The most badly affected provinces like

Ayutthaya and Pathum Thani spent weeks under three metres of water. At least 815 people died and 65 of the country's 77 provinces were declared disaster zones. Several large industrial parks were flooded, shaking the confidence of foreign investors – particularly the Japanese – in Thailand's viability is a manufacturing base. The World Bank estimated the value of the damage at THB1,425 billion (US$45.7 billion). The opposition tried to blame the calamity on Yingluck's administration, which they alleged had failed to deal with the problem decisively. But in the end, the opposition's attempts to politicise the issue fell on deaf ears: people saw that this was a tragedy, but not one that could fairly be blamed on Yingluck.

In 2012 and through to the middle of 2013, new anti-government groups sprung up to protest against the 'Thaksin regime'. These 'royalist' activists included 'Pitak Siam' ('Preserve Siam') and the so-called 'White Mask' group, who wore Guy Fawkes masks in imitation of the Occupy movement – amusingly oblivious to the fact that Fawkes had tried to kill the English king. Their rallies failed to come close to those of the PAD or UDD in either size or support. In August 2013, the PAD announced it was disbanding, its leaders noting that even if they succeeded in bringing down Thaksin's latest government, another would get itself elected sooner or later.

By that point many observers had come to believe that a 'grand bargain' had been struck between Thaksin, the army and other important parties. Army chief General Prayuth Chan-ocha studiously refrained from criticising Yingluck or appearing to support anti-government groups. The Department of Special Investigation, under its 'pliable' chief Tharit Pengdit, pressed murder charges against Abhisit and Suthep. At the same time, the country remained fiercely divided and Thaksin was still widely loathed in Bangkok and the South.

The government didn't help its case with some clumsy policy-making. The opposition had long held that Thaksin's policies amounted to little more than short-sighted 'populism', and some of those implemented by Yingluck's government did indeed appear to be exactly that. The 'First Car' scheme offered a tax rebate of up to THB100,000 for first-time auto buyers. It had been intended to support Japanese car manufacturers whose confidence in Thailand had been shaken by the 2011 floods. But the scheme only served to worsen Bangkok's already nightmarish traffic by putting more cars on the roads. And when indebted buyers started to default on auto loans they could ill-afford, a glut of repossessed second-hand vehicles depressed prices and hit the margins of the very manufacturers the scheme was meant to help.

Worse still was the government's 'rice pledging' scheme. Aimed directly at benefiting Pheu Thai's base in the rice-farming villages of the Northeast, the scheme turned into a disaster. The government had planned to buy rice from farmers at well over the market price, then hold its stocks off international markets in the hope that a shortage of supply from the world's No. 1 rice exporter would push prices upwards. It would then sell its stocks at the higher rates and recoup its money. In the event, other major producers like India and Vietnam merely stepped in to fill the gap in supply, and prices failed to soar as the government had hoped. Billions poured out of government coffers – and Thailand lost its status as the world's biggest rice exporter.

It was easy to understand the Bangkok middle class's resentment at such policies. Only a small portion of the Thai population actually pay income tax – mostly the relatively rich residents of the capital. They felt their wallets were being raided, only for the money to be redistributed as ill-thought-out handouts to Thaksin voters.

But Thaksin's biggest mistake was to come at the end of 2013. A number of 'amnesty bills' had been proposed by MPs ostensibly aiming at healing the divisions caused by the political crisis. One, from Pheu Thai MP Worachai Hema, was selected as the party's frontrunner. The bill would see the dropping of all charges relating to the political conflict against ordinary people, regardless of which side they were on. It would exclude protest leaders and those in authority – not to mention people charged with lèse-majesté.

The Democrat Party claimed the bill was merely a mechanism to allow Thaksin to return to Thailand without having to serve his two-year prison sentence or face additional charges. While the initial wording of the bill, which passed its first reading in August, seemed to exclude this possibility, they were to be proved correct.

In late October, a parliamentary scrutiny committee altered the wording of the Amnesty Bill so that it would include leaders in the conflict. This was generally understood to mean that Thaksin would benefit, as well as UDD and PAD leaders and politicians like Abhisit and Suthep. The result, unsurprisingly, was outrage: not only on the part of the opposition, but the red shirts themselves, who wanted justice for their comrades killed in 2010.

The Democrat Party took to the streets to oppose the bill. Under the Thai parliamentary system, a bill must pass three readings in the House of Representatives before it moves to the Senate for another round of scrutiny and approval. In a mammoth parliamentary session beginning on October 31, the government rammed the bill through its second and third readings in the Lower House, with 310 MPs voting in its favour. The Democrats had boycotted the vote. The sheer brazenness of the Pheu Thai move shocked many observers.

It seemed that Thaksin had spectacularly misread the situation, giving the hitherto rudderless Democrats an issue they could gain some traction on. Whether Thaksin had merely run out of patience, or been tricked by the 'establishment' into thinking he could get away with such an audacious move, remains unclear.

The opposition's street protests – which centred on Democracy Monument and the adjacent Ratchadamnoen Road – swelled to impressive numbers. They were joined by smaller anti-Thaksin groups who were already leading largely ignored protests in Lumphini Park and at Uruphong intersection. Every Thai protest needs a gimmick of some sort, and this was to be no exception. This time, protesters blew whistles, generating an almighty din supposedly representing the people's widespread revulsion at the corruption of the Thaksin 'regime'. Yellow shirts were replaced with black-

and-red T-shirts; faces were daubed with the Thai tricolour.

Sensing the public mood, Yingluck announced that if the Senate rejected the bill she would not continue to push it into law. On November 11, the Senate effectively killed the law, voting it down by 140 votes to 0. Many of the protesters went home. But perhaps seeing that he now had the excuse he needed to oust the government – and knowing full well he couldn't do it at the ballot box – Suthep elected to continue his rally. He announced that he and eight other Democrat MPs would be resigning to focus on leading the street protests.

The group renamed itself the People's Democratic Reform Committee and began a series of marches on government buildings, including the Finance Ministry and Government Complex at Chaeng Wattana, occupying them and claiming that they were ousting Yingluck in a 'people's coup'. While the protests were mostly peaceful, there were outbreaks of violence, particularly on the evening of November 30, when gangs of 'students' attacked buses and taxis on Ramkhamhaeng Road carrying red shirts to a UDD rally at nearby Rajamangala Stadium. At least four people were killed – one student, three red shirts – and many more injured.

Suthep issued a raft of decidedly undemocratic demands. The Yingluck government should be replaced by a royally appointed cabinet of 'good people', while parliament would be replaced by a 'People's Council' that would begin a wide-ranging reform process to purge the country of Thaksin's influence. Elections were meaningless – since Thaksin bought all his votes – so democracy was to be suspended for at least a year. Another demand was, rather fancifully, for a complete end to corruption. There was a generous helping of irony with all this – Suthep himself had faced a rap sheet of corruption allegations as long as his arm.

The police obtained an arrest warrant for Suthep on charges of 'insurrection', and warrants for other leaders on charges of invading public property among others. But perhaps fearing violence, they declined to arrest any of the ringleaders. The protesters made determined efforts to get into key buildings such as Government House. The police responded using standard riot control measures: tear gas, rubber bullets and water cannons. During the melees, live bullets were fired and some protesters hit. Both sides denied they were responsible.

What seemed clear was that the protesters were aiming to foment nothing less than a complete breakdown in the functioning of the state – potentially inviting the intervention of the army. What seemed equally obvious was that should they succeed in their aims, the conflict would only get more dangerous. The 15 million Thaksin voters – and the UDD – were not likely to take the destruction of 'their' government lying down.

On Sunday December 8, all 152 remaining Democrat MPs resigned. The 'Democrat' Party had clearly lost patience with democracy. Suthep announced that the next day would be yet another 'victory day', and that millions of Thais needed to flood the streets to oust the government. In a bid to ease the crisis, that morning Yingluck announced that she was dissolving parliament and calling fresh elections. This wasn't enough for the protesters, at least 250,000 of whom flooded the streets of the capital. Suthep demanded that Yingluck immediately relinquish power so that the 'People's Council' could begin its 'reforms'. The premier pointed out that under the constitution, her cabinet was required to continue as interim government until elections took place.

At the time of writing, the polls were scheduled to take place on February 2. The Pheu Thai Party said it was ready to fight the election and 'let the people decide' who should rule Thailand. But it looked doubtful that the Democrats – surely fully aware that they would lose another election – would take part. Should the army stage a coup, the UDD has made it very clear that it would resist the removal of the democratically elected government. Predicting the future course of the crisis is impossible. But we can surely expect, as the Chinese curse has it, some 'interesting times'.

Understanding Thai politics

The nuances of Thai politics can be difficult for foreigners to grasp. A common mistake is to see it through the prism of the left/right dichotomy we tend to apply in the West. Even in Western countries, this kind of analysis is overly simplistic. It's even more so in Thailand, where it's much like trying to fit a square peg in a round hole.

In Thailand, political parties have traditionally been built from the bottom up, rather than from the top down. Influential people in the provinces become politicians, politicians band together into factions (*phuak*), factions band together into parties. Most politicians are amoral creatures – not unlike the invisible spirits that many Thais believe reign over the land. Individual politicians or whole factions can be bought and their allegiances transferred from one party to another.

Vote-buying remains rife in Thai elections, though it's a more complicated issue than it may at first seem. Studies have shown that voters often take bribes from several politicians, then vote for their preferred candidate anyway. At the same time, patron-client relationships remain important in Thai society, and people who have benefitted from a local person of influence's largesse often feel a strong obligation to support them. This isn't to say that voters don't pay attention to national politics when voting. They do. But the politicians themselves and their local profiles are hugely important.

In more developed democracies, political parties represent coalitions of interests. But they also represent competing ideologies: the ideology of 'equality' versus that of 'freedom', for example. In Thailand, ideology plays a much smaller role. Those Thais who do see politics through an ideological prism tend to be restricted to the relatively well-educated, metropolitan elite. But the red- and yellow-shirt movements, for all their faults, have served to raise the importance of ideology in Thai politics.

Most foreigners who have lived in Bangkok for an extended period have an opinion on Thaksin and the political crisis. This may be based on their own idiosyncratic beliefs, though it's often influenced by the milieu of Bangkok society they find themselves in. Middle- and upper-class Bangkokians tend to err on the 'yellow', Democrat side. For them, the red shirts are nothing less than the rabble who tried to burn their city down. Expats who find themselves in their company often soak up their views.

Thailand's two English-language national newspapers, the *Bangkok Post* and *The Nation*, take a pro-Democrat, anti-Thaksin line. This, too, likely rubs off on foreign readers. Another segment of the foreign community, not usually bothered about politics, loathes Thaksin for his authoritarianism. His 'social order' campaign took the fun out of 'their' Bangkok. He also made it harder for less well-heeled foreigners to live in Thailand.

The red shirts and, to a lesser extent, Thaksin himself, have their sympathisers too. Many foreigners end up marrying women from Thaksin's stronghold provinces in the North and, particularly, the Northeast. They can be swayed by their new Thai family's genuine love for the man, or stories of family members whose lives were saved by Thaksin's 30-baht health scheme. Left-liberal foreigners have a tendency to favour the poor underdog in politics, and while painting the crisis as a battle of 'rich versus poor' would be simplistic, it's true that the red shirts are more representative of Thailand's rural poor than their opponents.

One way to view the political crisis is as a battle over resource distribution. There's an obvious split between the geographic bases of the two main parties, Pheu Thai and the Democrats. In broad strokes, the former takes its support from the North and Northeast, the Democrats from the South and Bangkok. Thaksin's governments channeled more investment into the North and Northeast than had gone before. This benefited not only the poor in those regions, but the rich, too. It's a mistake to assume that Pheu Thai doesn't represent the interests of its own segment of wealthy people.

To many observers, Thaksin himself is as much a symptom as a disease. If the Bangkok establishment hadn't neglected the North and Northeast for decades, Thaksin likely wouldn't have been able to win so much support in those areas. His genius was to spot what other political leaders had failed to understand: that the voters in the backwaters of Thailand's fledgling democracy could be made to count. If Thaksin never existed, can we be sure another politician wouldn't have taken his place?

CITY OVERVIEW

Climate

In his 1913 book *Chequered Leaves from Siam*, Eric Reid, a former British vice-consul of Siam and editor of the *Siam Observer*, had a character describe Bangkok's climate: '... every place has its drawbacks, and Bangkok's is the possession of the devil's own particular brand of warming apparatus. And the rain! When you ain't being slowly grilled at a thousand in the shade, you are sousing in floods, or the house is falling about your devoted ears in a thunderstorm.'

A century later, that still seems to sum things up nicely. Bangkok is one of the hottest major cities in the world. Thailand is supposed to have three seasons: hot, rainy and cool. In Bangkok, the latter is something of a misnomer. It is always hot in Bangkok. The average high in December, the

coolest month, is 31°C, with an average low of 20.8°C. The hot season runs roughly from March to May, when the rains tend to start. April is the hottest month, with an average high of 34.9°C. The urban heat island effect – roughly 2.5°C during the day and 8°C at night – ensures the city is hotter than other cities at the same latitude.

Talking about the weather in Bangkok usually boils down to talking about the heat. A simple 'ron' ('hot') makes a good opening conversational gambit with a Thai person most days of the year. Avoiding the heat, and particularly, the glare of the sun, is something of a citywide obsession. Young women, fearful of the skin-darkening effects of the rays, walk with umbrellas on days when there's not a cloud in the sky. Motorcyclists hide from the sun in the shadows cast by larger vehicles.

The rainy season generally starts in May or June and lasts until November. It usually doesn't get into its stride until August and September. It can, nevertheless, rain on any day of the year, with violent 'summer storms' not uncommon during the hotter months. Drizzle is rare, torrential downpours the norm. Parts of the city are prone to flooding, with the suburban sprawl of areas like Ladphrao being particularly vulnerable. Rain also ensures that the traffic situation – and your chances of finding a free taxi – goes straight down the drain.

The Seal of Bangkok

The seal of the city, which also appears on its flag, depicts the Hindu god Indra riding in the clouds atop a divine white elephant known as the Erawan. The seal was based on a painting by Prince Naris, a brother of King Chulalongkorn.

Planning #fail

Look out on the Bangkok cityscape and it's impossible to identify anything resembling a central business district. No Canary Wharf or La Défense here. Skyscrapers can and do sprout up anywhere, dwarfing whatever else happens to be in the neighbourhood. You'd be forgiven for wondering if Bangkok even has a planning department. As it turns out, it does. The Bangkok Metropolitan Administration includes a Department of City Planning, though you might wonder if its bureaucrats bother getting out of bed in the morning.

It's not as if there aren't planning regulations. The problem is one of enforcement, which will always be the case in a land of underpaid bureaucrats and widespread tolerance of corruption. Money talks, and when money wants a 30-storey tower in a residential neighbourhood, it gets one.

Developers are watching the case of the Aetas Hotel on Soi Ruamrudee carefully. In February 2012, the Central Administrative Court ruled that the building should be demolished after local residents brought a case against the property. The hotel had reportedly been built in defiance of a planning regulation specifying the maximum size of

Bangkok's lax planning enforcement means skyscrapers can sprout up almost anywhere. To the left of the picture is Rangsan Torsuwan's Sathorn Unique, one of the towers abandoned following the 1997 economic crisis.

a building that can be built on a street less than 10 metres wide.

Indeed, several tall buildings have appeared on Ruamrudee over the past 15 years, all relying on a certification by the local district office that the *soi* was wider than 10 metres. The trouble is, it isn't – as testimony in the trial proved. Nevertheless, the hotel owners and the Bangkok Metropolitan Administration (BMA) are appealing the verdict and, at the time of writing, the Aetas was still taking reservations.

But it's not just the mega-rich who flout zoning regulations. Wherever people live or work, street vendors follow, erecting stalls that narrow the pavements and cause pedestrian bottlenecks. Every second Monday, the BMA forces the vendors off the streets, which can feel like a breath of fresh air. Still, few Bangkokians would want the city to go the way of Singapore, which has forced its vendors into 'hawker centres', akin to Bangkok's shopping mall food courts. Vendors give the Bangkok streets their vital character. For now, chaos reigns.

Rangsan Torsuwan

Standing close to the junction of Charoen Krung and Sathorn Road, Sathorn Unique is a remarkable building. Never finished, this soaring neoclassical absurdity stands as a 47-storey monument to hubris. When the 1997 financial crisis hit Thailand, the baht plummeted and credit lines went up in smoke, the building was one of hundreds abandoned by their developers. Today, it is a ghost of a building. Its trash-strewn floors are open to the elements, and it serves mainly as a place of pilgrimage for adventurers.

The story of the architect behind Sathorn Unique, Rangsan Torsuwan, is no less interesting. Having graduated from the Massachusetts Institute of Technology and after spending years as a lecturer at Chulalongkorn University, Rangsan set up his own architectural firm in 1969, before moving into development in 1987. He was extremely successful, and his instantly recognisable work has made an indelible mark on the Bangkok cityscape.

His signature is a kind of exultant post-modernism, architectural pastiche in which styles and eras are thrown together without any signs of restraint. Neoclassical features are a trademark. Typical of his style is Sathorn Unique's larger sibling, the 68-floor State Tower on Charoen Krung, one of Bangkok's tallest buildings. It's capped with a distinctive golden dome sitting on top of classical columns – Ancient Greece meets Southeast Asia.

It's interesting to imagine what Bangkok might look like if Torsuwan had been given the mandate to build the whole city, as Baron Haussmann was with Paris. I can only picture an Ancient Greek city transported in time to the modern age of the skyscraper, and in space to the Chao Phraya river basin.

In 1993 came Rangsan's fall from grace. In June of that year, he was arrested by the Thai police. His alleged crime: plotting to murder none less than the president of Thailand's Supreme Court, Pramarn Charnsue. Rangsan was one of four men arrested for the plot, which never actually took place. He was alleged to be the mastermind. After a month in jail, he was granted bail.

The case dragged out for 15 years, having been heard by dozens of different judges. Only in 2008 was there a verdict. South Bangkok District Court sentenced Rangsan and the other three defendants to death. It commuted the sentences because two of the men had confessed and the plot was never carried out. Rangsan's sentence was reduced to 25 years. All four appealed.

And then came a remarkable turnaround. In September 2010, the Appeals Court acquitted all four men of the crime. The next year, Rangsan filed a THB3 billion lawsuit against the Royal Thai Police, the Office of the Attorney General and the Prime Minister's Office. So goes the story of one of the most influential minds behind the making of Bangkok.

Linear development

London is often said to be a collection of villages. As the city developed and these 'nodes' expanded, they eventually merged, creating the metropolis we know today. Development in Bangkok has followed a very different pattern, and one which has everything to do with the way Thailand has been ruled over the past couple of centuries.

In the Thai capital, development has been characterised as 'linear', meaning it has concentrated along its major thoroughfares. Thus, the neighbourhoods in Bangkok tend to be named after roads: Sukhumvit, Silom, Yaowarat, Sathorn, Ladphrao, Ratchada. Many of Bangkok's most important streets started life as canals that irrigated the farms of the aristocracy stretching out to the city's east. The same land-owning families kept hold of this land when the canals were filled in and turned into roads as the 20th century progressed.

But relatively little attention was placed on the areas lying between these large thoroughfares. Thus, rents along the sides of these roads remained high – ensuring the established elite continued to benefit. But the swathes of land between them remained difficult to access, and filled up with slum housing. Connections between the city's large arterials – such as Phahonyothin and Rachadaphisek, or Sukhumvit and Phetchaburi – remain poor, mostly networks of small lanes that become heavily choked with traffic. The concentration of power in the hands of a relatively small elite has ensured little has been done to change the situation.

Rattanakosin and Dusit

More than any other part of the city, the story of Bangkok is written into the built fabric of Rattanakosin. This artificial island, bounded by a meander of the Chao Phraya to the west and a canal to the east, is where the current king's great-great-great-grandfather, Rama I, chose to found his new capital, safer from Burmese attentions than Taksin's Thonburi and plundered Ayutthaya, behind the protective sweep of the river.

The glittering spires of the Grand Palace remain *de rigueur* on the tourist's Bangkok itinerary. Although it's no longer the

home of the royal family, they continue to hold their most important ceremonies on its grounds. Reigns will begin and end here. Within the walls is Wat Phra Kaeo, the royal family's private temple and home of the Emerald Buddha, the kingdom's most sacred Buddha image.

Rattanakosin also tells the story of King Chulalongkorn's modernising reign. Here, and in Dusit district to the north, we see the European architectural facade Rama V erected over his Siamese city in the late 19th and early 20th century. His goal, foisted on him by the threatening imperialist projects of Britain and France, was to convince the West that Thailand was 'siwilai' – a civilised nation not fit for colonial subjugation.

One of the Grand Palace's most impressive structures is the Chakri Maha Prasart Throne Hall, designed by English architects John Clunich and Henry Rose, and originally intended to be a Renaissance-style building topped with domes. In the end, Rama V decided to cap the building with golden spires and Thai-style roofs. The building has been called a 'farang wearing a Thai hat'. The symbolism of the

Thai features of the building being *above* the Western ones is also important, given Thai beliefs about elevation reflecting merit (*see page 131*).

Rattanakosin is also home to Thammasat University, the country's second-oldest higher education institute after Chulalongkorn University. Founded by Pridi Banomyong, one of the leaders of the 1932 'revolution', Thammasat's students have long been at the forefront in demanding changes in Thai society. This has often literally put them in the firing line, most notably on October 6, 1976, when at least 46 students protesting against the return to Thailand of ex-military dictator Thanom Kittikachorn were massacred by right-wing thugs (*see page 33*).

Sanam Luang, the 30-acre field to the university's east, on which many of the victims of 1976 were killed, is doubly linked with death. It was established by Rama I as the royal cremation ground, a function it continues to serve today. Still, the casual visitor wouldn't be able to guess its morbid history from its appearance. It's been popular with kite flyers since its earliest days. At night, the area changes character again, when it becomes a haunting ground for street walkers.

At Sanam Luang's southeast corner is the beginning of Ratchadamnoen Avenue, Bangkok's Champs-Élysées. The road, the name of which means 'Procession of Kings', follows the eastern flank of the field as 'Ratchadamnoen Nai' ('Inner Ratchadamnoen') to its northeast corner, where it crosses the first moat at Phan Phipop Lila Bridge and turns into 'Ratchadamnoen Klang' ('Middle Ratchadamnoen'). The road then heads east.

Slap-bang in the middle of Ratchadamnoen Klang is a reminder that it wasn't only kings who shaped Thailand's history – not in the 20th century, anyway. Democracy Monument is an impertinent interruption to the 'Procession of Kings'. Built in 1939 at the orders of the anti-monarchist dictator Phibunsongkhram, the monument is a tribute to the 1932 'revolution' that ended absolute monarchy. It's often served as a focal point for political protests over the years, including during the red-shirt protests in 2010.

At Phan Fa Lilat Bridge, Ratchadamnoen crosses the second moat and heads north into Dusit district as 'Ratchadamnoen Nok' ('Outer Ratchadamnoen'). It's here that the road is at its grandest. But Chulalongkorn's boulevard is crowned not with a mini Arc de Triomphe, as in French-colonial Vientiane, but the Ananta Samakhom Throne Hall, the beautiful Renaissance-style reception hall of his Dusit Palace complex. The king was to die in 1910, five years before its completion. Today, it's open to the public as a museum.

There's much more to be seen in Inner Rattanakosin, which is bounded by the Chao Phraya River to the west and Khlong Lot to the east. To the west of Sanam Luang is Wat Mahathat, home of Thailand's oldest university for Buddhist monks. Meanwhile, to its west, on Maharat Road, Bangkok's chaotic vitality gets expression in the form of the streetside amulet market, an intrusion of popular Buddhism on the royal isle.

Inner Rattanakosin is also home to Wat Pho, better known as the Temple of the Reclining Buddha, after the 46m-long statue of the founder of the Buddhist faith it houses. While it's taboo for the layperson to display the soles of his feet, those of this effortlessly relaxed enlightened being are inlaid with mother-of-pearl depictions of 108 characteristics of their owner. Wat Pho is also famous for its massage school. Having outgrown its premises in the temple's grounds, the Chetawan Wat Po Thai Traditional Medical School can be found at the end of Soi Phen Phat and offers courses in traditional Thai massage and other strains of massage.

Banglamphu

Just a stone's throw away from the royal grandeur: braids, Sangsom buckets and fisherman pants. Banglamphu, the area of Outer Rattanakosin to the north of Sanam Luang, is Bangkok's backpacker haven. Its most famous thoroughfare, Khao San Road, remains, as Alex Garland had it in *The Beach*, 'the gateway to Southeast Asia' – at least for young Westerners, anyway.

It's tempting to bash Khao San, the first syllable of which is often mistakenly pronounced to rhyme with 'grow', rather than 'Mao'. But, as the saying goes, it is what it is. Spend a few hours here and you'll always meet new people. True, conversation can often deteriorate into tiresome contests over who's been travelling the longest, or who survives on the most piffling daily budget, but not everyone passing by is a 'travel bore'. And if you don't feel like chatter, you can always just take a seat, tune out, and watch the human show walk by.

The backpacker scene has long burst the seams of its most famous road. Soi Rambuttri, which parallels Khao San before crossing Jakraphong Road and snaking round Chana Songkhram Temple, boasts a more relaxed vibe – though only barely these days. A small *soi* leading off Rambuttri where it parallels the river, emerging onto Phra Athit Road, caters to a relatively bohemian Thai crowd. On the corner of Phra Athit, where it turns into Phra Sumen Road, two landmarks face off: the stained white battlements of Phra Sumen Fort, and Roti Mataba, a legendary little restaurant that pairs roti with some excellent Indian curries.

Khao San Road remains the city's backpacker hub – and an excellent spot for people watching.

Thonburi

In today's Thonburi there's little evidence that the town used to be the capital of the Siamese empire during Taksin's 15 years of rule, though a monument to the 'mad' king stands near the western end of Rama I Bridge. It was erected in 1953 during the dictatorship of Phibunsongkhram. The statue depicts Taksin mounted not on an elephant, which would be realistic, but a horse. Some scholars have wondered if the erection of the statue was meant as an affront to the Chakri dynasty by Phibun's hostile regime.

Thonburi's most famous landmark is Wat Arun, 'The Temple of Dawn'. The temple served as Taksin's royal temple during his dynasty, and housed the sacred Emerald Buddha before it was moved to Wat Phra Kaeo. Its most obvious feature is its towering Khmer-style *prang*, which resembles those at Cambodia's famous Angkor Wat. The temple also features intricate Chinese-style decoration and Hindu iconography – a true Bangkokian mish-mash.

Thonburi is mostly suburbia. The area is more affordable than Bangkok itself, and thus is a frequent destination for expats who want to settle down and buy property in the city. It's also become much more easily accessible since the BTS Skytrain network was extended over the river to Wongwian Yai Station. The highlight of the area, though, is its canals, which are lined with greenery and houses, both ramshackle and grand, and serve as a reminder of how Bangkok used to look and feel – before the age of the motorcar transformed it into the concrete monster it is today.

Yaowarat and Pahurat

When Rama I moved his capital over the river to Rattanakosin, the Chinese merchants who were already living there were forced east to Sampheng. Today, the area remains at the heart of Bangkok's Chinatown, which is often referred to simply as Yaowarat, the name of its main thoroughfare.

Yaowarat was one of many roads Rama V ordered built in 1891. Unlike many of Bangkok's streets, which were built on top of canals and boast an almost Roman straightness, Yaowarat takes an unusually curved path through the city. Locals say it resembles the body of a dragon, making it – according to the principles of *feng shui* – an excellent place to do business. In fact, its construction was heavily resisted by the residents of the area, and the success of some landowners in that battle forced the road to snake its way round their properties.

In the 19th century and much of the 20th, the area was known for its vices: opium, prostitution and gambling. While the Teochew might have made up the largest group of Chinese immigrants in 19th-century Chinatown, there were migrants from many parts of China, all with their own customs, dialects and loyalties. They were organised into secret societies known as *angyi*. Control of the lucrative businesses of the area fell to these societies. In 1889, rivalry between the groups turned into all-out fighting, and the army and navy had to be called in to restore peace.

The area has since been 'cleaned up'. While most of Bangkok's Thai-Chinese population is well integrated into the population (*see page 86*), there remain Chinese-speaking families here and the area feels like no other part of the city.

Warrens of narrow streets are lined by small shophouses, the open ground floors of many offering glimpses into homes and business. At times you'd be forgiven for thinking you were in Phuket or Penang.

Yaowarat Road proper is a much grander affair. The area was Bangkok's first real business district, and the first to get tall buildings, which remain impressive after the modest shophouses of Rattanakosin. Huge vertical signs splashed with Chinese characters line the road and burst into life at night when the juice gets switched on. Most are for gold shops, the gold business having always been a Chinese business. Today, the opium dens may be gone, but the food is almost as addictive, whether on the street or in the many Thai-Chinese restaurants that line the road.

Charoen Krung

In typically confusing fashion, Bangkok's 'New Road' happens to be its oldest. When Charoen Krung, whose name means 'prosper the city', was built by King Mongkut in 1862, the city still lived up to its nickname as 'the Venice of the East'. The lack of roads wasn't something the city's expat community could get used to, so they petitioned the king for a road on which to ride their horses and carriages and 'get some fresh air'. The aquatic city, they complained, was making them sick. It seems complaining expats are not a new phenomenon.

Charoen Krung starts at the northeast corner of Wat Pho before heading over the two moats of Rattanakosin and into Chinatown. At Songsawat Road it lurches south into Bang Rak district, the riverside portion of which once formed Bangkok's European 'colonial' zone. That legacy is still visible. The Portuguese Embassy, the first Western diplomatic mission in Bangkok, is still here. The French Embassy is close by.

Here, a flavour of the colonial age lingers. It's in this zone that many of Bangkok's art galleries and antique shops can be found. The colonial collector and exporter of Oriental art is alive and well. Here, too, are some of Bangkok's most famous hotels, including the Shangri-La and The Oriental, which opened in 1879.

Much of The Oriental has been rebuilt as a rather ugly modernist structure, though some of the original building survives as the Author's Wing, which boasts suites named after some of its most famous guests, including Joseph Conrad, Somerset Maugham and Noel Coward. The colonial-style Author's Lounge still serves English afternoon tea and makes an excellent place to while away a Sunday afternoon, while the hotel also houses Le Normandie, perhaps the city's swankiest French restaurant. One hundred metres away from the hotel is the pretty Romanesque structure of Assumption Cathedral, Thailand's most important Roman Catholic church.

In the first half of the 20th century, Charoen Krung took over from Yaowarat as Bangkok's premier business zone. Taken as a whole, the buildings that line the road are a ramshackle jumble of styles and eras. Much of its 1960s architecture has long lost its lustre and the road was replaced by Silom as the city's most important commercial area from the 1970s.

The city's Bang Rak district hosts some of its most luxurious hotels. In the centre is Rangsan Torsuwan's State Tower, which hosts the upmarket Lebua Hotel and its rooftop bar, Sky Bar. To the left and right are the two curving halves of the Shangri-La.

Silom and Sathorn

The Silom and Sathorn roads started their lives as canals in the city's lazy agricultural hinterland. Sathorn is unusual among Bangkok's 'canal roads' in that its former life has been preserved in the form of its central drainage channel. Today, the two roads serve as bases for a variety of large Thai and international companies: banks, consultancies, accounting firms, law firms and insurance companies. It's no coincidence, then, that the area is also where many of the city's most exclusive condominium projects are based.

Rangsan Torsuwan has made his distinctive mark here in the form of State Tower, which towers over the area in its golden crown (*see page 61*). Its upper extremities are occupied by the 357-suite five-star hotel, Lebua. Its roof, with its neoclassical golden dome, hosts Sky Bar, which amusingly claims on its website to be 'unanimously accepted as the coolest bar in Bangkok'.

Perhaps no road in Bangkok has changed as much as Silom, once a canal surrounded by orchards and country villas, today one of the city's busiest roads. The superimposition of a Skytrain line gives the road an oppressive subterranean feel, while the road's most famous attraction, if you can call it that, is Patpong, as much as 'Nana' a byword for Thailand's sex industry.

Pathum Wan

Pathum Wan may be named after a temple, but it's best known for its shopping. At its heart is Wat Pathum Wanaram, a royal temple that hosts the ashes of Prince Mahidol Adulyadej, father of King Bhumibol and his brother Ananda (Rama VIII). The temple attained notoriety on May 19, 2010, the day the red-shirt protests ended. Six people sheltering in its grounds from the carnage on Rama I Road were shot dead by snipers on the nearby Skytrain track.

The temple stands between the Paragon and Central World, two of the city's flashiest shopping malls. The Paragon, located at the centre of a cluster of shopping malls, is directly served by Siam BTS station, the Skytrain networks central hub. Beside the Paragon is Siam Centre, one of the first shopping malls in the country, while on the southern side of Rama I Road is Siam Square, a shopping area known for its boutique clothes shops.

The area throngs with students from nearby Chulalongkorn University, which was the first to open in Thailand. Chula, which was founded by King Rama VI in 1917, owns the land Siam Square stands on, and the rents ensure it is well-financed. Siam Square also features the Lido and Scala, two old cinemas known for specialising in the kind of independent films that don't make it into the megamalls. A third well-known cinema, the Siam Theatre, burned down in 2010 during the red-shirt protests.

To the east, at the huge intersection between Rama I and Phayathai Road, is MBK, perhaps the best-known mall in Bangkok. MBK, which stands for 'Mahboonkrong', is pretty rough around the edges these days, though therein lies the appeal. Combining the feel of a Thai street market with the indoor mall experience, MBK remains a staple of tourist itineraries. It's full of tat, of course, but its IT floor remains

One of Bangkok's best-known shopping malls, MBK combines the feel of a Thai market with the air-conditioned mall experience you'll likely come to appreciate.

Legendary adventurer Jim Thompson disappeared in strange circumstances in 1967, but his exquisite teak house and art collection remain.

the place to pick up a second-hand phone and its vast food court includes some legendary stalls.

Close to MBK is the Jim Thompson House, the old home of the American businessman of the same name. Thompson is something of a Southeast Asian legend, following his mysterious disappearance in Malaysia's Cameron Highlands in 1967. Thompson revitalised Thailand's silk industry, founding the Thai Silk Company in 1948. In the 1950s and 60s, Thompson collected several old teak homes from around the country and had them rebuilt on one site beside the Saen Saep canal. Today, the beautiful buildings serve as a museum displaying Thompson's extensive collection of Asian art.

To the southeast of Pathum Wan is the 142-acre Lumphini Park, one of Bangkok's highlights. Built in 1925 by King Vajiravudh, the park features an artificial lake, pathways and playgrounds. In the morning it throngs with joggers and tai chi classes; in the evenings the aerobics crowd get their turn. Lumphini is named after the birthplace of the Buddha, and that's fitting: the park is a much needed space for quiet reflection in this city of endless chaos.

In its own way Lumphini has served as a source for its own brand of turmoil. In 2005–6, it was where PAD leader Sondhi Limthongkul first started whipping up his yellow storm of protest against Thaksin Shinawatra. It's remained the yellow shirts' protest ground of choice ever since.

Ratchathewi

North of Pathum Wan is the district of Ratchathewi, named after one of King Chulalongkorn's royal consorts. Phra Nangchao Sukhumalmarsri Phra Ratchathewi, as her name and title went, was the great-grandmother of MR Sukhumbhand Paribatra, the current governor of Bangkok. In the southern part of the district, to the north of Khlong Saen Saep, is the area known as Pratunam ('Water Door'), named for the gate used to control water levels on the canal.

Like nearby Pathum Wan, the focus in Pratunam is shopping, though things are a lot more rough and ready. Pratunam Market is a large, scrappy clothes emporium attracting traders from around the world. In particular, the zone around Baiyoke Tower II, Thailand's tallest building, is probably the most diverse part of Bangkok. Its motley cosmopolitanism makes it worth a visit, if only for the people-watching.

On Phetchaburi Road itself are more malls, including Platinum, an enormous warren of budget boutiques. Foodies know the area for Khao Man Kai Pratunam, probably the city's most famous Hainanese chicken rice stall. But IT mall Pantip Plaza is the stretch's most notorious emporium. It's a veritable cathedral of copyright theft, and as such attracts busloads of tourists. Despite Hollywood's best efforts, Pantip is still going strong as the city's premier knock-off destination. (There's legit gear to be had, too.)

In the northern part of Ratchathewi is Victory Monument, a phallic commemoration of the Thai victory in the Franco-Thai war erected by Phibun in 1941. Today Victory Monument is best known as a transport hub. It's served by one of the city's busiest BTS stations, which connects commuters to minibus services that take them north of the city. To the south of the monument, on the east side of Phaya Thai Road, is Soi

Rangnam, a residential street boasting a number of good restaurants and popular with foreigners. Overlooking the BTS station on the corner of Rangnam is the Skytrain Jazz Club, a reliably fun place to get a sundowner – if you can be bothered to climb the endless flights of steps.

Sukhumvit

It's no coincidence that Thailand's most famous road happens to include what is arguably the most nakedly commercial strip of land in Thailand. It's on Sukhumvit Road – and its Rama I and Phloenchit incarnations – that the city takes the business of squeezing baht from its visitors most seriously. For many foreigners, Sukhumvit *is* Bangkok.

A century ago the road was little more than a muddy trail extending across an irrigated agricultural plain. Khlong Saen Saeb, running parallel to the north, was the area's main thoroughfare. Smaller *khlong* and irrigation channels criss-crossed the route. In 1782, Rama I, then General Chakri, returned to Thonburi down this road from Cambodia to take the Siamese throne from Taksin and found Bangkok.

In the first half of the 20th century, Sukhumvit became fashionable among the aristocratic and commercial elite,

Huge parts of Bangkok are occupied by slum dwellings, many of which line the city's waterways.

who built spacious homes in the area. In 1950, the road was paved and widened into a highway extending all the way to Trat, following a coastal route through Pattaya and Thailand's eastern seaboard. It was named after Phra Pisansukhumvit, the chief engineer of the project.

Over the 20th century the *khlong* that crossed Sukhumvit were gradually filled and replaced with *soi*, though some of these canals lasted into the 1960s. It's this mode of development that explains the impractical 'design' of this part of the city. Sukhumvit's connections to Phetchaburi and Rama IV, the major roads to the north and south, are nowhere near adequate. The narrow connecting *soi* are often painfully choked with traffic. It's all because the network still to this day mirrors the old *khlong* network.

Rows of shophouses came to line the roads. The Condominium Act in 1979 also changed the character of the area. From the 1980s, luxury condominium blocks began to appear, increasingly housing foreigners doing business in the region. Sukhumvit began to be thought of as the city's foreign ghetto. Much of the land along the road is owned by Thai-Indian families, and the trendy bars and restaurants of the area almost always host at least one table of affluent Sikhs.

Lower Sukhumvit, which turns into Phloenchit Road at the Chalerm Mahanakorn Expressway and extends to Asok intersection, boasts a curious demographic makeup. It serves in part as the centre of the low-rent foreign-oriented sex industry. It's also the base for the city's Middle Eastern community, many of whom come to the city for treatment at Bamrungrad, the luxury hospital on Soi 1. Thus the streets of the area throng with a curious combination of libidinous vacation men, working girls and Arab families. Lord knows what the latter say when the children enquire about the tables brazenly laden with erectile dysfunction tablets, dildos and plastic vaginas.

In particular, Soi 4 (South Nana) is a rancid eye-opener of a road, and thus, like Khao San, an excellent spot for people-watching. Here, the local fauna is a motley mix of hookers (many surgically enhanced, others surgically diminished), beggars, drunks, vacationing single men, more Middle Easterners and the occasional European family with kids in tow, no doubt cursing the travel agent who booked them into one of the local hotels.

Soi 3 (Soi Nana) and its smaller neighbour, Soi 3/1, are very different. This is Bangkok's Islamic quarter. Soi 3 is now lined with Middle Eastern and African restaurants. The Grace Hotel, an emblematic establishment from the Vietnam R&R era, fell into disrepair in the 1980s but was bought by a Saudi investor and now serves an Arab clientele to great success. The smaller, parallel Soi 3/1 – referred to by some locals with a striking lack of political correctness as 'Soi Bin Laden' – is lined with Middle Eastern restaurants, complete with patrons sipping mint tea and blowing shisha smoke into the balmy air.

Many of Thailand's richest families still own properties along Sukhumvit's *soi*, which turn more genteel as you move away from the main drag. And there remains at least one quiet public spot: Chuvit Garden. It was here that the troubles of Chuvit Kamolvisit, the famous massage-parlour-owner-turned-politician, really began, after he was arrested for having the area the park stands on cleared by a mob of hired goons (*see page 301*).

Asok is a busy hub, coming at the intersection between Sukhumvit and the monstrous Ratchadaphisek ring road. It's also where the BTS Sukhumvit line and MRT meet. The intersection itself is now serviced by another megamall, Terminal 21.

Things get classier on Upper Sukhumvit, east of the junction. The neighbourhoods of Phrom Phong, Thonglor and Ekkamai, are home to large numbers of *farang* expats, Japanese and wealthy Thais. As a result, Upper Sukhumvit is where much of the city's best foreign cuisine can be found. The Thai food, particularly the street food, tends to be overpriced and underwhelming.

Soi Thonglor, Sukhumvit 55, has earned the nickname the 'Beverly Hills of Bangkok', owing to the fabulous wealth concentrated in the area. It might not match the glitz of the LA suburb, and the main drag isn't exactly glamorous, but the lanes extending off the road are where many of Bangkok's celebrities and super-rich choose to live. Together with the equally exclusive Soi Ekkamai, the area is also the city's high-end party district.

Khlong Toei

The vast port-side slum of Khlong Toei, named for a canal long since filled, is easy to miss. Almost hidden from view from the roads that surround it, the sheer size of the slum is impossible to gauge – it's almost hidden from view. In fact, it's home to around 100,000 people. When the port opened after the Second World War, stevedores and their families settled in the area.

The growth of Sukhumvit to the north fuelled growth of the slum further. Many of its residents come from the Northeast of Thailand, drawn by the promise of jobs. The cheap thrills of Bangkok's premier tourist draw keep them in work. There's huge poverty in the area, together with its attendant demons: drugs, prostitution, alcoholism, gambling, debt and violence. Khlong Toei is thus, in a certain sense, Sukhumvit's dirty little secret.

The slum itself is not a monolithic mass, but several connected communities in varying states of disrepair. Some of the buildings are unremarkable shophouses; others are shacks cobbled together from whatever their residents could find – shipping containers, pig pens and all. Much of the slum stands mostly on Port Authority land, and the residents have no legal rights to live there. Those who want to stay are frequently evicted from their homes.

The slum is also home to many of the city's pig slaughterhouses, staffed entirely by Christians. Thai Buddhists who love pork don't want the *bap* (bad karma) earned from killing animals. Khlong Toei wet market, meanwhile, is the largest fresh market in the city, and probably supplies a good portion of the food you'll eat while living here. Khlong Toei is also one of the city's 50 districts, including the area south of Sukhumvit Road between the Chalerm Mahanakorn Highway and Soi 52.

North Bangkok

Phahonyothin Road is named after Phot Phahonyothin, the second prime minister of Thailand and one of the leaders of the 1932 coup that ended absolute monarchy. The road begins at Victory Monument and is covered by a Skytrain line up to BTS Mo Chit, the Sukhumvit Line's current terminal station. The road is one of Thailand's four major highways and takes traffic north, all the way to the Burmese border in Chiang Rai.

Phahonyothin Soi 7 is known as Soi Ari, a pleasant residential area popular with expats. With its street-side food stalls, it nevertheless retains a Thai feel. Ari used to be known for its low-rise suburban feel and the area resisted the encroachment of large condo blocks until relatively recently. The decisive change was the recent construction of Noble Reflex, a monstrous grey carbuncle that towers ominously over the neighbourhood like some kind of terrestrial Deathstar. (Disclosure: This book was mostly written from one of the apartments in said monstrosity.)

Heading north on Phahonyothin takes you through the Saphan Khwai neighbourhood and on to Chatuchak district,

The gargantuan Chatuchak Weekend Market is the place to go to find bargains – so long as you don't mind the crowds and the heat.

with its most famous attraction, Chatuchak Weekend Market, supposedly the world's largest of its kind. With at least 15,000 stalls, you can find practically anything here, at rock-bottom prices. Next to the market are three conjoined parks: Chatuchak Park, Queen Sirikit Park and Suan Rot Fai Park.

Heading North eventually takes you to the sprawling suburbia of Don Muang district, home of Bangkok's second airport. After Suvarnabhumi opened in 2005, Don Muang was closed for a time before reopening in 2007 as the city's low-cost airline airport.

To the east of Chatuchak district is Ladphrao district, a huge middle-class residential neighbourhood serviced by Ladphrao Road and intricate networks of small *soi*. The traffic here is terrible, as is the flooding. Almost completely Thai, it's a great place to go for Thai cuisine. Chok Chai 4 night market is one of Bangkok's best-kept secrets for excellent street food.

PEOPLE

AN OLD SAYING CLAIMED, 'If you throw a stone in Siam, you will either hit a prince, a monk, or a dog.' If you throw a stone in 21st-century Bangkok, there's no telling who you'll hit. The princes, monks and dogs are all still here, of course, but the population of the city gets more diverse by the year. Khon Kaen *som tam* vendor, Ugandan clothes merchant, Malay-Muslim Ramkhamhaeng student, Japanese salaryman, Thai-Indian nightclub owner, Mon construction worker, Sino-Thai investment banker, English writer – all can be found living and working in Bangkok.

Almost a quarter of the kingdom's population – 14.6 million souls – live within the Bangkok Metropolitan Region, which includes the five adjacent provinces of Nakhon Pathom, Pathum Thani, Nonthaburi, Samut Prakan and Samut Sakhon. The 2010 census estimated the population of Bangkok province at 8.3 million, though only 5.7 million of that number were registered residents of the city. The remaining 2.6 million were Thais from other parts of the kingdom and foreigners. The real population is probably larger than this, but illegal migrants don't tend to talk to census-takers.

Thailand is said to consist of four regions: Centre, North, Northeast and South. Most of Bangkok's Thai migrants are from the poor Northeast, better known as Isarn. This huge, mostly flat expanse is Thailand's rice-growing heartland, and the most populous of the four regions. Migrants from its sleepy farming villages head to the capital each year to work in the service industries, drive taxis and build the fabric of the city. Many divide their time between home and the capital, heading back to the rice fields when help is needed for the harvest.

The city's slums, including the vast port-side conurbation of Khlong Toei, are a testament to its economic magnetism. Easily dismissed as tragedies, they're equally places of opportunity, where the poor can live in proximity to the jobs they need. Yet Bangkok is also where the money is, and the home of the wealthiest Thais. According to the National Statistics Office, in 2007 the average monthly household income in Thailand as a whole was THB 18,296. The figure for Bangkok was almost twice that, at THB 34,514. As a result, Bangkokians are more likely to have been educated abroad or to have travelled overseas, and to have gained exposure to foreign ways of thinking.

A Thai travel agent I knew in Chiang Mai many years ago once told me: 'Bangkok is not Thailand. The real Thailand is here in Chiang Mai.' At the time, not knowing much about the country, all I could do is nod. Surely, I thought, the real

Eating is as close to the Thai heart as activities get, and Bangkok is a fabulous place to do it.

Thailand was not to be found in that vast, traffic-clogged metropolis.

A Bangkokian might well have it the other way: only in the city of the palaces, of the Thai court, can you find real Thai culture. There's a tendency for the city's natives to see themselves as sitting at the pinnacle of Thai society, and to view provincial Thais as yokels. In his memoir *Bangkok Found*, Alex Kerr quotes Professor Vithi Phanichphant, an expert on Thai culture: 'Bangkok people basically see all the others as hill tribes. Above Nakhon Sawan is Lao. Below Nakhon Sri Thammarat is Khaek (Muslim). Beyond Prachinburi is Khmer.' Anyone who has lived in the capital will know there is more than a little truth in this. Bangkokians, like Londoners, New Yorkers and Parisians, can be a haughty bunch.

MINORITIES

You only need gaze at the Thonburi riverfront from royal Rattanakosin to see evidence of the long history of immigrant communities in Siamese capitals. In *Reading Bangkok*, Ross King notes that from south to north an informed observer can make out the Gong Wu Chinese shrine, the Kuwa Til-Islam Mosque, the Santa Cruz Portuguese school and church, and Wat Arun, with its towering Khmer-style *prang,* Hindu iconography and Chinese decoration. The capital may have crossed the river since Thonburi's day, but that cosmopolitan character remains.

The Thai state has pushed the idea that Thailand is a homogeneous nation, but Thais – and particularly Bangkokians – are of much more mixed lineage than official dogma suggests. Mon and Khmer people lived in Siam long before any Tai set eyes on the Chao Phraya. Their blood and cultural influence lingers.

And Bangkok has always gathered migrants. Ban Yuan in Samsen is the home of the city's Vietnamese community, and has been since the Rama III era (1824–1851), when Christian refugees poured into Siam to escape the wars between Vietnam and Cambodia. Makassarese, from Sulawesi in Indonesia, had fled to Ayutthaya in the 17th century when their kingdom was annexed by the Dutch. When Bangkok became the capital, they based themselves in the area still known today as Makkasan.

Not all migrants came by choice. From the founding of the city in 1782, Rama I and his Chakri successors began deposing local rulers in surrounding states, taking control of territory running from the Malay peninsula to the northern reaches of Chiang Rai. Some of the conquered people would then be transported to Bangkok as slaves and made to carry out public works such as digging canals. After a certain period of bondage, they were allowed to establish communities.

Hence the origin of many of the city's Thai-Muslim neighbourhoods. The Muslim population of Bangkok is estimated at anything from 260,000 to more than half a million, with at least 165 mosques. Their communities are often located beside canals, or roads that were built upon them. One of the most famous canals – or *khlong* as they're known in Thai – is Saen Saeb, which slices through Sukhumvit Road's northern, odd-numbered *soi* and still serves as a thoroughfare for river taxis today. It was dug during the Rama III period by Malay-Muslim prisoners of war, and their descendants still live along its banks. (The use of Muslim slave labour to construct Bangkok's canals still features in anti-Siamese propaganda in the Deep South to this day.)

Chinese

Bangkok, it could be argued, is not a Thai city. Its essence is captured more aptly as 'Sino-Thai'. In this respect, the capital has more in common with the Chinese towns of the Thai South, places like Phuket Town, Hat Yai and Trang, than much of the Thai hinterland. It was Thai-Chinese property developers who built the endless terraces of shophouses that line so many of the city's roads. It's Sino-Thai businesses that provide the main thrust behind the economy. And while the Chinese have assimilated with the indigenous population better in Thailand than in any other country in the region, it's possible to discern differences between them and their

Bangkok's Chinatown is centred around Yaowarat Road and Charoen Krung Road.

countrymen. They are likely to be more driven by the Confucian values of filial piety, diligence and thrift.

It's believed that more than half of Bangkok-born Thais have at least some Chinese ancestry, while around 10 per cent identify as Sino-Thai. A Who's Who of Thailand would be dominated by Sino-Thais. Recent prime ministers Yingluck Shinawatra, Abhisit Vejjajiva, Samak Sundaravej, Thaksin Shinawatra, Chuan Leekpai, Chavalit Yongchaiyudh and Banharn Silpa-archa are all of Chinese descent. So too are the Chearavanonts, Chirathivats and Sirivadhanabhakdis, listed by *Forbes Asia* magazine as the richest families in Thailand. Even HM the King has some Chinese blood.

The Chinese have long served as Siam's commercial class, though they weren't always so politically influential. A Chinese merchant community was already living on Rattanakosin when Rama I moved his capital there in 1782. They were displaced to Sampheng, which remains the city's Chinese quarter today. The ancestors of most Sino-Thais came to the country in the 19th and early 20th centuries to escape poverty and ethnic strife in China. More than half of the Sino-Thai population trace their ancestry to Chaozhou (in Guangdong province), better known as Teochew. It's been claimed that these migrants were so influential that the Bangkok accent is inflected by the sounds of Teochew. Many Sino-Thais also identify as Cantonese, Hakka, Hokkien and Hainanese.

As you might expect of a disproportionately wealthy ethnic minority, the Chinese haven't always been well-accepted in Thailand. While early immigrants were usually men who found native wives, by the 20th century female immigrants were arriving too, and assimilation slowed. There were at least a couple of periods in the past century when anti-Chinese sentiment boiled over. King Vajiravudh (Rama VI) once denounced them as the 'Jews of Southeast Asia' in a vitriolic essay, despite himself being partly of Chinese lineage.

Later, the dictator Phibunsongkhram tried to reduce Chinese influence in the country, restricting immigration and changing the name of the country to Thailand, partly a heavy-handed attempt to emphasise that the country was Thai, not Chinese.

Even *phad Thai*, reportedly invented by Phibunsongkhram's household and promoted by the strongman as the country's national dish, was a Thai appropriation of something quintessentially Chinese: the noodle.

Today, the Chinese population of Thailand is almost uniquely assimilated, and those less tolerant times mostly forgotten. Sino-Thais have adopted Thai customs in a way that never happened in neighbouring countries like Malaysia. They celebrate Songkran and Loy Krathong, while giving their children *ang pao* (red packets) at Chinese New Year and worshipping their ancestors. Many also observe the annual Vegetarian Festival in October, in which they refrain from eating meat, drinking alcohol and having sex for nine days (in theory, at least). The Thai-Chinese of today still know of their origins, of course, but identify first and foremost as Thai.

Indians

The Indian influence on Thai culture has deep roots. It was Indian traders, among others, who spread Buddhism to Southeast Asia. The ancient Indian language of Pali still serves as the liturgical language of Thai Buddhism, while the Thai language itself is full of Sanskrit derivations. The rites practised in the Thai court are derived from Hinduism, or more precisely, Brahmanism, and were adapted from the practices of the Khmer monarchy.

Today, the Indian community is centred on Pahurat, to the east of Chinatown, though Thai-Indians can be found living all over the city. They are, in the main, a wealthy sub-community, with a long history of involvement in trade. Much of the hyper-valuable land around Sukhumvit Road is owned by Thai-Indian families. The most famous of these landowners was A.E. Nana, a turn-of-the-20th-century Indian-Muslim merchant and developer (*see sidebar*).

Thais often refer to Indians and other South Asians as '*khaek*', which literally means 'guest'. While not exactly insulting, Thai-Indians tend to consider this pejorative – those who were born in Thailand object to the implication that they aren't permanently welcome in their own country.

A.E. Nana

Ahmed Ebrahim Nana was an Indian-Muslim commodities trader who lived in Bangkok at the turn of the 20th century. Taking the helm of his family's firm in 1890, Nana led the business as it moved its rice and opium trading business from Ayutthaya to Bangkok's Pahurat and Sampheng districts, today's Chinatown.

Through an uncanny ability to secure debt financing, Nana was able to move into property development, competing with rich Chinese and the Thai aristocracy. As Ross King explains in *Reading Bangkok*, Nana's success owed something to the fact that he was a British subject. This gave him treaty protection and access to British consular services, though being Indian he was spared the suspicions normally held of Westerners.

By the time of his death in 1934, Nana had acquired vast plots of land along what is now Sukhumvit Road. By repute, the whole road was almost named after him, though he 'politely declined' and it was instead named after Phra Bisal Sukhumvit, the first Thai graduate of the Massachusetts Institute of Technology and the man who supervised its construction. Still, Sois 3 and 4 did become Soi Nana and Nana Tai respectively and thus his surname eventually became shorthand for the stretch of Sukhumvit ranging from those soi up to at least Soi 11.

These days, of course, Nana is ground zero for Bangkok's low-rent foreign-oriented sex industry. Thus, Nana's name has become world famous, the area bearing his name a centre of libidinous pilgrimage for scores of ageing debauchees from across the globe. One can only imagine what he would make of it all.

Starting out as a restaurant and shopping hub, Nana Plaza morphed into a sex emporium in the 1980s.

Other foreigners

Foreigners have been living in Bangkok since the founding of the city, and their influence on its development is more significant than proud Thai official history tends to acknowledge. To take just one example, the aristocratic Bunnag family are descendants of Sheikh Ahmad, a Persian merchant who established himself in Ayutthaya around 1600. By the time of Chulalongkorn's coronation, in 1868, they were in almost complete control of Siam.

Some of the city's most important institutions were founded by Westerners. Henry Alabaster, a British diplomat who arrived in Siam in 1857, became an advisor to King Chulalongkorn and founded the country's post office and first national museum at the Grand Palace. He also supervised the building of Charoen Krung, the country's first paved road. The country's stock exchange was founded by William Bird, an army colonel and Office of Strategic Services (OSS) man from Philadelphia.

An Italian sculptor, Corrado Feroci, was responsible for some of the city's best known statues and reliefs, including those at Democracy Monument and Victory Monument. Feroci changed his name to Silpa Bhirasi and became a Thai national in 1944, before founding Silpakorn University, the country's premier arts education institution. Meanwhile, the *Bangkok Post* was founded in 1946 by ex-OSS officer Alexander MacDonald. Visit its offices in Khlong Toei today and the portraits of its earliest editors seem to tell a story: a parade of white American men with the wily faces of spooks.

Most of the foreigners you'll see in central Bangkok are tourists – 13.8 million visited the city in 2011, according to the Tourism and Sports Ministry. But hundreds of thousands more live and work in the Thai capital. The 2010 census counted about 82,000 Japanese, 56,000 Chinese, 117,000 other Asians, 48,000 Europeans, 23,000 from the Americas, 5,000 Australians and 3,000 Africans. Those figures don't include workers from Thailand's poorer neighbours, who come to the city to do the low-paid work few Thais want to do. Of them, 304,000 are Burmese, 63,000 are Cambodian and 18,000 Lao. Many are here illegally. If you're wondering why that Sukhumvit DVD vendor speaks Thai with an odd accent ('*ha si bah*'), it's because he's from Karen State.

The lexicon of immigration is loaded the world over: 'expats' are rich, 'immigrants' less so, 'migrants' worse off still. This is certainly true of Thailand. While most foreigners are referred to politely as '*tang chat*' ('different nation'), people from Burma, Cambodia and Laos have a special term, '*tang dao*' ('different land'), reserved for them. It's tempting to wonder if this implies a certain yearning for the days when the latter two were Siamese vassals, not nations in their own right. This may be a fine linguistic point, but it certainly reflects the reality that these migrants receive very different treatment compared to visitors from more affluent parts of the world.

'Expats' can be found in every neighbourhood of the city in varying concentrations, though Sukhumvit Road, from Phloenchit up to Ekkamai, is undoubtedly the 'expat zone'. There's a long and rather boring debate to be had over who qualifies as an 'expat', rather than a 'tourist'. Many foreigners only spend part of the year in Thailand, sweating out the

Sukhumvit Soi 3/1 is the centre of the city's Middle Eastern community. Head here when kebab cravings strike.

balmy 'winter' months in Bangkok to escape the biting cold of their home countries.

Communities have staked out sections of the Sukhumvit ghetto for themselves. The Nana area may house the sex industry, but it's also the centre of Bangkok's Middle Eastern population. Soi 3/1 is the place to go to enjoy shawarma, houmous or a good toke on a hookah pipe. Sukhumvit Plaza, close to Soi 12, is the city's Koreatown, while the area from Phrom Phong to Ekkamai is where the city's Japanese community can be found. Westerners seem to spread themselves across the stretch.

VALUES AND BELIEFS

Family

The family is where Thais learn duty, obedience and consideration for others. It's a source of identity and serves as a model for other kinds of relationship in wider society. Thais refer to each other, even total strangers, by familial names: *phi* (older sibling), *nong* (younger sibling), *lung* (uncle), *pa* (auntie) and many more. The king and queen are styled as the father and mother of the nation, and their birthdays double as Father's and Mother's Day.

In the Anglo-Saxon West, the young may continue to live with their parents through their twenties, though it's regarded as something slightly shameful – like a World of Warcraft habit or not being able to drive. In Thailand, young people frequently live with their parents until they're married. This is particularly true in Bangkok, since there's little incentive to move away from home when you already live where all the jobs are.

The mother, in particular, occupies an exalted position in Thai thinking as a symbol of pure moral goodness. Young Thai children tend to be pampered and taught to depend on their parents, whom they develop a powerful sense of duty towards. Parents' love should be unconditional, of course, though children are expected to repay them in later life. To fail to do so is a grave sin.

Most Thais find the idea of letting their parents spend

their last years in a nursing home abhorrent, though such institutions do exist. Pensions, too, are a relatively alien concept. Many Thais save for retirement, of course, but it's nevertheless expected that their children will ensure they're taken care of in their dotage. Parents in the West can feel uncomfortable at having to be looked after by their own children. That's not considered a shameful thing in Thailand – merely a return of *bunkhun* (kindness).

Actions taken for the benefit of the family are easy to justify. 'I did it for my children,' is a reason every Thai can understand. There is a relatively high tolerance for corruption in business and public life in Thailand. The mafia godfather, the corrupt bureaucrat, the rich man who buys his criminal son's freedom – these figures are not celebrated, but their behaviour is well understood.

It goes without saying that showing a lack of interest or respect towards your own parents will not impress your Thai friends or partner. It's polite to show interest in their families, too – and always a good source of chit-chat. Remember, if you marry a Thai person, you aren't just marrying them, you're marrying their family. You may be expected to help them out financially, especially if you're significantly wealthier than they are. Refusal to do so could put a strain on your relationship.

Hierarchy

In the minds of the Thai, no two Thais are equal. From the poorest farmer to the king himself, every Thai has his or her place on the ladder: below one person, above another. In this sense, Thai society is more a tower than a pyramid. Thais can instinctively size up their peers to decide whether to show them deference, or to expect it. The calculus involved in this evaluation is, for the *farang*, very difficult to learn. Certainly, wealth and age count, as well as hazier factors: prestige, spiritual advancement, family name.

From a Thai perspective, this isn't something to lament, just the natural order of things. As Niels Mulder explains in *Inside Thai Society*, within the family or close community, hierarchy is merely 'the recognition of wisdom, leadership, benevolence and relative age'. In wider society, it's an acknowledgement of something that holds sway in all civilisations: the uneven distribution of power. In this way, perhaps, Thai society is more honest than some others.

Hierarchy is at work everywhere: in language; in the position of the hands and the head in a *wai* (*see page 134*); in who dishes out the rice at dinner time (the least senior) and who picks up the tab (the most senior); in the quiet consent of young employees when a senior colleague makes a questionable proposal. It's least apparent, perhaps withering to nothing, when younger Thais get together with their friends. They may still call each other '*phi*' and '*nong*', but close friends will socialise more or less as equals – and share the tab.

Patron-client relationships remain crucial to the functioning of Thai society. Those of lower status may perform services for a more powerful patron, and give him or her their loyalty. In return, the patron provides support to the client, in the form of influence, protection or money. At elections, such relationships are at their most visible, as politicians dole out money and promises of future largesse or support to citizens in exchange for votes. (This is less the case in Bangkok, where people are less likely to know the politicians in their districts, than in provincial Thailand.)

Hand in hand with this hierarchical view of the world comes the feeling Thais call '*kreng jai*'. There's no easy way to translate *kreng jai* into English – foreigners familiar with the concept tend to use the Thai term. A simple rendering might be 'consideration for superiors'. Essentially, *kreng jai* means thinking about the feelings and convenience of your 'betters' and adjusting your behaviour accordingly. Thus, a mechanic fixing your air-conditioning might refuse to ask you for a glass of water, despite being thirsty. A junior colleague might keep his need to use the bathroom to himself, rather than asking you to stop the car. In both cases, the subject is putting your needs ahead of his own, because he feels *kreng jai* towards you. You can always protest – '*mai tong kreng jai na*' ('you don't have to feel *kreng jai*') – but words don't always trump deep-seated feelings.

At the same time, *kreng jai* is a two-way street. A 'superior' can be criticised for not fulfilling her side of the relationship, too. While Thais are expected to feel *kreng jai* to their 'betters', their 'betters' are expected to treat them with a degree of respect, and to offer them the protection and patronage that their position allows.

Sakdina

For hundreds of years Siam was governed by a system referred to today as '*sakdina*', meaning 'power of rice fields'. Under the system, which was codified by King Trailok in 15th-century Ayutthaya, every Thai was assigned a number according to his or her status in society. The number, measured in *rai* (a Thai unit of area), may have originally referred to the rice fields each person was permitted to farm. Over time it lost this association, since every member of society was eventually incorporated into the scheme: monks, women, slaves and all.

The king, having dominion over everyone and everything in his kingdom, had infinite *sakdina*. The heir to the throne had 100,000 *rai,* while high ministers of state might have 10,000. All Thais with *sakdina* of less than 400 *rai* – the vast majority of the population – were either slaves (*that*) or commoners (*phrai*). Even the *phrai* usually had to spend six months of the year doing corvée labour – working without pay – for the noble who ruled them.

The system was intended to maintain social order by defining how people were to interact, including how they should address each other and how each person should bow. *Sakdina* also had legal consequences. In a court case, the testimony of someone with high *sakdina* outweighed that of someone of a lower rank. If a commoner committed an offence against a noble, he would be punished more severely than if it had been against someone with lower *sakdina*. At the same time, for some crimes, a person of higher *sakdina* would be punished more harshly than someone lower, since they were expected to live by 'higher' standards.

The system wasn't abolished until the reformist reign of King Chulalongkorn, Rama V, who ended corvée labour and slavery.

(continued overleaf)

But you don't have to look too deeply at Thai society to see that cultural vestiges of *sakdina* remain to this day. As we have seen, Thailand is still a very hierarchical society. The complex set of pronouns in the Thai language and different types of *wai* all speak to this sort of thinking (*see pages 93, 134 and 276*), and are direct descendants of *sakdina*.

In 2008, the People's Alliance for Democracy (PAD), known colloquially as the 'yellow shirts', called for a 'new politics' in which parliament would mostly be appointed. The rural masses, the PAD explained, lacked the political maturity to elect 'good' politicians. To some critics, this was nothing more than an 'old politics' – that of the *sakdina* system, in which some Thais' votes would count for more than others.

The PAD's red-shirted political opponents, the United Front for Democracy Against Dictatorship (UDD), later invoked the *sakdina* period themselves by claiming to be the *phrai* of the modern era. The Bangkok elite, by contrast, were like the oppressive feudal lords of the past, they claimed. Some observers noted that the red-shirt movement and their financial backers included their own fair share of 'lords' – albeit wearing '*phrai*' T-shirts – too.

Or consider the moral panics that occasionally erupt when, for example, it's found that university students are involved in informal prostitution to fund their studies. Commentators fret about the disintegrating morals of Thai youth; the students are usually humiliated and punished. And yet every night of the week, in the red-light zone of Patpong, young women from the poor Northeast perform acts far more degrading than anything these middle-class girls get up to. The moral panic, however, is absent. It is hard to avoid comparison to the days of *sakdina*, in which those of noble birth were punished more severely than the *phrai* for the same crime, since 'more' was expected of them.

Hi-so

Like '*farang*', '*sanuk*', '*soi*' and '*khlong*', the Thai expression '*hi-so*', short for 'high society', can become so familiar you forget it isn't standard English. In the loosest sense, you might translate it as 'posh'. A woman showing up to work looking particularly well-dressed might be met with calls of '*hi-so na!*' from her colleagues. Meanwhile, foreigners talk of '*hi-so* Thais', the immaculately dressed types that fill the slick bars and clubs of Thong Lor-Ekkamai, some, alas, displaying that brand of standoffishness that new wealth tends to bring.

As has been common for at least a century, the Thai elite continue to send their children to be educated abroad. Some attend boarding schools, generally in the US and UK. Others are educated in Thailand before being sent to Western universities, returning with the international finish and English fluency needed to land today's most sought-after jobs – no longer in the bureaucracies, but at international corporations. These Thais are completely fluent in English and Western customs. You don't need a cultural guide to learn how to interact with them.

But being genuinely *hi-so* – being a society type, in other words – is about more than being seen in the right bars, clubs and restaurants. It's remarkably easy to find yourself rubbing shoulders with the rich and famous in Bangkok; door staff are nervous about turning guests away, for fear of making someone important lose face.

Where the elite *really* want to be seen is the pages of the society press: publications like *Thailand Tatler*, *Prestige*, *Hi!* and the Hi-So Party website. The gatekeepers of *hi-so* are thus not doormen but the journalists and owners of such publications. 'You're not *hi-so* unless we say you are,' is the unwritten mantra. Perhaps most coveted of all is a listing in *Society*, *Tatler*'s annual run-down of Thailand's 500 top society people – a 'top-of-the-posh', if you like.

But as Naphalai Areesorn, editor of *Thailand Tatler*, says, these days it's harder than ever to decide who's *hi-so* and who isn't. And with this new emphasis on being seen – rather than being 'suitable' – society damsels can come out of nowhere. 'Nowadays you can have a person who suddenly bursts into society. You've never seen this person before. She's always very beautifully or extravagantly dressed so she draws attention. All the photographers flock to her and her picture's used in most of the publications – and all of a sudden she's become *hi-so*.'

Having said that, not just any riff-raff with cash to flash can find themselves in the society pages. 'To be *somebody*, you should also be a decent person, who does a lot of charity work, who's never been convicted,' adds Naphalai. 'You've got politicians who are very well off. Some of them we wouldn't include in *hi-so*.'

WHAT'S IN A NAME

You can know a Thai person for months, even years, without ever knowing their real name. All Thais are given nicknames, a tradition aimed at confusing the evil spirits believed to take an interest in harming newborns. In most settings, their nickname is the name they will go by. Even the king has one ('Lek', though referring to him as such is a no-no).

Some nicknames refer to size: 'Lek', 'Noi' and 'Jiw' all mean 'small'. Others are beastly: 'Mu' (Pig), 'Kop' (Frog), 'Mot' (Ant). Nicknames seem to get more outlandish by the year, as foreign languages and brand names are plundered for material: 'Donut', 'Bonus' and 'Benz' are recent favourites. In *Very Thai*, Philip Cornwel-Smith notes some even stranger specimens, taking in the confusing ('Yes') and the somewhat immodest ('God').

The existence of Thai nicknames is a relief, since real Thai names can be very long, and murder to pronounce. When written in the Roman alphabet, they're frequently subject to the Idiosyncratic System of Transcription (*see page 279*), which makes working out how they're supposed to sound nigh-on impossible. Charoen Sirivadhanabhakdi, anyone?

In the office, Thais will often use their nicknames but may also be referred to by their first names preceded by the word 'Khun' ('Mr' or 'Mrs'). 'Why is Khun Somsak so late today?' you might ask. This custom has been carried over to foreigners too: expect to be called 'Khun Dave' or even 'Mr Dave' in such settings.

Thai surnames are a relatively new phenomenon, and one that has never fully caught on. Only made a legal requirement in 1926 by King Vajiravudh, they were intended to aid bureaucracy as Siam modernised. Every family had to choose a unique name – or have one bestowed on them by the King. As a result, any two Thai people with the same surname are likely to be closely related. The Thai-Chinese tend to have the longest surnames, often featuring their old Chinese name as the first syllable. Hence the preponderance of names beginning with 'Wong' and 'Tan'. Media mogul and People's Alliance for Democracy (PAD) leader Sondhi Limthongkul's surname, for example, derives from the Hainanese name 'Lim'.

Descendants of aristocracy are easy to spot. The grandchildren of kings are considered royalty. More distant descendants become commoners, though they retain titles. The great-grandchildren of kings take the title 'Mom Rajawongse' and write the initials 'MR' before their name. MR Sukhumbhand Paribatra, the governor of Bangkok, is a great-grandson of Rama V. Great-great-grandchildren are called 'Mom Luang' and take the initials 'ML.' Lower descendants append 'Na Ayutthaya' to their surnames, while the descendants of aristocratic families from other parts of Thailand may have the surname 'Na [place]'. Deputy Prime Minister Kittirat Na Ranong, for example, is a member of the Na Ranong clan, who trace their ancestry to Khaw Soo Cheang, the first governor of the Andaman province.

Double standards

One day in July 2007, Kanpitak 'Mu Ham' Pachimsawat, the 18-year-old son of a millionaire businessman and a former Miss Thailand, crashed his Mercedes-Benz into a public bus in Bangkok. Mu Ham was angry. He got out of his car, then proceeded to smash a rock into the face of the offending bus driver. Not content with that, he got back in his Merc and drove it into a crowd of people waiting at a nearby bus stop. One woman was killed, seven others were injured.

Two years later, Mu Ham received a sentence of 10 years and one month in jail for manslaughter and attempted murder. He got bail immediately. In March 2013, that sentence was slashed to two years, suspended. The court agreed with the defence's argument that Mu Ham had a 'mental problem' that meant he couldn't be expected to control his temper. He never spent a night in prison.

(continued overleaf)

'One rule for the rich, another for everyone else,' is a common refrain in Thailand, usually expressed pithily in the phrase '*song matarathan*' ('double standards'). Nowhere is this more starkly obvious than in the legal system, in which money, status and personal connections matter. The wealthy never seem to go to jail, regardless of the strength of the evidence against them – or the public outrage at the injustice of it all.

You could fill a chapter with tales like that of the odious Mu Ham. We might point to the incident in 2001, when Duangchalerm Yoobamrung, son of the infamous politician Chalerm Yoobamrung, allegedly shot a police officer in the face in a crowded nightclub. Witnesses, of which there were scores, proved strangely reluctant to testify against him, and he was eventually acquitted.

More recent is the case of Vorayuth Yoovidhaya, grandson of Red Bull founder Chaleo Yoovidhaya, who killed a policeman in a hit-and-run accident in September 2012. He was allegedly driving his Ferrari at 170 kph at the time (and tested positive for alcohol and cocaine). That case is ongoing, though with Vorayuth out on bail and failing to show up to several indictments, it looks unlikely to go anywhere anytime soon.

Howl at the injustice of it all, but bear in mind that it's illegal to criticise Thailand's courts. As scholar David Streckfuss writes in *Truth on Trial in Thailand: Defamation, Treason, and Lese-Majeste*: 'The courts are a public body that cannot be criticised. Even legal experts are unclear about exactly what comments can be made concerning the courts. Court decisions examined in this study suggest that it may be illegal to say that the courts are unjust. This is not a moot question because a perceived insult can result in up to seven years' imprisonment.' Words to remember.

ON THE SURFACE

It was the night before an election and I was staying on Khao San Road. On such days the authorities ban sales of alcohol, fearing voters might be plied with drink and shepherded to voting stations by wily party canvassers. My friends and I, being disenfranchised foreigners, set out into the night in the hope of getting some 'refreshments', eventually finding a bar that was open. There were plenty of people inside, but not a single item of glassware to be seen. Instead, everyone was drinking from coffee mugs.

On the surface, the law wasn't being broken. The 'revellers' were merely enjoying hot, midnight beverages – as you do – and the police were doing their job. In Thailand, how things look on the surface is considered, in a sense, to be reality. So long as everything appears to be functioning smoothly, everyone is smiling and conflict is unseen, all is well. Appearances are everything.

In *Inside Thai Society*, Niels Mulder writes: 'A smile may indicate agreement, or self-confidence, but may also be a means to gently express one's opposition or doubt. A person on the defensive may smile, and one may smile when sad, or hurt, or even insulted.' The point is to keep smiling: to keep up appearances, to project the image that all is well – what lies beneath be damned.

Linked with this idea is the notion of 'face', a concern Thais share with most other Asian societies. Since appearances are a kind of reality, it's as important to *appear* successful as to *be* it. Hence the noticeable Bangkokian tendency towards conspicuous consumption and flaunting success.

A middle-class family might have an expensive German car, which everyone gets to see. (Making sure they do is worth spending a little extra time stuck in traffic.) Not everyone, however, will get to see the family's far more humble abode.

The number of expensive smartphones you see on the Skytrain might be surprising, given their cost and the average monthly income in Bangkok. But they're considered an investment worth making. And any given Starbucks will be full of people using expensive hi-tech gadgets. Frequently, those tablets aren't being used to read, write, or manage a business, but to play games. Even the expansive body art that covers some bargirls' backs is its own form of conspicuous consumption: tattoos aren't cheap.

'Don't think too much'
It's not uncommon to get this piece of advice from Thai friends or partners – that or the similar 'Don't be serious'. You may hear this when you make a social blunder, by acknowledging

a relationship conflict with someone, for example. More often, though, it's because you're simply being too analytical, trying to think your way through problems in a world which will always be characterised by change and suffering.

Thais are as aware as anyone that there are hidden mechanics below the surface of things. They're just less inclined than Westerners to try to uncover them. From a Buddhist perspective, the Western post-Enlightenment drive to understand how everything works is not the best use of energy. Chaos and complexity are a given. The truth cannot be known, except through the practice of meditation and eventual enlightenment. 'Don't think too much' might be impossible advice for some *farang* to follow. But ask a depressed person – it's not without merit.

Hot hearts and cool hearts

A Thai is expected to remain *jai yen* ('cool heart') no matter what life throws at him. To get flustered or angry is to lose face. It shatters the sheen of surface harmony that Thai society demands. A Buddhist is expected to follow the Middle Way (*see page 113*) and to respond to life's vagaries, whether good or bad, with equanimity – or to try to, at least.

Open conflict is to be avoided, for a number of reasons. Thai culture evolved from village life, where animism was used to explain a dangerous world. Human anger was believed to attract the anger of spirits. As Robert Cooper explains in *Culture Shock! Thailand*, when provoked the spirits could visit all sorts of misfortune on a village, whether 'floods, droughts, epidemics, or attacks by bandits'. The cooperation of the whole community was needed to solve such problems. Tolerating conflict meant the community was less able to protect itself, potentially with fatal consequences.

Of course, staying calm in all situations takes energy, and since burdening your friends with your deepest anxieties and frustrations isn't socially acceptable, pressure can build. Most Thais rarely lose their cool, but on occasions when they do, many don't go for half measures. The tabloids are filled with a daily litany of tragedies: perceived slights, affairs and other humiliations met with violence.

The Phra Sri Ratana Chedi, at the Temple of the Emerald Buddha in the Grand Palace, is said to house a piece of the Buddha's breast bone.

Lumphini Park is a rare oasis of green in the centre of Bangkok.

MBK Centre, close to the National Stadium BTS station, may not be the most upmarket mall in Bangkok, but is possibly the most famous.

Chatuchak Weekend Market, open only at – you guessed it – the weekend, is one of the largest weekend markets in the world, with more than 15,000 booths. It's a great place to pick up Thai handicrafts and cheap clothes, not to mention more outlandish products.

Men play *takraw* on a makeshift court. A foot to the head would normally be considered a grave insult, but the 'rules' are frequently waived for practical reasons.

Alcohol is frequently involved, and when booze comes into play, pretence can be dropped. Those who spend a lot of time in bars will eventually run into the spectre of the malevolent drunk who harasses those around him, looking for insult and an excuse for a fight. (The best way to deal with these situations is to be polite and respectful and wait for the man to leave.)

Martial flavour

There's an unmistakeable martial flavour to Thai society – at least when it comes of officialdom. Twice a day, at 8am and 6pm, the national anthem blasts from speakers in parks, schools, BTS stations and all kinds of public facilities. Loyal citizens are expected to stand at attention, and while no one says anything to oblivious tourists who keep moving, it's polite for foreigners to observe the custom too.

Since absolute monarchy ended in 1932, the Thai military has launched 18 coups and ruled the country for the majority of its recent history. The generals haven't been in charge

for some time (with the exception of the year following the coup that ousted Thaksin Shinawatra in 2006, a military government hasn't been in power since 1992), those decades under military rule have left their mark.

Cultural vestiges abound, particularly in the government bureaucracies. Bureaucrats pose for photographs in military regalia. Uniforms are everywhere. Even the security guards at malls and condominiums salute those they protect as they come in and out. (It is best to avoid succumbing to the temptation to turn your head and bark, 'At ease!')

Fashion and fads

If Charles Mackay came back from the dead to write a new edition of his 1841 classic, *Extraordinary Popular Delusions and the Madness of Crowds*, he'd find plenty of material in Bangkok. Take the opening of Thailand's first Krispy Kreme donut franchise at Siam Paragon in September 2010. Before the store had even opened, huge queues had formed that snaked out the doors of the shopping mall, doubling and tripling back on themselves. Weeks later it still took half an hour to reach the counter.

This being Bangkok, of course, a black market sprang up, with enterprising vendors buying up dozens of boxes of the donuts and selling them on the streets of the city at a profit. In the latter months of 2010, there was only one brand of cream-filled dough ball to be seen with, and that was Krispy Kreme.

Bangkokians are a faddish bunch, and keeping up with the zeitgeist is something of a citywide obsession. In the West, just as no self-respecting hipster would ever admit to being a hipster, the label 'trendy' carries a pejorative connotation: of being a little too concerned with the fickle vagaries of human taste, and thus lacking real character. To be 'trendy' is to lack authenticity.

In Bangkok, trendiness is something to aspire to openly, something to flaunt. Being up-to-date is as essential to one's image as success, wealth and beauty. Westerners are just as concerned with fads and fashion as Thais – they're just more likely to kid themselves that they aren't.

Advertisements for upmarket condominium blocks rarely fail to point out the development's fit with the audience's 'trendy lifestyle'. One project went further and simply named itself after the quality it aspired to be. Hence The Trendy Condominium on Sukhumvit 13, 'an ultra chic, super hip, multipurpose development comprising private homes, offices and a shopping plaza'.

If anything speaks of the Thai love of fashion, it might be this: the winter collections rolled out each year by the city's trendier clothes stores. Selling hooded tops, jackets and sweaters in a city where 'winter' temperatures rarely drop below 20 degrees is surely a feat of salesmanship of ice-to-eskimos proportions. Then again, the air-conditioning in some Bangkok establishments, as well as the meat-locker-on-rails commonly referred to as 'the Skytrain', can justify an extra layer.

Hitler chic

Find the odd one out: Superman, Batman, Captain America, the Incredible Hulk, Adolf Hitler. Got it? In July 2013, Thailand's top university, Chulalongkorn, was forced to issue an apology after some of its students erected a painted billboard on its campus showing the aforementioned 'superheroes'. Needless to say, the international media was more than a little incredulous that the Nazi leader had made it into this pantheon of *übermenschen*.

This wasn't the first time the media had picked up on 'inappropriate' uses of Nazi imagery in Thailand. Only a couple of weeks earlier there was another outcry when pictures surfaced on the web purporting to show a Bangkok restaurant called Hitler Fried Chicken, complete with logo showing the Führer dressed as Colonel Sanders. The restaurant turned out to have been in Ubon Ratchathani and had closed years earlier, but the incredulity at its crassness was real. In September 2011 a school in Chiang Mai held a 'Nazi parade', with school kids wearing meticulously replicated uniforms. Anyone who has lived in Thailand for a while will know that T-shirts with swastikas on them are far from an uncommon sight.

(continued overleaf)

What's going on? Firstly, these incidents seem to derive from a certain obliviousness to (Western) history, rather than a desire to offend. The holocaust still isn't taught on the Thai school curriculum. Nor, for that matter, is the Khmer Rouge genocide, which happened only a few hundred miles from Bangkok. History teaching in Thailand focuses on Thailand.

But here, too, is the Thai focus on the surface of things, rather than their deeper meaning. The meaning of the swastika, of goose-stepping SS troops, of Hitler himself, is left unprobed. What might the Nazi project resemble to someone who hasn't factored the piles of bodies into their calculus? A bunch of well-drilled soldiers in snappy uniforms, led by a leader with 'iconic' facial hair and represented by a distinctive symbol with Eastern origins. In short: imagery ripe for use in marketing or fancy-dress competitions.

Needless to say, not all Thais are ignorant of European history. After the outrage over the Hitler superhero mural, some Thais wrote on news-site comment sections asking why they *shouldn't* support the Nazis, or at least recognise their successes. The holocaust had been terrible, they admitted, but pointed out that Thailand itself had historically been bullied by the British and French empires. Why shouldn't Thais support Germany, then, when it took on the old imperialists? After all, their allies, the Japanese, had effectively ended European imperialism in Southeast Asia.

Is expecting a Southeast Asian nation to be respectful of Western sensitivity over the Holocaust a type of cultural imperialism? It's worth noting that these incidents of cross-cultural offence-taking go both ways. In January 2013, Thai Buddhists started a Facebook campaign against a Dutch company. They were angry after coming across Internet images of portable public toilets in Brunssum that had been decorated with the image of the Buddha. The Dutch embassy made the company aware of the campaign and the firm promptly withdrew the offending loos. Perhaps, then, what we're witnessing isn't cultural imperialism, but the steady homogenisation of world cultures, driven by communications technology – or more specifically, the Internet.

Techno joy

Queues for the newest iPhones rival those for the newest donut chains. In 2012, Bangkok overtook Jakarta as the world's No. 1 Facebook city, while the same year, Suvarnabhumi Airport and Siam Paragon took the top two spots in Instagram's list of the most photographed locations on the service worldwide. It's perhaps not surprising that of all Bangkok's landmarks, these particular sights placed highest. Think of the face-boosting implications of being seen flying abroad or shopping at one of the city's most upmarket malls. A society concerned with status is made for social media.

An openness to technology, a susceptibility to fads and a love of *sanuk* ('fun') make Thai cyberspace the ideal breeding ground for Internet memes, which spread like wildfire among the city's Facebook-addicted masses. In 2013, you had to look hard to find a company or government department that hadn't made a Harlem Shake video. The year before, it was Gangnam Style parodies, while 2011 was the year of planking (the act of being photographed lying face down in unusual settings, in case you're too old or too sensible to pay attention to such things).

This enthusiastic adoption of new technologies, fashions and fads speaks of a certain self-confidence, of the Thais' ability to absorb foreign influences without losing their souls. At least, that might apply to the people themselves. The society's supposed cultural guardians are less secure. Almost every new craze is accompanied by warnings from conservative corners about the erosion of 'Thai culture'. Indeed, disapproval of modernity is practically institutionalised in the form of the Ministry of Culture's dystopic-sounding Cultural Surveillance Centre.

Even planking fell foul of the bureaucrats' attentions after a fully robed monk was pictured taking part in the craze. Conservatives launched a counter-meme urging young people to photograph themselves sitting in the traditional Thai *'pubpeap'* stance, in which both legs are folded to one side of the body. The meme's Facebook page managed to gather an impressive quarter of a million likes. Still, it failed to capture young imaginations as much as the incomparably more silly, and thus *sanuk*, planking had.

White is beautiful

It would have escaped the attention of most of the tourists in MBK, but a few years ago I was taken aback by a banner ad for a whitening cream hanging in the main atrium. The slogan? '*Phio khao phio suai*': 'White skin is beautiful skin'. In much of the West, those words might be classed as hate speech. In Thailand, they're less an assertion of racial superiority, more a banal expression of something nearly everyone believes. The idea that white skin is more attractive than brown skin is depressingly prevalent – and accepted by people of all skin tones. 'I'm not beautiful; I'm black,' is a common refrain from pretty Thai women with the kind of golden complexions many Western women would kill for.

If you based your knowledge of Thailand entirely on Thai TV, you'd be forgiven for thinking the country was populated almost exclusively by lithe, beautiful Thai-Chinese and *luk khrueng* (Thai-Caucasians). Casting pays little attention to the presence – not to mention feelings – of the country's silent, dark majority. Browner Thais do surface on television now and again, mostly as baddies or 'the help' in *lakhon* (soap operas). Otherwise they're *jok* (comedians).

Pretties – attractive young women hired to promote products in shopping malls and exhibition centres – must not be dark. Anaemic is also the rule on the catwalk and lily-white faces smile from every magazine cover and roadside hoarding. If the models aren't white when the photograph is taken, they sure are after Photoshop has done its work.

Thus, in Bangkok, two types of weather bring out the brollies: rain and shine. Caught without umbrellas, young women scurry out of the blazing sun, handbags or magazines held aloft to block the rays. Pools and beaches are to be enjoyed fully covered, naturally. In 2011, *The Nation* reported that 14 per cent of Bangkokians suffered from sunlight deficiency – in one of the hottest cities in the world.

So if you're naturally brown? Get whiter, of course. The cosmetics industry gleefully encourages colour prejudice in advertising – and rakes in millions of dollars in sales of whitening products every year. In the skincare sections of convenience stores and pharmacies it can be hard to find a product that *doesn't* bleach you white: whitening soap, whitening shower gel, whitening deodorant… and that's just for the men. Women, of course, must go further. There are feminine products that bleach armpits and, yes, even the nether regions.

In dating, the playing field is uneven. You may see dark-skinned men with light-skinned society maidens. But the opposite is rare. The reality is that rich Thai men tend not to be interested in women with dark skin. Social-climbers too dark to mask their complexions with creams and powders often gravitate towards foreigners. This seems to suit most Westerners just fine.

The preference for lighter skin is hardly unique to Thailand – the same applies across Asia. Dark skin has long been the preserve of those who toil in the sun: of the farmer and the labourer. Lighter skin is associated with wealth, prestige and class. However, the ideal skin tone *has* become whiter over the past century. The Thai used to regard a 'golden' hue like that of the Burmese as the ideal. As the prestige of the northern, paler nations rose, both inside and outside Thailand, anaemic became the look of success.

The situation shows no sign of changing. The poor still work outdoors, whether they're hawking, labouring or riding motorcycle taxis. Bangkok society remains economically and politically dominated by Thai-Chinese. And while the cultural cachet of the West may be in decline, the rising nations of Asia also prize the pale. Thai teens obsess over Korean soaps and K-Pop. It's the *kimchi* look that many teenage girls aim for: doe eyes, bee-sting lips and, yes, lily-white skin.

Sanuk

Thailand wouldn't be Thailand without the Thai lust for *sanuk* ('fun'). All cultures dabble in this thing we call 'fun', of course, though some seem 'funner' than others, and Thais are among the most committed seekers of *sanuk* around. If it isn't fun – at least a little bit – it isn't worth doing.

Behind the temple fair, the silly movie, the underground lottery, there it is: *sanuk*. Perhaps, too, we see it in the 'cutesy' aesthetic evident in all sorts of unlikely corners of Thai culture – the cops sitting under giant toy-town police helmets at every other intersection, for example. At times, there are mass outbreaks of *sanuk*. At Songkran, it envelops the whole nation. The world boasts few countries in which almost every citizen would be willing to drop everything for a day – or 10 – to take part in a boisterous water fight. I couldn't see the English doing that – and not just because of the weather.

You don't celebrate Songkran, you play it (*'len Songkran'*). Indeed you play a lot of things in Thailand that are taken more seriously, at least linguistically, elsewhere. You don't *use* the Internet, you *play* it. You can *'doen len'* (to play walk; to amble), *'kin len'* (to play eat; to nibble) and *'phut len'* (to play speak, to joke), though this only goes so far. You don't, for example, *'len hong nam'* ('play toilet').

It's normal to ask someone if they find their job fun: *'tham ngan sanuk mai?'* It's usually expected to be – even if that simply means finding plenty of time over the course of the day for gossiping and group snacking. Political protests are expected to be *sanuk*, too: witness the political street games ('stamp on so-and-so's face!') and ribald speeches that characterise your average red-shirt 'shindig'. Even funerals can be *sanuk*. Once the monks are out the door, things rapidly turn into a party.

But for some foreigners, there is such a thing as too much fun. After years in Thailand all the *sanuk* can start to seem, well, *'mai sanuk'* ('not fun'). Many flee the country at Songkran. Others feel that all eight hours of a tour bus ride to Udon Thani need not be accompanied by loud *luk thung* karaoke music. And others – this writer among them – lament the selections of movies at the multiplex. Only the most *sanuk* – which frequently means daft – movies seem to make the major screens. Few Thais expect movies to offer serious depictions of life's tribulations; cinema is for escape, not analysis. 'Did you enjoy it, darling?' you might ask your girlfriend after forcing her to sit through *Requiem for a Dream*. 'No. It was *mai sanuk*,' might come the reply. Well, yeah.

Every city has its share of grafitti; Bangkok is no exception. This makeshift *takraw* park in the Ratchathewi area features some of the city's best pieces.

But *sanuk* is a more subtle phenomenon than many people give it credit for. Perhaps that's due to the difficulty of translating between languages as different as Thai and English. Imagine a nation obsessed by 'fun' and you might picture a country of happy-go-lucky buffoons who turn everything, from funeral to financial market, into a game. But the Thais could hardly have built their country into the flourishing 21st-century nation it is if they couldn't take skyscraper construction or air-traffic control seriously.

Instead, perhaps it's better to think of *sanuk* as meaning 'enjoyment' or 'satisfaction'. At heart, *sanuk* is about being happy with one's station in life – a Buddhist's way of seeing the world. Why be a slave to ruthless ambition? Content yourself with wringing enjoyment out of wherever your humble background has landed you. You might not choose, perhaps, to work as a maid – but since that's where you are, you may as well make the most of it. And make it as *sanuk* as you can. A phrase we should all take to heart might be K.I.S.S.: Keep It *Sanuk*, Stupid.

Money and luck

Take the Buddhist notion of karma (you get what's coming to you), add a certain devil-may-care attitude to future planning, throw in an unquenchable lust for *sanuk*, and what do you get? A nation of gambling-lovers. Gambling is illegal in Thailand, with the exception of the state lottery and horse-racing (the stock market seems to have avoided sanction too). That doesn't stop the proliferation of illegal gambling dens, which occasionally make the headlines when they are broken up by police. The six-digit state lottery ('*huai*'), meanwhile, is drawn on the 1st and 16th of every month. Ticket sellers are a common sight in Bangkok, either set up on stalls by the roadside or roaming the streets, wooden ticket cases around their necks.

But more popular still is the 'underground lottery', illegal as it is. Around one-third of Thailand's population is believed to play it, and for a simple reason: you have much higher chances of winning. The draw offers more gambling options than the government's lottery – players can, for example, bet on the last two or three digits of the state draw. Another popular draw is based on the last two digits of the figure the Stock Exchange of Thailand closes at.

It's a pretty serious business, and gamblers resort to all sorts of methods to try to divine winning numbers. The sacred, the strange, and even the tragic, are all believed to lead to fortune. There's a reason why newspapers report the licence plate numbers of cars involved in fatal accidents. The births of abnormal animals – pigs with two heads, five-legged buffalo – fill the pages of the newspapers. Numbers related to such happenings, such as the date of the creature's birth and the house number where it happened, are then gathered to glean winning combinations.

Indeed, numerology is something of a national pastime. Thais may share this fixation with the Chinese, though the digits thought lucky in Bangkok aren't necessarily the same as those sought after in Shanghai. In the Thai capital, it's all about the number 9, which has associations with religious and kingly ritual and a sonic resemblance to the word '*kao*', meaning 'progress'. Thus when it comes to telephone numbers, licence plates and other digit-bearing accessories, the more 9s the better. It's not uncommon to find Thais standing at the 7-Eleven counter, sifting through SIM card numbers for the best-looking digits. Where else but Thailand could a number be described as 'beautiful' (*boe suai*)?

SPIRITUAL BELIEFS

Buddhists and more

Buddhism brings colour to Bangkok – literally. Amid the drab expanses of blackened concrete that characterise much of the cityscape, the Buddhist temples, with their soaring golden roof finials and curved eaves in bright red, terracotta and green, are vibrant citadels of the spiritual in a sea of modernist grey. On the morning streets, as workers in muted office-wear stream by, the bright saffron robes of the monks on their alms runs seize the eye – a reminder that Bangkok has changed, and hasn't changed at all.

Around 95 per cent of the population of Thailand identify as 'Buddhist'. But Thai Buddhism is a hybrid creed. There are at least three components to Thai Buddhist belief: Theravada Buddhism, which arrived in Thailand from Sri Lanka; the Hindu rituals imported from Cambodia practised in the Thai court; and animism, the Tai practice of spirit worship which predates the former two by millennia.

Most readers will be familiar with the central tenets of Buddhism: that nothing in the world is permanent, that life is characterised by suffering, that suffering is caused by desire and can end only when desire is abandoned. Suffering does not end with death, because before long the self is reincarnated. How one is reincarnated is determined by karma – one's actions but, more importantly, the intention behind those actions. In Theravada Buddhism, emphasis is placed on the individual's own quest for self-liberation. In Mahayana Buddhism, practised in China, Japan and Tibet, among other places, there is more emphasis on helping others.

Buddhists aspire to following the Noble Eightfold Path, also known as the Middle Path or Middle Way – the Buddha's instruction manual on how to live, essentially. The eight components of the Middle Way, all including the word 'right', are the right view, right intention, right speech, right

Making it official

Perhaps surprisingly, Buddhism is not the official state religion of Thailand. While the king is required to be a Buddhist, the Thai constitution guarantees freedom of religion for all Thais, without prioritising the Buddhist faith. That doesn't sit well with some of the faithful, however, and there are frequent calls from some quarters to have Buddhism constitutionally enshrined as the official religion. In 2007, hundreds of monks marched into Bangkok to pressure the government to include such a clause in the latest constitution, which was then being drafted. Accompanying the monks on their journey to Parliament – at the height of the hot season – were nine elephants, causing headaches for the police, who feared the beasts might go berserk and harm onlookers. In the event, the monks failed to achieve their demands and the 2007 constitution, still in force, does not declare Buddhism as Thailand's official faith.

action, right livelihood, right effort, right mindfulness and right concentration. Buddhism, then, is both a philosophy and a method.

The Buddhist temple (*wat*) stands traditionally at the heart of Thai village life. Its monks' virtuous practice and devotion to meditation brings merit to the whole community, and helps to keep evil spirits at bay. As well as a home to monks, the temple is a meeting place, community centre, counselling centre and house of learning. Before Thailand established its modern education system, it was only at temples where poor Thai boys could get an education.

All Buddhist men are expected to be ordained as a monk or novice at some point in their lives. This used to mean donning the robes for at least the three-month period of the rainy season known as Buddhist Lent. Today, a dwindling number of Thai men are prepared to make such a commitment, and while they continue to be ordained at some point in their lives, a stretch as short as a week or two is becoming the norm.

There are a few reasons for being ordained: doing so earns you much merit. Yet it also bestows merit on one's parents and is often seen as a way to repay them – particularly the mother, who cannot herself be ordained – for the selfless kindness they showed in bringing you into the world. A man might choose to become ordained to make amends for an act of wrongdoing, to gain an education – or even to escape the law.

Thai monks are supposed to live an ascetic lifestyle, to shun material possessions and the distractions of everyday life in

LAHIDE LIBRARY
8704430

favour of a life of pacific contemplation. While lay Buddhists are expected to observe five precepts, monks are held to 227. These rules vary in severity. The least serious can be forgiven if the monk confesses his transgression to another monk. They include such misdemeanours as damaging a plant, sitting alone with a woman, hiding another monk's robe or bowl ('even as a joke') and 'tickling with the fingers' (the devil finds work for idle hands). There are four offences that result in a monk being automatically defrocked: having sex, stealing, killing a human and lying about achieving an advanced spiritual state.

Buddhist precepts

The Buddhist precepts are the code of ethics that those who call themselves Buddhists are expected to live by. Lay people observe five – or are supposed to anyway. The more devout observe eight, while monks are expected to follow 227. Precepts differ from Christian commandments in that they're more like recommendations than rules. This allows a degree of flexibility, which most Thais duly take advantage of. The first five Buddhist precepts are:

1. Do not take life.
2. Do not steal.
3. Do not commit adultery.
4. Do not lie.
5. Do not consume intoxicating substances.

Taking life

The Biblical 'Thou shalt not kill' may apply to humans, but in Buddhism the prohibition against taking life applies to animals, too. A few Thais take this seriously to the point of refusing to kill mosquitos, though most don't: electrified insect-frying tennis racquets do a roaring trade. The vast majority of Thai Buddhists eat meat, reaching for justifications that at times skirt absurdity: 'The chicken was dead when I bought it' or 'I took the fish out of the water but it died of its own accord'.

Even monks eat meat, arguing that they're required to consume whatever is put in their bowls without pleasure or disgust. (I did wonder if the monk I recently saw standing with his alms bowl in front of a fried-chicken stall might have been pushing this principle a little far.) Nevertheless, the first precept explains why most of those who work Bangkok's slaughterhouses are Muslims or, in the case of the pig abattoirs of Khlong Toei, Christians.

Thailand retains the death penalty for crimes such as drug trafficking and murder. At the time of writing, no one has been executed since August 2009. Charovet Jaruboon, the so-called 'Last Executioner' of Bangkok's maximum security Bang Kwang Prison, executed 55 people using a machine gun over the course of his long career (the method was changed to lethal injection in 2003). Charovet, a Buddhist who died in April 2012 aged 64, was unsurprisingly concerned with questions of karma. He discussed the subject with monks at length, telling interviewer Don Linder, 'Their opinion is the same – the convicts on death row are swamped in bad karma and the executioner is doing them a favour by sending them on to the next incarnation for a chance to redeem themselves.' Thai Buddhism is nothing if not flexible.

Hit squads

With a murder rate of 4.8 per 100,000 people per year, murders are roughly as common in Thailand as in the United States. Business disputes and love triangles tend to lie behind most killings, though the person who pulls the trigger is rarely the person who wants the victim dead. Rumours abound on exactly how much contract killers charge; expats love scaring new arrivals with stories of how little it costs to have someone killed. Certainly, it depends on the social status of the target. An article by security analyst Anthony Davis written in 1997 claimed it cost US$12,000-$40,000 to hire a three- or four-man hit squad. Needless to say, this is not a subject the average visitor to Thailand needs to worry about – as grimly fascinating as it might be.

Stealing

The vast majority of Thais obey this precept, though those that don't make their presence felt, particularly in tourist areas, where signs often warn of pickpockets. Like their colleagues the world over, *khamoi* (thieves) operate in crowded places, particularly markets and tourist hotspots such as Khao San Road. Having said that, for every thief there are many more Thais who are scrupulously honest. Tales of taxi drivers returning large sums of cash left in their cabs to absent-minded passengers abound.

Adultery

Thais are publicly faithful to their partners, but behind closed doors adultery is common. Love motels, in which rooms can be rented by the hour and curtains are on hand to draw round cars and protect licence plates from prying eyes, are everywhere. In 2009, a survey of 29,000 people in 36 countries by condom maker Durex claimed that Thai couples were the most unfaithful in the world, with 54 per cent of Thais in relationships admitting to infidelity. The survey, which didn't reach the levels of rigour expected in the social sciences, sparked a furore in the Thai media, with commentators lining up to rubbish the claims. To take just one example, the deputy director of the Mental Health Department, Dr Tawee Tangseri, told *The Nation* he 'doubted Thai women often cheated on their partners because they adhered to tradition and preserved their purity.'

Lying

Show me a human who never lies, and I'll show you a bodhisattva – or a dead man. The fourth Buddhist precept forbids fibbing, yet Thais undoubtedly have a facility for being 'economical with the truth'. The word 'lying' seems heavy-handed. When a Thai person bends the truth, there is often a respectable, or at least non-malevolent, motivation for doing so: the need to preserve social harmony. Most, I suspect, would agree that everyone getting along is more important than sticking scrupulously to the truth.

Intoxicating substances

The fifth precept forbids the consumption of alcohol and other intoxicants. Given the obvious popularity of drinking in Bangkok, it might surprise to learn that the World Health Organisation reported in 2011 that 62.9 percent of Thais over 15 do abstain from boozing: 40.8 per cent of men and 81.3 per cent of women. Bangkok is notably less conservative in this area than the countryside. Those who do drink are partially redeemed by the fact that Buddhism doesn't consider the consumption of intoxicants *inherently* evil, merely that doing so makes it more likely you'll break the other precepts. But perhaps the truth is even simpler: avoiding booze would violate another less official Thai commandment: 'always seek *sanuk*'.

Making merit

If the ultimate purpose of Buddhism is escape from *samsara*, the cycle of birth and death, for most Thai Buddhists the faith boils down to a more modest goal: the pursuit of happiness. By doing good deeds, the faithful make merit ('*tham bun*' in Thai), which they believe will be repaid in good fortune in the current life, as well as the next. What goes around comes around.

The most common merit-making activity is to donate alms (usually food) to monks, who are expected to rely on charity to survive, owning nothing save the robes on their backs and their alms bowls. From just before dawn to as late as 8am, monks can still be seen on the streets of many Bangkok neighbourhoods, their saffron robes vibrant reminders of Thailand's spiritual endowment in a materialistic metropolis.

Some people remove their shoes before placing food in the monk's bowl. The monk then blesses the donors, who stand still or prostrate themselves, their hands in a high *wai* befitting of the monk's spiritual advancement (*see page 136*). Monks are not supposed to make eye contact with those giving alms, particularly women. Neither are they meant to say thank you, which once caused an intoxicated friend of mine to snatch a freshly donated THB1000 note back from a monk's hand. In some parts of the city, the ritual has been refined with steely capitalist efficiency: stalls sell ready-made food packages that the faithful may buy before donating them straight to the monk standing nearby.

Still, with Buddhism you get out what you put in. More merit is gained by making the food yourself. Intention matters too: giving is not supposed to be accompanied by thoughts of future returns. Nevertheless, it often is, and all Thais know which gifts bring which rewards. Give life-giving rice, and your life will be happy and healthy. Give soap or cleaning products, and your skin will be clear and silky smooth. Those with dental issues, meanwhile, would be well-advised to donate toothbrushes, toothpaste and toothpicks.

Naturally, some Thais are more dedicated to the task of merit-making than others. The anonymous freedom of the big city leads many young Thais to neglect thoughts of their karmic balance. Away from the guiding influence of family, young migrants are more able to do as they please – and this frequently doesn't include getting up at five in the morning. And the shift to homes in high-rises increasingly divorces people from community life. Perhaps alms runs along condo corridors would be fruitful for enterprising clergymen.

Still there are many ways to make merit. New homes and new years are inaugurated with merit-making ceremonies, in which monks are invited to a property – preferably in auspicious groups of nine – to receive alms, chant in Pali and push the host's karmic ledger into the black. Donating to build or renovate temples, visiting Buddhist shrines and observing the precepts all bring merit, too. But nothing improves your

Buddhist monks making their morning alms rounds remains a daily spectacle in many neighbourhoods of the city.

karma like becoming a monk, or having a son become one, as we've seen.

The more spiritually advanced the beneficiary of your acts, the more merit you earn. Monks, then, make the best recipients. Feeding a dog will do little for you; feeding a beggar is better, though not by a lot, since his own stock of merit must be low. That is the corollary of the idea that your station in life can be improved by being 'good', that the least fortunate in society have brought their fate on themselves, either by acts of evil in this life or in those that came before. Equally, the successful enjoy a virtuous sheen – you don't get rich unless, in the view of the cosmos, you deserve it.

In decline?

You could hardly find two more opposing creeds: Buddhism, which preaches that desire is the root of suffering, and the ethos of late capitalism, in which 'greed is good' and desire celebrated as the driver of prosperity. In Bangkok, where these two forces square off in dialectical opposition, the latter seems to have gained the upper hand. As Phra Paisan Visalo, one of Thailand's most respected monks, frankly admitted to *The New York Times* in December 2012, 'Consumerism is now the Thai religion. In the past, people went to temple on every holy day. Now, they go to shopping malls.'

While barely a year goes by without a new mega-mall opening its doors, temples find themselves increasingly empty – both of parishioners and clergy. Officially there are around 200,000 monks in Thailand, but Phra Paisan admitted to the *Times* that the number had dropped to no more than 70,000. The truth is that in 21st-century Thailand, an increasingly prosperous country on the cusp of 'developed' status, the monkhood has less to offer men than in times gone by – certainly, at least, by today's materialistic standards.

Traditionally, entering the monkhood was guaranteed to put a roof over a poor man's head, and food in his belly. Today, even Thais of humble backgrounds aspire to more than that – and stand a good chance of getting it. And while getting ordained used to be the only way a man without means could gain an education, today the state provides every Thai citizen with at least 12 years of free schooling.

Demographics, too, play a role. Thai couples are having fewer children than ever before. Between 1970 and 1990, the average number of children per Thai woman plummeted from six to two. The figure now stands at around 1.5. While a family with six children might easily spare a son for the monkhood, few parents want their only male child to shun a lifetime of income, and thus the ability to look after them when they're old.

Scandals don't help. The reputation of Thai Buddhism still has a long way to fall to match the crisis in trust faced by the Catholic Church, but barely a week goes by without a defrocking splashed across the papers. Monks deal drugs, hire prostitutes, shack up with women (and men), defraud parishioners – you name it. Bad monks are nothing new, retreating into the anonymity of the monkhood has always been popular with criminals looking to hide out from the law (and makes some karmic amends while they're at it). But now the penetration of mass media means the antics of these 'bad apples' are much more visible.

Still, although Thais have less and less time to spare the temples – and fewer sons – they are giving them much more of something befitting of the age: money. Donations are pouring in and *wats* are in better repair than ever. The public's rising largesse, unfortunately, brings its own challenges for Thai monks: avoiding the temptation to give in to material pleasures. In June 2013, a video surfaced showing two young monks sitting in a private jet wearing pricey-looking aviator sunglasses, a Louis Vuitton bag in shot. One of them, Luang Pu Nen Kham, is now reportedly facing investigation by the DSI – Thailand's FBI – after it emerged he had a cool THB200 million sloshing around in several bank accounts. Worse allegations later surfaced: that he had fathered several children, including one with a 15-year-old girl.

It goes without saying that such tales aren't typical, and the upstanding members of Thailand's clergy haven't yet given up on the lapsed Buddhist masses. Recognising that the faith's teachings – and particularly the benefits of meditation – still have value for people stressed out by today's busy urban lifestyles, they hope to repackage Buddhism for the modern age. As Phra Anil Sakya told *The New York Times*: 'People today love high-speed things. We didn't have instant noodles in the past, but now people love them. For the sake of presentation, we have to change the way we teach Buddhism and make it easy and digestible like instant noodles.'

Spirits and power

Thais regard the spirit world in much the same way as they do the human world. Both revolve around power. Some spirits are amoral entities whose power can be harnessed for human benefit, given the right persuasion. Others are evil, and protection must be sought against their malevolent attentions. Certain places and objects attract concentrations of spiritual power, or *saksit*: religious items, shrines, temples, amulets and things of mystery and synchronicity – two-headed piglets, white elephants, unusually shaped rocks and trees, for example. Spirits infest the urban jungle as much as the wild one. Bangkok is a City of Angels and a City of Ghosts.

Every piece of land is believed to have a spirit that rules over it, the *jao thi* ('lord of the place'). These invisible potentates must be respected. They are easy to anger and worthy of fear. When Thais prepare to build on a piece of land, they invite its guardian spirit to move to a certain part of the plot. There, they build a spirit house – known as '*san phra phum*' or '*san jao thi*' – for the *jao thi* to inhabit.

Even in Bangkok, these bright little palaces on pedestals can be seen everywhere, if you keep your eyes open. Regular offerings, which can be of incense, water, food and even cigarettes, must be made to the spirit to keep it content. Some believers make an offering every day. Others are less conscientious, though many will be sure to do so every *wan phra* (Buddhist holy day), of which there are four every lunar month.

The bigger the building, the larger the spirit house that is required to house the local *jao thi*. Large structures such as hotels, government offices and department stores require a different kind of shrine entirely: a *san phra phrom*, or shrine to Brahma, the four-faced Hindu god of good fortune and

The Erawan Shrine, dedicated to Brahma, is one of the most revered shrines in Bangkok. It stands at Ratchaprasong Intersection in the centre of the city's upmarket shopping district.

protection. The most famous of these is the Erawan Shrine, which sits outside the Erawan Hotel at Ratchaprasong Intersection. Here, in the busy centre of the city's shopping district, devotees flock to make offerings to the deity, ensuring that the surrounding air is always thick with incense, and the nearby garland vendors do a roaring trade.

And in this land of the deal, even spirits are open for business. Spirits and gods (*thewada*) can be cajoled through ritual into granting the wishes of the living. It is a quid pro quo: the devotee makes an offering, tells the spirit what he or she wants – to win the lottery, to get the girl – and promises to return with a second, larger offering once the wish has been fulfilled. This could be anything from flowers, to a pig's head, to a performance. Failure to fulfil your side of the bargain would be deeply foolish: it would anger the spirit, which may punish you for your treachery.

Perhaps the most lurid example of this deal-making phenomenon – I just can't help myself – is the Chuchok Shrine in Bang Khen District in the northern suburbs of Bangkok. Here, Thais come to ask Chuchok, an old Brahmin beggar from Buddhist scripture, for wealth or success in business. If the spirit, by legend a lecherous old man, gives them what they want, they return to put on a real-life show for him: a sexy dance by a troupe of scantily clad 'coyote' dancers.

The temples may be emptying out, but such shrines are ever popular. As Alex Kerr notes in *Bangkok Found*, 'While Buddhism mostly offers teachings about facing the facts and living with them, the Hindu gods provide hope of changing those facts of your life.' It seems no coincidence that the popularity of these deities rises as consumer capitalism tightens its grip on the Thai psyche, and that the Erawan Shrine stands just metres from stores selling the most expensive of European luxury brands.

Evil spirits

Not all spirits are as helpful as Chuchok. Some are entirely malevolent. Evil spirits may haunt particular places but more frequently roam the land like bandits. With them come sickness, misfortune and death. Babies get nicknames to confuse such entities, who are believed to be drawn to newborns. (How else would a hunter-gatherer explain the sudden death of an infant?) For the same reason, it's considered dangerous to call a baby 'beautiful' or 'cute'.

Thai ghosts

Here are some of the most well-known types of Thai ghost:

Krasue: The fearsome *phi krasue* manifests as the disembodied head of a beautiful young woman, her internal organs dangling from her neck like the tail of some kind of hellish kite. Flying through the night and cursed with constant hunger, the *krasue* seeks blood and flesh to devour, often drinking the blood of cattle and chicken.

Krahang: A *phi krahang* is a male ghost that flies through the night and is believed to haunt the same areas as the *krasue*. The *krahang*, which may have feathers and uses wicker rice baskets for its wings, likes to eat filthy things: rubbish, excrement and even human placentas.

Mae Nak: The tale of Mae Nak Phra Khanong ('Lady Nak of Phra Khanong') is one of Thailand's most famous ghost stories. The story concerns a beautiful young woman, Nak, who dies during childbirth while her husband is recovering from a war injury. When her husband comes home, she has become a ghost. He only realises she is a spirit when she stretches her arm unnaturally to pick up a lime. He flees, and Mae Nak turns into a vengeful, bitter spirit. There is a shrine to Mae Nak at Wat Mahabut in Phra Khanong in Eastern Bangkok.

Pop: This kind of ghost is believed to be able to take possession of the living. It usually inhabits a sorceress's body, leaving it during her sleep and heading off into the night. If it possesses someone else, it will try to eat their intestines, and is often blamed for sudden deaths in country villages. Spirit doctors exorcise such ghosts by performing a kind of spinning dance that draws the spirit out of its victim's body.

Pret: *Phi pret* is a male 'hungry ghost' with a ravenous appetite he can never satisfy. Standing very tall and thin, but often with a huge distended belly and swollen genitals, the *pret* has a mouth the size of a pin prick. Unable to sate his desires, he cries in agony as he roams the land in permanent suffering. *Prets* are thought to be the souls of people who were greedy or selfish or committed a great sin in a previous life.

Instead, you should point out how ugly it is. Parents know to take this as a compliment.

Call these entities 'evil spirits', call them 'ghosts' – most Thais believe in them. Few are willing to live in a house in which somebody is known to have died. Ghost movies – some serious, some silly, some veering from one to the other from scene to scene – are a staple of the cinema screen, and Thai belief provides filmmakers with a rich seam of colourful spooks to draw from. Unlike the West, where ghosts rarely deviate from the transparent-dead-person-who-walks-through-walls template, Thais have an extensive taxonomy of spooks, each one more bizarre than the last.

Monks and professional spirit doctors are called to exorcise such entities. As Mulder explains, 'The latter specialises in localising the spirit, then subduing it by trapping it in a pot, or chasing it away by evoking strong annulling forces. These fiends can sometimes also be dealt with by politely placating them and asking them to go away in return for a gift – essentially a pay-off.'

You can also protect yourself from these spirits using *saksit* objects. Amulets (*phra khrueang*) that contain a statue of the Buddha, coins etched with the likenesses of famous monks and Pali inscriptions are common defences, and it takes a monk or spirit doctor to make them. Or you might go for something more permanent: a protective tattoo based on Buddhist or Hindu symbols.

Amulets and tattoos

The world is a dangerous place, and it isn't just the eldritch attentions of the *krasue* that you might seek protection from. Misfortune of all kinds can be warded off with the right kind of *phra khrueang* strung round your neck. There are at least four types: natural charms such as unusual seeds, teeth, tusks and stones; images of Buddha or monks; enchanted talismans such as sacred diagrams, folded leaves and phalli; and plant roots used in black magic and medicine.

It's a custom dating back past the Buddhist era to the Thais' earlier origins as animist hunter-gatherers. Today, amulets most commonly take the form of small clay tablets embossed with the image of the Buddha or a powerful monk. Older specimens may have been excavated after being buried hundreds of years ago, their makers hoping to preserve Buddhism for posterity. But temples still make them today, their monks using the proceeds to fund social projects (at least that's the theory).

It's an industry worth hundreds of millions of dollars. Aesthetics, rarity, age and the supposed power of the talisman – closely connected to the stature of the monk who made or blessed it – are all factored into the price. While a mass-produced specimen might cost as little as 100 baht, the most valuable run into the hundreds of thousands or even millions of baht. Several magazines are dedicated to the subject, their pages chock full of images of worthy specimens and true-life tales of bearers saved from death through the wearing of the right *phra*. Bangkok's largest market is on several small *soi* leading off Maharat Road in Rattanakosin.

For many Thais, one amulet is enough. For others, collecting these defensive tokens becomes an obsession. You don't need to take many taxi rides in Bangkok before running into a common type: the driver who can't be too careful, his rearview mirror festooned with amulets and garlands, Buddhas on the dash, and famous monks gazing down from posters on his car's ceiling. Men with too many amulets can fall under suspicion by polite society – if you need so many, you must be up to no good, goes the thinking.

Sacred tattoos – *sak yan* – serve the same protective purpose. Applying them is an ancient practice that owes something to animism, Brahmanism and Buddhism – the elements that inform Thai Buddhism, in other words. A tattoo must be applied by a monk or magic practitioner. They usually combine geometric *yantra* (a Pali-Sanskrit word meaning 'design', pronounced *'yan'* in Thai) with spells written in one of a variety of scripts. After the Thai conquered the Angkor Empire in the 15th century, they began using the Khmer *khom* script for tattoo spells in Central Thailand.

There are huge varieties in design. A tattoo might be as small as the simple 'nine spire' *yantra* below the nape of the neck, or a huge, intricate diagram covering the whole back. But here, size doesn't matter: it's the power of the spell and its caster that counts. It's said that every male member of the Chakri dynasty has received a *sak yan*, including King Bhumibol. Until 2003, the practice had been in decline, fuelled by bourgeois Western-informed notions that tattoos were not for 'decent people'. However, since 2003 – when Angelina Jolie famously received a *sak yan* tattoo – it has thrived again.

FITTING IN

THE TITLE OF THIS CHAPTER IS IRONIC, given the unavoidable reality of a *farang*'s life in Thailand: you will never fit in. No matter how well you speak Thai and understand customs and beliefs, you will be thought of as different. Even if you're married to a Thai person, your children are Thai and can't eat pasta without dousing it in fish sauce, you will not be considered Thai. For some foreigners, this is torment – to have so much invested in this country and still be thought an alien, followed everywhere by the word '*farang*' as if it were their name.

But there's good news, too. Since you're an outsider, Thai people won't expect you to understand their hard-to-grasp culture and customs. This means you'll get less blame when you commit social faux-pas – and commit them you will. We might call this '*farang*'s privilege', a sort of 'get out of jail free' card ready to be played in tricky social situations of all kinds. If it's annoying to be singled out as a foreigner 'yet again', remind yourself that if you were thought of as Thai, you'd be expected to conform to the rules that govern Thai society, including the deference to status and all the rest of it. Is that what you really want? And if it is, are you capable of it?

Some foreigners revel in *farang*'s privilege, using it to their advantage in all manner of situations – even when they secretly know better. But while Thais will be far more tolerant of a foreigner breaking the rules than one of their own, there are lines that shouldn't be crossed. And you'll impress the

Thai people by trying to be more culturally aware. Nobody says anything to the *farang* who struts down the streets with his top off, but that doesn't mean people approve. Even 'get out of jail free' cards get dog-eared from overuse.

HIGH AND LOW

The vertical hierarchy of Thai society is reflected in a more general belief that the higher something is, the more worthy it is. The sky is sacred, the ground profane. The head is holy, the feet unclean. North trumps south, front beats back, and woe betide she who hangs her framed pic of Ananda Everingham above her portrait of Rama V.

As the highest part of the body, the head is the most sacred part, and is believed to house a person's *khwan* (spirit essence). It's taboo to touch a Thai person on the head, which is why a hairdresser will usually *wai* before cutting your hair. Still, this rule is often cast aside in more intimate relationships. Lovers are no respecters of it, nor is the dad who tousles his son's hair.

The feet are the lowest part of the body, both literally and spiritually. Never point your feet at a Thai person or use them to point at objects. The feeling of insult probably derives from feudal times, in which slaves were required to grovel before their masters and could be given orders through foot gestures. In an airport check-in queue, it's always tempting to kick your bag along the floor. No one will say anything if you do – indeed, most people probably won't care – but it will reflect better on you in some eyes if you summon the effort to move it by hand. Yes, it's hard being culturally respectful sometimes.

It's no coincidence that the Thai greeting, the *wai*, involves temporarily lowering one's head ('I am lower than you'), while raising one's hands ('you are higher than me'). This process is taken to the extreme in the custom of prostration (*krap*), an ancient practice often still performed today before royalty, monks and images and statues of the Buddha or revered clergy.

Photographs and portraits of monarchs, found in most houses, offices and businesses, must be the highest images on the wall. In newspapers, pictures of members of the royal family must be highest on the page. Of course, in the Internet age, Facebook feeds, blogs and Tumblrs have an endlessly scrolling procession of posts, meaning it's quite possible that such images can end up below those of less sacred beings. This is tolerated. The 'rules' in Thailand can be waived when there's good practical reason for doing so.

The elevation of other objects is important, too. Books, which are semi-sacred, should not be placed on the floor. Indeed, Thais will avoid placing almost anything on the floor, if it can be avoided. On a train, most passengers will try to hold their bag on their lap, rather than placing it on the ground, though this isn't an inviolate rule.

Similarly, a shoe's place is on the floor. I once got a light telling-off on a tour bus for stashing a rucksack with shoes sticking out of the side pockets on an overhead shelf. Gesturing at an old lady sitting in front of me, the conductor pointed out that my trainers were 'above grandma's head'.

Finally, don't step over people who are sitting on the floor, or over food. If people are in your way, say '*kho thot*' ('sorry', 'excuse me'). As you pass a sitting person, it's polite to crouch slightly, as if to apologise for towering over them.

DRESS AND MODESTY

Your standing in a status-focused society is reflected in what you wear, and by 'dressing the part' you let others know how they should treat you. This is part of the reason uniforms are so popular in Thailand (*see page 104*). Having said all that, Thais are also a fashion-conscious bunch, a trait which can conflict with the older values that are being eroded as the country develops.

Go back 200 years and there was no difference between the dress of ordinary Siamese men and women. Both sexes would wear little but a *phanung* – a length of cotton wrapped around the waist. Bare female chests were common well into the 20th century.

It was only following decades of concerted modernising drives by the rulers of Siam, from Chulalongkorn (Rama V) onwards, that Western modes of dress were adopted and ideas about female 'propriety' in dress took hold. By 1941, dictator Phibunsongkhram was issuing decrees banning Thais from dress that would 'damage the prestige of the country', including wearing loincloths or appearing in public without a shirt or blouse on.

These days, things are more relaxed. Nobody worries too much about the minishorts favoured as casual dress by many young women – though there are occasional moral panics over the ever-shorter skirts sported by university students. Older standards are still applied strictly in the more famous temples, including the Grand Palace, where the shoulders and legs of both sexes must be covered.

Still, take a relaxing midnight stroll around the Nana area any night of the week and what you'll see is anything but modest – call this another case of Thais putting practicalities first. Prostitutes mostly exist in their own subcultural bubble in Bangkok. When they return to their home towns, where they too are members of polite society, most wouldn't dream of wearing their work clothes.

Another long-standing tradition in Thai society is to avoid wearing the colour black, traditionally a colour for mourning and funerals. Today, a walk down any busy Bangkok street will take you past dozens of people wearing the colour, while at a rock concert you'd be hard-pushed to find anyone in anything else. At least when it comes to the new generation, this is one cultural rule we can declare dead and buried.

WHY *WAI*

In January 2013, the rapper Snoop Dogg – or Snoop Lion, as he now calls himself – landed in Phuket to film a music video. While staying at the luxurious Sri Panwa resort, he was snapped by local paper *The Phuket News* making a *wai* for the camera. Or at least trying to. The elbows in a *wai*, the famous prayer-like gesture that Thais use to greet each other, should be kept close to the body; Snoop's were sticking out to his sides in what looked more like an Indian *namaste*. The *Bangkok Post* ran the photo of the legendary rapper under the distinctly uncharitable headline 'Snoop Dogg/Lion tries to *wai*, fails'.

You might take two lessons from this snippet: one, that the *wai* isn't easy to get right; and two, that Thai people are unforgiving of those who get it wrong. On the first point you'd be right. The *wai* is more complex than meets the eye – there are actually several different types of *wai* – and few foreigners manage to master the custom.

On the second point, you'd miss the mark. Thais are very tolerant of foreigners messing up their *wais*; indeed, they expect it. They know their culture isn't easy for outsiders to grasp. At best, they will be happy you are making the effort. At worst, they might simply be amused at your mistake. The *Post*'s reaction was untypically nasty, and perhaps betrayed more about the editor's feelings for rap music than about Thai culture.

Prostration

In centuries past, when subjects were brought for an audience with the king, they had to crawl in his presence. As Robert Cooper explains in *Culture-Shock! Thailand*, 'In those days, the wretched subject could not look at the king and, being too low to speak to him directly, had to say words to the effect that "my head beneath the dust under your feet addresses you".' This is the origin of the first person singular pronoun used by men, *phom*, which literally means 'hair'. In 1873, King Chulalongkorn abolished prostration, writing in the Royal Gazette that it 'reaffirms the existence of oppression which is unjust'. As part of a concerted effort to re-sacralise the monarchy in the second half of the 20th century, the practice was revived in certain settings.

The *wai* is intimately connected to the Thai concern with status and hierarchy (*see page 93*). People of lower status are expected to initiate *wais* with those of higher status, not the other way round. There are different types of *wai* depending on the relative status of the two people concerned. The general rule is that the higher the status of the receiver, the higher the hands move and the deeper you bow.

There are plenty of situations demanding of a *wai*. As well as a greeting, it's used to say goodbye, to show gratitude or respect and to apologise. Ever-conscious of the invisible spirit potentates of the land, Thais *wai* shrines and spirit houses as they pass by, whether walking, sitting on a bus or sometimes even driving. They hold their hands in a *wai* while being blessed by a monk, for example after donating alms.

In general, failing to return a *wai* is rude – not unlike leaving someone's hand hanging in the air without a shake. To receive a *wai*, the hands are held in front of the chest, without a bow. But there are exceptions. There is no need to *wai* anyone who is serving you. To restaurant and store staff, for example, a nod and smile will suffice. Monks and royalty are always exempted from having to return a *wai*. Instead, they can receive the *wai* by simply nodding or raising their right hand.

Can't *wai* properly? Even Ronald knows how to do it.

Charmed by the custom and eager to 'have a go' at Thai culture, foreigners who are new to Thailand frequently go overboard with the *wai*. A friend of mine from the US Midwest who's spent the best part of a decade in Thailand these days recounts how, in true democratic spirit, he spent his first few months in Thailand *wai*-ing absolutely everybody, including the staff at his local 7-Eleven. The Thai response to a misplaced *wai* from a 'superior' is less likely to be 'Thank you, what a touchingly egalitarian gesture' than 'Why is he *wai*-ing me? Crazy *farang*.'

How to *wai*

Start with your palms and fingers pressed together, your elbows tucked into your body, with your forearms at a 45-degree angle off vertical. Then bow your head while raising your hands slightly. With a social equal, the tips of the fingers should be at nose level with the head slightly bowed. The important thing is to *feel* the *wai*. It is not just a gesture of the hands, but one of the heart. To a social superior, the tips of the thumbs should be level with the nose and the fingertips reaching the brow. The bow should also be deeper. With a monk, the thumbs should be at eyebrow level, with the fingertips at least at the hairline. The head should be bowed to an angle of almost 90 degrees. To receive a *wai* from an inferior, the hands are held together at chest level, without a bow.

THE 'F' WORD

Years ago a friend was working as an English teacher at a school in Sri Racha in Chonburi province, not too far from Pattaya. One of the other teachers, an older American man, complained to the management about the language the Thai teachers were using when talking about the foreign staff: namely, their constant use of the word '*farang*', which has two meanings in Thai – 'guava' and 'white person'. This teacher thought the word was racist. The management listened to his concerns and, surprisingly, banned the Thai teachers from saying it in the school. But in the following days, my friend noticed the Thai teachers were now using a new word a lot: '*haksida*'. He asked his Thai girlfriend what it meant. 'Oh,' she laughed. 'It's Isarn language for "*farang*"'.

'*Farang*' will probably be one of the first words you learn in Thai, being one of the select few Thai words that foreigners use when speaking English. While some people suppose it must be short for the Thai word '*farangset*' ('French'), it's believed by scholars to derive from the Persian '*farangi*', which in turn refers to the Franks, the Germanic tribe that ruled Western Europe in the Middle Ages, and from whom France gets its name. A black person from the West may be referred to as '*farang dam*'.

If you're white, Thai people will use the word in your presence, whether you like it or not. And they'll say it a lot. Most Thais argue that the word *farang* isn't racist, and simply means a person of European descent. And they're basically right. There's nothing inherently wrong with the language having a word that means 'white person'. And unlike some of the racial epithets that are considered offensive in polite Western society, there's no history of oppression lurking behind '*farang*' that makes it offensive. The vast majority of *farang* in Bangkok live lives of relative privilege. An oppressed minority they are not.

Having said that, the word is probably overused. If it's used for the purpose of distinguishing you in a crowd, it's reasonable: 'Who ordered the *phad Thai*?' 'The *farang* in the corner.' But in some people's speech, it can seem to take the place of the third person pronoun when a foreigner is present. They won't ask their English-speaking friend what '*he*' said, but what 'the *farang*' said. And when you're the only person in the shop and *still* being referred to as 'the *farang*', it can seem like you're having your *farang*-ness rubbed in your face a tad unnecessarily.

Some foreigners, like the man in the anecdote above, take exception to this. They start to consider the word to be a sort of racial slur, and demand they're described as '*khon tang chat*' (literally, 'different nation person') or '*khon tang prathet*' ('different country person'). This is going too far. What grates on these expats – usually those who are married to a Thai, whose children are Thai nationals, and who expect to spend the rest of their life here – is the way the word functions as a constant reminder of the fact that they're considered different. But that's an idea you just have to accept, or you won't be very happy in Thailand.

Farang for sale

My friend Eric recounts something that happened to him while with his Thai wife in Isarn a few years ago: 'I'm on a bus sitting in a gas station in Khon Kaen when this fruit vendor motions to me [through the window] that he's got fruit for sale. I indicate to him that I'm not interested. He makes a beeline for the bus anyway and all I hear when he gets on is, "*farang, farang, farang*". I turn to my wife and say, "Damn it, I told him I don't want anything. Why does he assume the white guy wants his shit?" My wife turns to me and says: "Calm down. He's selling guava. And he's trying to sell it to the entire bus, you idiot."'

KEEPING YOUR COOL

You'll expend a lot of effort in this sweltering city trying to keep cool. But if you're to master the art of living here, you'll probably need to get better at keeping your emotional cool, too. There are few hard-and-fast rules that apply to living in Bangkok, but one is this: never lose your temper.

Outward expressions of anger are disliked by Thais for a number of reasons. Losing your temper is not considered socially acceptable for almost any reason. Thais are well aware that many foreigners have a tendency to be *jai ron* ('hot-hearted', 'quick to anger'), but unlike other aspects of foreign culture and attitudes, this is one area in which you can't expect much tolerance.

By getting angry, you lose face and cause those around you to lose respect for you. If you lose your temper with a Thai friend or colleague, it may not be easily forgiven. If you need more of a reason to avoid losing your cool, there's a practical one: it's counter-productive. In many parts of the world, aggression can cause others to take your concerns more seriously or help you get your way. This is simply not the case in Thailand. Getting angry will get Thai people's backs up, put them on the defensive, and potentially cause them to strike back against you.

A second, related piece of advice: never make a Thai person lose face. Try to be aware of the potential for losses of face in your social interactions. If you need to tell an employee off, do it in private. If you feel someone has ripped you off, don't turn the conflict into a public spectacle. Even in restaurants, forget 'the customer is always right'. Complaints should be made calmly, even with a smile.

Of course, you're bound to find yourself in some frustrating, even maddening, situations in Bangkok. Cross-cultural communication problems only exacerbate the stresses and conflicts that are part and parcel of everyday life. But regardless of the situation, deep breaths and measured words beat raised voices and angry glares.

Expat web forums are chock-full of tales from foreigners about being 'screwed over' by Thais and extended diatribes about Thailand or its people. I don't want to cast aspersions on all people with such stories, some of whom have good reason to be angry. But the No. 1 characteristic that seems to be shared by people who get chewed up by Thailand is their inability to adapt to this aspect of Thai culture, their inability to stay *jai yen* in the face of provocations or injustice, either real and imagined.

Losing your temper in Bangkok can end very badly indeed. In July 2013, an American expat, Troy Lee Pilkington, was hacked to death by a machete-wielding taxi driver. Pilkington reportedly thought the driver, Chidchai Utmacha, had rigged his meter, and when he refused to pay the THB51 fare, an argument broke out. Chidchai claimed that it was only after Pilkington threw his cup of coffee at him that he got out of his cab and pulled a 12-inch knife out of the boot.

Without wishing to blame the victim for the murder – there's only one person seriously at fault here – the story illustrates how conflicts can escalate. Bangkok is generally a safe and welcoming place to live, but if you want to make it dangerous, losing your temper is the best way to go about it.

SPEAKING AND LISTENING

Politeness is important to Thais, which should come as no surprise given the value placed on status and the maintenance of social harmony. To obey the rules of politeness is to show that you know your place – and that of others. There are exceptions to this: bargirls, for example, will frequently come across as decidedly rude. But that's a special case, a world in which social norms and graces are temporarily abandoned.

As in every culture, politeness is partly expressed through verbal language and partly through body language. In Thailand, there seems to be more emphasis on the latter than in the West. To show deference to someone is to become physically submissive by lowering your height. In a restaurant, a polite waiter will duck down as he collects the plates from your table, bobbing repeatedly in a kind of apologetic supplication.

The Thai language has an array of particles that can be added to the end of a sentence to indicate levels of formality and respect. You'll quickly learn the two most common ones – 'kha', used by women, and 'khrap', used by men. When you talk to someone new in Thai, it's polite to add these words to the end of the first two or things you say to them. Doing so is so ingrained in some Thai people that they will even do it when speaking English.

Having said that, some Thais won't say 'kha' or 'khrap' much. This isn't necessarily a sign of rudeness. Many of those who do this will be from the Northeast of Thailand. Their first language will not be Central Thai but a version of Lao, which does away with 'kha' and 'khrap' entirely.

If you have to repeat yourself to make yourself understood with a Thai person, try to avoid the temptation to raise your voice. This could be misinterpreted as a sign of anger. When speaking Thai, it's best to err on the side of over-politeness. After some experience with the culture you should get a feel for when the strictures of politeness can be loosened.

Thai people often seem to hold foreigners to higher standards of linguistic politeness than they do themselves. Thai has a variety of pronouns that indicate differing levels of status and formality. Two in particular, 'ku' ('I', 'me') and mueng ('you'), are frequently used between close friends. When used with strangers, they sound highly arrogant. If someone you don't know calls you 'mueng', expect trouble. These words are best avoided by foreigners, even with close Thai friends. At the very least, they're unlikely to take your use of these words seriously.

Indirectness

Unlike in the West, in which plain speaking – 'telling it like it is' – is generally admired, Thais tend to prefer a more indirect, less confrontational approach to conversation. For example, when faced with a request they can't fulfil, some Thai people will try to avoid giving a straight 'no' for an answer.

If a member of a gym asks for the air-conditioning to be switched on, a staff member under strict orders to use the fans only might say 'Here, we use the fans more'. In other situations, they might say 'yes', but add a caveat that defers having to grant the request, which can then be quietly forgotten. 'Can I borrow THB10,000 from you?' 'Ask me again next month.'

There's nothing particularly unusual about this kind of indirectness, as far as cultures go, of course. Some are more direct than others. Think of the speech of the English: 'I was just wondering whether you'd perhaps be able to turn the air-conditioning on in here, or...' You wouldn't hear that kind of dancing around the subject coming from an American.

It's important to point out that this, as ever, is not a hard-and-fast rule and not all Thais fear directness. Some pride themselves on a reputation for *phut trong-trong* – straight talking. In general, such people tend to enjoy positions of relative power.

Speak of the king

As noted earlier, many Thai people revere King Bhumibol and the topic of the monarchy is highly sensitive (*see pages 29–31*). Even ignoring the legal aspects stemming from Article 112, it's a subject that should be broached with care. Many Thais will not tolerate anything that sounds like criticism of the king or the institution. Others are more relaxed. Some very gentle probing should reveal which camp they're in.

Thais love to gossip, and the palace is as much a subject of rumour as any other section of society. It's quite possible to find yourself privy to such talk when you get to know Thai people well. Indeed, many young Thais are not particularly circumspect about the subject at all. The safest policy is to allow Thais to take the lead in such conversations. Once the subject has been raised, you are usually on safe ground to ask questions, though you may wish to keep your opinions to yourself. Of course, you may be asked for them directly. So long as you reply with sensitivity, you can generally be fairly honest in your response.

You're free to say more or less what you like about other monarchies – and you won't fall foul of the law. Some Thais will feel uncomfortable if you talk critically of your own royal family, and may be quick to point out that what might be true in other countries isn't true in Thailand. Others will be interested to hear a different take on the institution.

The Thai love for their king can prove seductive to many foreigners. In a world in which cynicism about politicians is the norm, many are surprised to encounter a leader who has apparently laboured hard for his people and is loved for it.

Expressing admiration for the king is an easy way to please friends in certain circles.

Perhaps the ultimate example of this phenomenon is Alan Bate, a British expat who cycled round the world as a tribute to King Bhumibol. Bate, who was pictured prostrating himself in front of the monarch's image in locations on five different continents, has described the king as 'one of the world's last real role models'.

Contrary to official dogma, the monarchy is not without its critics – as anyone who has taken a few taxi rides in Bangkok can attest. Many observers have noted that politicians' widespread use of the lèse-majesté law – as well as their constant invocations of the institution to claim political legitimacy – has only served to erode its reputation.

Foreign journalists working in the kingdom must self-censor or face the consequences. The ethics of filing copy in such an environment has been the subject of debate. Andrew MacGregor Marshall, a former Reuters journalist who left his job to publish '#thaistory', an analysis of Thailand's ongoing political crisis using thousands of leaked diplomatic cables, argues that all stories coming out of Thailand that relate to the monarchy should be prefaced with a 'health warning' making it clear the report has been filed under the restrictions imposed by Article 112. Marshall, who continues to publish work that would almost certainly get him arrested in Thailand, lives in Singapore.

The shelves of Bangkok's book stores are packed with books on the king, almost all hagiographic in tone. Academic texts, meanwhile, tend to be treated more leniently by Thailand's book-suppressing functionaries, probably because the abstractions of academese render them less threatening.

Of the books that cannot be found in stores within the kingdom, the best known is probably American journalist Paul Handley's critical biography of Bhumibol, *The King Never Smiles*. Handley, unsurprisingly, is no longer welcome in Thailand. One Bangkok-based writer, Ron Morris, meanwhile, took a different approach with the monarchy section in his book on Thai political culture, *The Thai Book*: 15 pages were left blank, except for the legend 'REDACTED BY THE AUTHOR'.

Thailand talk

The monarchy aside, some people will take offence if you are too critical of Thailand. There's nothing unusual about this – most people, the world over, dislike hearing direct criticism of their country from foreigners. Basic manners dictate that you talk respectfully about the country you're living in. Nevertheless, that doesn't mean to say you can't draw attention to or comment on aspects of Thailand that concern you, or that you shouldn't be honest when a friend asks you a direct question about a particular issue.

There's always a way to frame things tactfully. For example, complaining about 'how corrupt Thai people are' will not win you friends. You can, however, get away this kind of observation if you're more specific. Nobody is going to mind too much if you complain about politicians or the police. Indeed, they'll probably congratulate you for noticing – unless, perhaps, they're politicians or police themselves.

Compliments

Thais are inveterate flatterers and masters of the well-chosen compliment. Such chatter is just how small-talk is done in Thailand, and very pleasant it can be too. But don't take it too seriously. When you're regularly told how well you speak Thai, and how smart and good-looking you are, it can go to your head. You might even develop a case of *cranium giganticus expatriaticus* – the inflated sense of self-regard that can afflict the unwary male foreigner in the early stages of exploring Thai culture.

Taking the fat with the thin

While Thais are inveterate flatterers, if you put on weight your Thai friends won't be shy to let you know about it. Being told in matter-of-fact tones that you 'look fat' or have 'gained weight' can come as a shock to Westerners, both male and female, but it's something you'll probably need to get used to in Thailand – if you have a tendency to put on weight, that is.

It's rarely meant cruelly, and calling someone fat isn't seen as insulting in the same way as in the West. Getting upset or angry is, naturally, the wrong reaction. It's much more dignified to laugh about it. What's more, while many Thais aren't afraid to comment on you putting on the pounds, the same people are just as quick to point out if you lose weight, too. So learn to take the rough with the smooth – or, in this case, the fat with the thin.

Favours

Favours are a way to cement social bonds, particularly in patron-client relationships. While it's obviously good practice as a human being to be grateful for the things others have done for you, in Thailand it's worth paying particular attention to favours and acts of generosity performed for you by Thai friends. One day, they might ask you to repay their *bunkhun*, and to fail to come through for them is considered very poor form.

Gift-giving

Thais rarely unwrap gifts in public, which is considered bad manners. Unwrapping them in private removes the potential for embarrassment. Nevertheless, Western gift-giving practices are becoming more common, with Thais frequently exchanging birthday and sometimes Christmas presents too. 'Secret Santas' are making their way into workplaces, together with the public unwrappings that go with them. So choose your gifts wisely.

VISITING SOMEONE'S HOME

As with many countries, Thais pride themselves on their hospitality, and if you're invited to a Thai home, expect to be treated very well. A full belly is a very likely outcome of the visit. It's polite to bring a small gift with you. In times past, this might have been some homemade food or fruit. Today, alcohol is just as appropriate if you know your host drinks.

When entering a home, always take your shoes off. Your host may tell you there's no need to do so, in a polite accommodation of what they think to be your culture. Remove them anyway. You may also be expected to remove your shoes when entering a business's premises. Lines of shoes in front of the door will tell you when this is the case.

Another old Thai belief is that it is bad luck to step on the threshold of a house. This is because it is one of a few parts of the home that has its own guardian spirit, and to step on the threshold would offend it. So take your shoes off, step over the threshold, and enjoy the hospitality.

FRIENDLINESS

Thai people are friendly – or so goes the stereotype. In provincial Thailand, this is mostly true. It's relatively easy to get invited into a stranger's home, or to be asked to join a *wong lao* – drinking circle – for rice wine or a few whisky sodas. In Bangkok, people are cooler. The city is not the sea of smiles some of the brochures might like you to think.

As a foreigner, you are nothing unusual here and are not likely to attract much unsolicited attention, except from touts. As in big cities the world over, people's default mode in public is to have their guard up, 'to keep themselves to themselves'. With a hybrid Sino-Thai culture, Bangkok people are, perhaps, more focused on getting ahead than getting friendly.

Still, smile at someone and, 90 per cent of the time, they will smile back. Ask someone for directions and they'll almost always do their best to help. And outright rudeness is rare. The city compares favourably with most other Asian capitals in this respect. When TripAdvisor commissioned a poll of 75,000 people on the world's cities, Bangkok was voted the seventh-friendliest, beating every other East Asian city except Tokyo. It must be doing something right.

MAKING THAI FRIENDS

The Thai have a saying: 'A friend to eat with is easily found, a friend to die with is hard to find.' To form a superficial friendship with a Thai person, one which might involve drinking or eating together now and again, is easy. To form a deep and lasting one, finding what Thais call a *phuean tai* ('die friend', 'friend to die with'), is something many – perhaps most – foreigners never accomplish here.

It's a phenomenon a number of foreign writers have noted and pondered the reasons behind. Most obviously, the cultural gap between Thais and Westerners is wide and difficult to bridge. Finding common ground and shared experiences to talk about can be hard. And the large differences between the English and Thai languages make things harder still. Few Thais who haven't been at least partly educated abroad can speak English well enough to understand all your jokes.

There may be differences in these cultures' definitions of what a friendship even constitutes. For example, while Westerners tend to feel that good friends can and perhaps should burden each other with their deeper anxieties and problems, Thais are less likely to feel the same. Their need to save face and to project a positive image of themselves works against that. Family is where Thais can really be themselves.

To many Thais, a good friend is primarily someone you can rely on to come through for you when times are hard. This can involve loans of money, and requests of that sort can come at a point in a friendship earlier than many foreigners are comfortable with. If the foreigner is significantly better off than a Thai friend, this can lead to anxiety about the motives of the Thai person in pursuing the friendship.

A number of foreign writers, including Niels Mulder, author of *Inside Thai Society,* and Robert Cooper, who wrote *CultureShock! Thailand*, have noted how rare it is for foreigners to form deep friendships with Thai people. Of course, not everyone has the same experience. Novelist Lawrence Osborne says he's found it quite easy to make close Thai friends. 'You have to be able to join their flow, I suppose, and maybe it only goes so far because in the end they are hardly even aware of us. They couldn't care less. Of course, I like that! I don't need a host population to care about me.' If you *do* need the host population to care about you, perhaps big cities aren't for you.

CLASS

For better or worse, Thailand is a class-conscious society. While recent decades have seen a rapid rise in social mobility, and the emergence of a new, aspirational lower-middle class, Thais still tend to 'know their place' in social terms. They frequently have a strong ingrained sense of who they're meant to fraternise with and who they aren't.

Foreigners, whose background and status is more difficult to glean, are harder to place hierarchically. Having said that, most foreigners – from 'developed' countries at least – will likely find themselves promoted a rung or two on the social ladder. And so long as you're reasonably well turned out, you can expect to form friendships with Thais of all sorts of background. One night, sip Black and soda with *hi-sos* in a fancy bar; the next, share a bottle of Sang Som with your security guard friend.

On the other hand, bringing Thai friends of different social classes together rarely seems to bear great results. Often, they're unused to finding themselves thrown together in social settings, other than in patron-client situations – the boss treating his staff to a celebratory dinner, for example. Don't be surprised if, after introducing themselves politely, your executive friend and office secretary friend studiously ignore each other. Once you've spent some time in Thailand, you'll get better at gauging the relative social standing of your Thai acquaintances. And you'll likely learn which of them are socially compatible.

THAI-*FARANG* RELATIONSHIPS

It's a pretty safe bet that most people reading this book have had a relationship with a Thai person, or will do in the future. Most Western men who come to live in Thailand form relationships with Thai women. It's less common for Western women to get involved with Thai men, though many do. The subject of Thai-*farang* relationships is one that already has dozens of books devoted to it, and it's only possible to scratch its surface here.

For many foreigners, the gulf between their own background and Thai culture is part of the attraction. A relationship with a Thai person is not just about 'getting to know you', but 'getting to know your culture' too. This, for many, adds a fascinating extra dimension to the relationship. A former colleague of mine who has been married to a Thai woman for 20 years told me that cultural differences were among the things that kept his marriage interesting. 'She's unpredictable,' he said. 'Even after all this time, I'm still discovering new things.'

Thai-*farang* couples – particularly *farang* men with Thai women – can face prejudice, both from Thais and foreigners. Outsiders often assume such marriages are essentially nothing more than financial arrangements. The sketch in the British show 'Little Britain', depicting the relationship between slimy Englishman Dudley Punt, with his buck teeth and comb-over, and his grasping Thai wife Ting Tong Macadangdang, who eventually turns out to be – fancy that! – a ladyboy, might typify the laziest attitudes to such relationships.

Such stereotypes are not without basis, but there are also plenty of successful Thai-*farang* marriages. Still, another happily married friend told me that after 15 years, he and his Thai wife still had anxieties about how people perceived their relationship. When they met new people, they often found themselves quickly dropping the story of how they met – while both were working for a prominent international aid organisation – into the conversation.

Communication can be a problem for any couple. It's much more of a challenge when you're trying to bridge a linguistic gap as wide as English and Thai. While even couples who hardly speak a word of each other's language may 'find a way' to communicate and express their feelings to each other, things become more difficult in social situations. Either partner can find themselves completely at sea when socialising with their partner's friends.

There are also significant differences in the ways that men and women socialise in the West and in Thailand. In Thailand, single men and women are less likely to 'hang out' together than in the West. They will more frequently socialise in couples, or in single-sex groups. Women often go out with gay men. It's less common to find mixed groups of singles socialising.

There are also different expectations surrounding the way men and women interact. Western men and women are more likely to treat each other the same way they'd treat friends of their own sex. This can cause problems with Thai partners.

The marriage of convenience

There's a stereotype of the Thai-*farang* couple known around the world: the older Western man who marries a much younger Thai woman. She has youth and beauty; he has money. It's real enough to be worthy of attention here. In such cases the woman is usually from a poor family in the Northeast of Thailand. She may already have a child from an earlier relationship with a Thai man. The man, on the other hand, has often divorced from a Western woman considerably later in life.

Such couples meet in any number of ways. These days the Internet is awash with Thai dating websites – some specifically aimed at bringing such couples together, others just like any other dating site. The couple may also have met in a venue associated with the sex industry. In her, the man sees a chance to spend his twilight years with an attractive young woman in a pleasant country. In him, she sees a way out of poverty, an escape from a life with few prospects except hard work and wages that don't last to the end of the month.

She will have not only her own welfare in mind, but that of her whole family. He might sell his house at home, using the money to buy a new home in the woman's village. Combined with his pension, he will likely have enough left over to give him and his wife a very comfortable lifestyle. It's a marriage of convenience, then, but not necessarily one that starts off unhappily.

But while some of these marriages no doubt work as hoped, they do seem to be prone to failure. Frequently, mutual understanding comes quite far down the list as the basis for the relationship, meaning that neither party knows entirely what they're getting into. And it's hardly surprising that a retiree from the West and a young woman from Thailand might have different priorities and visions of what they want to get out of life.

In 2007, *The Nation* reported comments from a judge at the Juvenile and Family Court in the Northeastern province of Khon Kaen, who told the paper that of 142 divorces filed in his province in a three-month period, 'most' were local girls looking to split from foreign husbands. 'He speculated that Thai girls had unreasonable expectations of a superior lifestyle and high incomes when they married foreign men – only to become sharply disillusioned quite quickly.'

If a man appears to be getting on 'too well' with a woman, it can result in jealousy and recriminations. The man may feel he's done nothing wrong, while the woman feels slighted.

DATING

Dating norms are changing. In times gone by, a woman on a first date with a man would generally be accompanied by one or more friends acting as chaperones. The man would be expected to pay for the date, friends and all. This custom – or perhaps 'precaution' is a better word – isn't completely dead, but in Bangkok it's now much more the exception than the rule.

Still, while the chaperones might have disappeared, the expectation that the man pay for the date remains common. Often, this is not unreasonable, since in the case of most – though certainly not all – Thai-*farang* relationships, the man is much better off than the woman. Nevertheless, some Thai women will insist on paying their way, particularly if they're keen to assuage the man's fears that she's only after money.

Sexually, things can progress quickly. Traditionally, a woman was expected to remain a virgin until marriage. Some women from 'upstanding' middle-class families still hold to this custom. Most don't. And many women living in Bangkok will be far from their families – and prying eyes. Thus, they do what they want.

Still, female virginity remains 'officially' prized in Thai society. This is one area in which public rhetoric is sorely divorced from reality. Each Valentine's Day, the Thai media gleefully stokes a moral panic over the young women who will choose the day to have sex for the first time. The attention is rarely directed at the men. As far as Thai society is concerned, boys will be boys.

THE SEX DIVIDE

There's an obvious sexual divide when it comes to the relationship experiences of foreign men and women in Thailand. The majority of straight men from the West living here are in relationships with Thai women, or have been in the past. While many Western women do start families with Thai men, they're vastly outnumbered by their male peers. At the risk of making an unseemly generalisation, relatively few Western women seem to find Thai men attractive, and the feeling is often mutual.

In *CultureShock! Thailand*, Robert Cooper explains that Thai men tend to think of women as falling into one of two categories: *priao* ('sour') and *wan* ('sweet'). A 'sweet' woman is one who conforms to the traditional Thai ideals of femininity – devoted to her husband, deferent, and with impeccable manners. A 'sour' woman, on the other hand, is more likely to be assertive and less concerned with etiquette.

Cooper asked some Thai men whether they felt jealousy over the number of Thai women who formed relationships with Western men. The answer was almost universally 'no'. They pointed out that Thai men had a preference for the 'sweet', while foreigners seemed to be more interested in

Sin sot

The Thai custom of *sin sot* – the paying of a so-called 'bride price' – is often misunderstood, and frequently a source of tension between Thai-*farang* couples when the prospect of marriage arises. Traditionally, a man wishing to marry a woman provides her and her family with two things: *khong man*, a gift of 24-karat-gold jewellery presented to the girl herself, and *sin sot*, a gift of money to the family.

Sin sot is practised at all levels of society, though richer metropolitan families are less likely to expect it these days. The more humble a woman's background, the more likely her family is to expect *sin sot*. The amount to be paid is negotiated with the bride's family by the groom or his representative. In typical Thai fashion, they're unlikely to be so crass as to demand a specific figure. Instead, they'll usually expect the groom to propose an amount. They'll make it clear if the amount is acceptable.

The amount of *sin sot* paid will depend on the family's wealth and status, the woman's age, occupation and whether she's been married before. The groom's means may also be taken into account. Poorer families might expect THB100,000, with THB200,000–500,000 going to middle-class families, rising to the millions if the family is wealthy. Every case is different, however, so it's difficult to lay down hard-and-fast rules.

To an outsider's eye, it might appear that the husband is 'buying' his wife from her family. This is the wrong way to think about the custom. By paying *sin sot*, the man is demonstrating to the family that he's financially able to provide for his wife. The parents will often return the money to the couple in some way, perhaps in the form of land or a house.

One friend of mine told me that he reluctantly agreed to pay THB400,000 for his wedding with his Thai wife. After the ceremony, his new mother-in-law offered to give him back the money, which he accepted with some relief. When he told his wife, she was furious, telling him that he was supposed to insist on her family keeping it. To my friend's dismay, his wife then insisted they give all their wedding gifts to her mother. They spent their first few days of marriage barely speaking.

Why talk when you can check your phone?

the 'sour'. 'So why be jealous?' his subjects asked. 'I should feel sorry for them!' Western women's lack of interest in Thai men is thus frequently mutual. From a Thai perspective, the former tend towards the 'sour' and don't appeal so much to the Thai 'sweet tooth'.

There's also a class aspect to all this – middle and upper class women are more likely to conform to the 'sweet' template than working class women, who tend more to the 'sour'. This isn't a theory that can be taken too far – human behaviour can rarely be divided into simple dichotomies like this. But it does help to explain some tendencies in Thai-*farang* relationships.

PUBLIC AFFECTION AND KEEPING UP APPEARANCES

Having seen the brazen sexuality on display in places like Soi Cowboy, Nana and Patpong, some travellers get the impression that Thailand is a sexually liberal place. Those with more exposure to mainstream Thai society begin to see it as conservative. The truth probably lies somewhere between these two views.

It's certainly true that in comparison with many Western societies, couples are expected to behave modestly in public. Making out on the BTS, for example, would be completely unacceptable. Traditionally, the opposite sexes aren't even supposed to touch in public, though this rule is fast becoming old-fashioned. And those elements of Thai society that appear to be conservative are frequently not as conservative as they look. The focus for any Thai person in public is to keep up appearances. What happens in private is your own business.

In 2011, a cultural stink was raised after a video surfaced on the Internet showing some girls dancing topless on Silom Road during the annual Songkran water fight. In typical fashion, the Thai Ministry of Culture condemned the girls for 'destroying the image' of Thailand.

There was plenty of irony in all this. A hundred years ago it was normal for Thai women to go bare-chested in public, and it was only after decades of determined 'modernisation' drives by Thai monarchs and military strongmen that Western standards of dress were adopted. What's more, at the very moment it was condemning the girls, the Thai Ministry of Culture turned out to have a large image of a painting entitled 'Thai Goddesses of Songkran' on its website. The picture featured three ethereal Thai ladies, all of whom were displaying their ample bosoms. The incident took place just down the road from Soi Patpong, the infamous sex district, in which infinitely more lurid things happen every day.

STAYING CLEAN AND THE SNIFF KISS

The Western-style mouth-to-mouth kiss is reserved for the bedroom in Thailand. How do Thais show affection for each other in public? Through the sniff-kiss, the act of putting your nose to your loved one's cheek or neck and inhaling deeply. Thais call this endearing gesture *hom*, which is also an adjective that means something smells good. It's a delight to be on the end of a *hom*, a validation of your partner's feelings for you, as well as confirmation that you – yes, you – smell fragrant.

It's no coincidence that Thais are highly concerned with cleanliness. Taking several showers a day is normal, including before going to bed. Both men and women make liberal use of baby powder. The result is that Bangkokians are miraculously clean and pleasant-smelling people, given the temperatures and the steamy, polluted air of the city.

But staying clean and sweet-smelling can be a challenge for foreigners. Most of us just aren't used to the heat, and just minutes outside can leave us drenched with sweat. Sometimes this can't be helped. But those who only take a single shower a day are definitely 'doing it wrong', as the saying goes. Take a leaf out of the locals' book: two or three showers a day, and a regular dusting with baby powder. Your Thai partner will appreciate it – and be more inclined to reward you with a *hom*.

MIA NOI AND MISTRESSES

The practice of taking a *mia noi* ('minor wife', 'mistress') is an old one but still fairly widespread in Thailand. In such arrangements, a husband remains married to his *mia yai* ('major wife') and continues to support her and the children. But he also supports a second, generally younger wife, putting her up in an apartment and giving her a regular sum of money. Sometimes he will have children with his *mia noi*, sometimes not.

Some *mia noi* are perfectly happy with this arrangement. It allows them to live a largely independent life without having to work or deal with the frustrations that can come from spending every waking hour with a husband. There's also little to stop her from taking a *kik* (*see below*).

The *mia yai* may know about the *mia noi*, though she may be kept in the dark. On finding out, she may accept the arrangement, so long as her husband continues to support her and her children. It's unlikely she'll be happy about the situation, of course, though she may reason that if she makes a fuss about the *mia noi*, her husband might leave her and the family. Today, the rising number of financially independent women means the *mia noi* is on the decline.

JUST FOR *KIKS*

Not a friend, not a lover, but something in between – it won't be long before you hear the term '*kik*' thrown about

Penis cutting

One day in 1997, Prayoon Ekklang, a taxi driver from Nakhon Ratchasima, awoke with a severe pain in his groin. Standing in front of him was his wife, La-ong. In one of her hands was a knife, in the other his severed penis. According to local newspaper reports, La-ong then attached the member to a bunch of helium balloons and released them into the sky, never to be seen again. One thing was for sure – Prayoon wouldn't be taking another mistress.

Despite the prevalence of infidelity in Thai society, Thai women have a fearsome reputation for jealousy, and not all are willing to accept their spouse taking a *mia noi* or *kik*. They have been known to exact furious revenge on philandering husbands. Severing the cheater's member, while hardly common, has happened often enough to make Thai surgeons world leaders in penis reattachment surgery.

As an *AFP* story from 2004 explained, severed penises have been boiled, buried and even fed to ducks. A frequent trigger for the attack is some sort of public humiliation of the wife through the husband's taking of a mistress – a loss of face, in other words. Add to that the penis's symbolic importance in Thai culture as a symbol of potency – it's often referred to as '*jao lok*', 'lord of the world' – and you have a recipe for this most vicious act of vengeance.

Surasak Muangsombot, a surgeon at Bangkok's Paolo Memorial Hospital, told *AFP* that his team alone had operated on 33 cases of severed penises. While the reattachment had always worked, the penis only assumed normal function half the time. Dr Surasak's hardest case required bribing a furious wife to reveal where she had hidden her husband's severed member. It turned out to be floating in a septic tank. Said Dr Surasak: 'I asked the nurse to clean it up well and warned the patient that he may get septicemia and he said, "Do your best and if it gets septicemia I will die with my penis."'

---

in Bangkok. You might even become one yourself. The origin of the term isn't certain, though some say it derives from '*kuk kik ju ji*', an onomatopoeic expression for the coos and murmurs exchanged by lovers.

Regardless, there doesn't yet seem to be agreement on the precise meaning of the word. Some take '*kik*' to mean a sexual relationship without commitment: 'friends with benefits' or 'fuck buddies' in the West. Others say a relationship with a *kik* doesn't have to be sexual. For some, a *kik* is someone you cheat on your partner with, and a single person can't have one. Others say you can 'make out' with a *kik* but not go as far as sex, which you reserve for your partner. Yes – it's confusing.

Is the *kik* new to Thai culture, or just a cutesy rebranding of something that's been around forever? An older word for someone you have an affair with, '*chu*', is much more threatening. It's common for men to be described as '*jao chu*', meaning a philanderer. The term is often worn as a badge of pride. In the same way that in the West, a man who sleeps around is a 'stud', while a woman who does the same is a 'slut', few women wish to be labelled '*jao chu*'.

Perhaps what's new about the *kik* is the level of mutuality implied. Both participants engage in a *kik* relationship for nothing more than the pleasure – sexual or otherwise – of the other person's company. A mistress, on the other hand, is frequently 'in it for the money'.

Ideally, a *kik* relationship can be broken off without any hard feelings on either side. The reality is likely to be messier. Some couples start off as each other's *kik* before graduating to something more serious – not so different from the way things work in any other part of the world, really.

PROSTITUTION

Pity the fat, sweaty, middle-aged white man. Not only is he fat, sweaty and staring his senescence in the face – he's also poster boy for Thailand's sex industry, sketched in a thousand articles in the international media as the typical client of the Thai prostitute. And while a stroll down Sukhumvit's Soi 4, one of Bangkok's sex industry epicentres, will take you past many gentlemen sitting in girly bars who match that description, you'll see men of all shapes, sizes, ages and races.

The Bangkok John could be anyone: the fat, sweaty middle-aged European of the clichés; a thin, young and actually rather dry American; a backpacker from Tokyo; a Chinese businessman; a programmer on holiday from Bangalore. 'He' could even be a 'she'. Or a 'they'.

But he's most likely to be a Thai male. The foreign-oriented sex industry is dwarfed by that catering for the domestic market. Prostitution is technically illegal in Thailand, but officially tolerated. Drive up Ratchadaphisek Road from the Rama 9 intersection and it's plain enough. Around the Huai Khwang area, vast, casino-sized 'massage parlours' line the

Girls of Soi Cowboy, complete with numbered badges.

road: Poseidon, Caesar's Palace, Emmanuelle. No one is under any illusions what these places are for – just ask Chuvit Kamolvisit (*see page 301*). It's an open secret that visits to these places are used by salesmen to grease the wheels of government and business.

Still, it's easy to overestimate the prevalence of prostitution in the city. In 2001, the World Health Organisation claimed the 'most reliable' estimate was that there were 150,000 to 200,000 sex workers in Thailand. That represents around 0.5–0.75 per cent of the female population, though this ignores the fact that many of the country's prostitutes are men.

Foreigners who are new to the city often find themselves in nightspots where working girls congregate, leading them to get an exaggerated impression of how common prostitution is. It shouldn't need to be spelled out, but here we go: the vast majority of Thai women are not prostitutes and should not be treated as such.

Having said that, exchanging money for sex or company is certainly less taboo than it is in the West. Prostitution in Thailand is more of a continuum than a dichotomy, and it can be hard to say who's a prostitute and who isn't. We might be confident saying a woman who works in a 'dodgy' massage parlour is in the profession, but what about a university student who meets a man in a nightclub and asks him for money if he wants to go home with her?

Most working girls in Bangkok are from Thailand's poor Northeast. A typical story: a poor young woman gets pregnant by a Thai man who wants nothing to do with the child. Abortion being illegal – and a heavy source of *bap* ('bad karma') – she has the baby, but has neither the education nor the connections to get a well-paying job to provide for the child. She thus turns to prostitution to pay for her child's upbringing. Frequently, she will be inducted into the industry through a family friend or someone from her village, who will arrange for her to move to Bangkok to work.

'Sexpats'

The term 'sexpat' is often thrown around in Bangkok circles to refer to foreign men who supposedly live in Thailand purely in order to exploit opportunities for cheap sex. There is, to be sure, a touch of reality to this, though frequently also a degree of hypocrisy in those who use the word. Some middle-class expats apply the term to their less well-heeled compatriots, while living lifestyles that aren't actually very different.

Novelist Lawrence Osborne, who sketched a number of Bangkok characters in his memoir *Bangkok Days*, says the term is meaningless. 'Very few people live in a place just for sex – that's insane,' he says, pointing out that people almost always have several reasons for living somewhere, often related to money. 'But the West is obsessed with the sexual angle – which Thais find baffling and vaguely pathetic but in some way humanly understandable. The reality is more prosaic than the myth.'

Her parents will look after her child, and she will send money home each month to pay for it. There may be a 'don't ask, don't tell' policy when it comes to the origins of the cash. The family knows the girl couldn't be making that kind of money in a factory or a legitimate spa, but a pretence will be maintained.

Some women go into prostitution because of a strong sense of duty to look after their parents. By providing for them, they also make merit. As Mulder explains in *Inside Thai Society*: 'As long as the woman cares for her relatives and recompenses the *bunkhun* of her parents with gifts and money, she can still see – and present – herself as a good person. When she has accumulated enough or when her fortunes turn, she may return to her village of origin to marry and be accepted with little or no stigma.'

In recent years the discourse about sex work has been conflated in the media with that of 'sex trafficking'. The prevalence of genuine sex slavery is overblown, as organisations like EMPOWER fervently argue, but there can be subtle, or not so subtle, pressures at work that can make a woman decide she has little choice but to sell her body. A customer, unless he gets to know her well, has no way of knowing the circumstances that drove her into the industry, and therefore precisely what he is complicit in – perhaps a transaction between two consenting adults, perhaps something murkier.

LGBT

When it comes to sexuality, anything goes in Thailand – so long as it takes place behind closed doors. Gays, lesbians and transsexuals are accepted in Thai society and violence targeting gays is unheard of. While much of the world is trying to move past the legacy of religious homophobia – or remains mired in it – Buddhism has nothing to say about homosexuality.

Still, while being gay has never been criminalised in Thailand and the age of consent remains equal for people of all sexualities, gay couples don't have special protections in law and it remains rare to find openly gay people in positions of power in Thai society. It's an open secret that at least one very prominent Thai statesman is gay, though it's not something that can be acknowledged publicly.

The multifarious nature of human sexuality is acknowledged in the Thai language, with an interesting range of slang. Gay men mostly identify as 'king' or 'queen' depending on their sexual role. Lesbians, meanwhile, go by '*tom*' (short for tomboy) and '*dy*' for the feminine role. There is some more unusual terminology too: an '*adam*' is a man who likes *toms*, while a '*cherry*' is a girl who goes for gays and ladyboys.

For foreigners, Bangkok is a great place to be a gay man. The nightlife, centred around Silom Sois 2 and 4, is lively and unpretentious. As with heterosexuals, many gays from the West find their sexual stock rises in Thailand, which at least partly relates to their relative affluence. Thai gays tend to be less flexible than Westerners when it comes to their role in relationships. They will usually prefer to be either dominant or submissive in every relationship.

Many of the cultural taboos that apply to heterosexual relationships apply to gay couples, too. Showing too much affection in public is frowned upon. Gay foreigners can make the mistake of thinking this indicates their Thai partner is not 'out'. It is just as likely due to the traditional tendency to modesty in public.

Lesbians, *toms* and *dys*

Lesbian couples are common in Thai society and, given their rigidly defined gender roles, very visible. The word 'lesbian' is mostly avoided by homosexual Thai women. While women who identify as such do exist, calling themselves '*les*' for short, most identify with other terms.

Butch lesbians call themselves '*tom*', short for the English 'tomboy', while femmes use the word '*dy*', pronounced like the word for 'good' but with a rising tone. *Toms* bind their breasts, cut their hair short and wear men's clothes. *Dys* tend to be dress very feminine. It's quite common for straight women to experiment with a relationship with a *tom* when they're in their teenage years or early twenties, before moving into relationships with men.

Generally *toms* try to play the role of the ideal partner in the relationship, spoiling their *dy* in every way, including taking her shopping, carrying her bags and paying for her every whim. *Toms* are expected to maintain their male role in bed, and will keep their clothes on during sex in order to maintain their male appearance, instead concentrating entirely on pleasuring their girlfriend.

The rigidity can be frustrating for foreign lesbians used to more fluid roles in relationships. Caitlyn 'Cee' Webster, an American expat who runs the website bangkoklesbian.com, advises foreign gay women to stick to the label 'lesbian': 'I've heard of many Western women referring to themselves as a '*tom*' or '*dy*', then to get in bed with a real Thai *tom* or *dy* and be frustrated with the lack of sexual fluidity. I've heard stories of Western lesbians attempting to touch a *tom* sexually or trying to take off her shirt only to have their hands slapped away in anger, ending with frustration with both parties. So, please describe yourself as a lesbian!'

Transsexuals/ladyboys

Famous the world over, Thailand's ladyboys ('*kathoei*'), form a very visible contingent in Thai society. Or perhaps – to the untrained eye – they're not so visible. Thai people's smooth skin and small frames seem to make them particularly well-suited to convincing gender reassignment surgery, and some Thai ladyboys achieve levels of feminine beauty most women can only dream of. Today, ladyboys can even undergo surgery to reduce the size of their Adam's apple and raise the pitch of their voice.

The word '*kathoei*' is still in widespread use, though its meaning is ambiguous, since these days it's often used by gay men, too. In comparison with most parts of the world, transsexuals are given the freedom to be who they want to be. At the same time, Thai Buddhists often view ladyboys as being born that way as punishment for past-life misdeeds.

They remain far from equal members of society. It was only in late 2011 that Thailand's first transsexual cabin crew took to the air, on airline PC Air, named not after 'political correctness' but for its owner Peter Chan. Thailand is yet to have a single transsexual MP or prominent business leader. Many nightclubs ban ladyboys from their premises entirely. News stories, whether in Thai or English, don't hesitate to point out that the perpetrators of crimes are ladyboys in their headlines. Ladyboys are unable to legally change their sex, meaning that even those who have undergone gender reassignment surgery are kept in men's prisons.

Many ladyboys end up as sex workers. A contingent of foreigners seems to have a particular appreciation for ladyboy prostitutes. There are bars in the major sex districts that are staffed entirely by *kathoei*. What these men look for in a ladyboy – the combination of a beautiful woman and a penis – isn't necessarily what ladyboys want for themselves. Many find that once they've had full gender reassignment surgery, they cease to be in demand with such men.

PRACTICALITIES

THE PROSPECT OF setting yourself up in Bangkok can be intimidating for the first-time visitor. Visions of a vast, steamy, anarchic city in which getting anything done takes a mastery of Thai, a suitcase full of cash and a letter of recommendation from your ambassador can be put to rest: in reality, there's little to worry about. Visas and work permits can be perplexing, but there are relatively few hoops that a foreigner has to jump through to start a life, or a chapter of one, in Thailand. Nevertheless, that doesn't mean a little extra knowledge won't make things easier.

WHAT TO BRING
What does the discerning traveller need to bring to this balmy megalopolis? The first thing to bear in mind is that there's very little you *can't* buy in Bangkok. So long as you have money, you could easily show up with nothing but the clothes on your back and a passport and buy everything you needed once you got here. Having said that, imported goods can be expensive. Prices for imported electronic gadgets such as cameras, lenses and computer products can be 15 per cent higher than in the United States. Liquor is also taxed heavily.

Foreigners with a work permit are allowed to bring in one air and one sea shipment of household goods into the country duty free. The shipments must arrive within six months of your entry to Thailand. Alcohol and vehicles aren't included in the scheme. For more information on the scheme, see www.customs.go.th. Some expats have their goods shipped to the port and then have trouble getting them through customs. The easiest thing to do is to get a quote from a reputable moving company, rather than trying to do it on the cheap.

Given that the Thai capital is one of the hottest major cities in the world, you might wish to pack some light clothing. Good-quality clothes that fit the larger frames of *farang* used to be hard to find, though it's becoming easier now that international clothing chains have branches in the more upmarket malls. One thin layer will serve you well any day of the year, though you should bear future travel possibilities in mind. In Chiang Mai, during the cold season of November to February, it can get cold enough at night to warrant a jacket. As you head north from Thailand into other parts of East Asia, chilly winters become the norm.

Mosquitos can be a pest in Bangkok during the rainy season, though the coating of most of the land in concrete and asphalt means they're less of a problem than upcountry. You won't catch malaria on Sukhumvit Road, though dengue fever infections aren't unheard of, so mosquito spray wouldn't go amiss.

The Bangkok sun can be fierce and if you're planning on being outdoors for extended periods, you should protect your skin. Still, mosquito spray and sun lotion are easy to find in the city – just go to any pharmacy or department store. Arriving packed with both is more a peace-of-mind measure than a necessity.

You may also wish to bring certificates of higher education. Some employers will want to see them as proof of your qualifications. If you plan to work as a teacher, a degree certificate is technically required to get a work permit, though an employer's relationship with the local Labour Office can result in 'exceptions' being made.

VISAS

To live in Bangkok, you'll need a visa. If you already have a job secured before you arrive, your employer will be able to advise you on what sort of visa you should apply for in your home country. Otherwise, you will need to learn to navigate the complicated and perplexing world of the Thai visa, a subject so complicated and perplexing it spawned a whole web forum dedicated to understanding it.

ThaiVisa

The ThaiVisa website (www.thaivisa.com) is probably the best place to find practical information about life in the city – if you can handle the bozos. It started as a forum for foreigners to exchange information about Thailand's baroque and constantly changing visa system. It's since expanded and today covers all aspects of life in the kingdom.

If there's anything you need to know about living in Bangkok, someone has probably posted it on ThaiVisa. Topics are searchable from the main forum page (www.thaivisa.com/forum). Naturally, you can also post your own questions. As with any web forum, be sure to check the subject hasn't already been dealt with elsewhere first.

Unfortunately, the cloak of anonymity seems to bring out the worst in some users of ThaiVisa and a depressingly large proportion are more interested in attacking people seeking information than helping them. One contingent in particular seems to despise everything about 'Thai's' [sic] and Thailand, despite choosing to remain in the country. As evidence, I offer the following threads posted on the forum (spelling and grammar have not been changed): 'What Is It About Thai's On The Telephone', 'Why can't Thai's give/follow directions?', 'Why Are So Many Thai's So Uneducated About Buddhism', 'Are Thai's Deaf?' and 'Double Standars For Thai's In Our Countries?'

There are certainly some unsavoury characters lurking on the site. No one I know was particularly surprised when it emerged in February 2012 that one of the moderators, a Norwegian man who went under the name 'Katabeachbum', had been arrested for murder. The man had allegedly killed his girlfriend before keeping her decomposed body in a bin filled with acid inside his home for two years. Now, obviously, I'm not trying to tar all ThaiVisa users with the same brush: there are some very helpful members who are happy to offer the confused newbie some good advice. Just know what to expect out there.

The Thai government occasionally changes the rules regarding visas based on the prevailing political winds. When the current policy priority is to 'encourage tourism', rules may be relaxed and fees lowered. If the government is pushing to 'crack down' on foreign undesirables, the opposite happens.

The policies of individual Thai embassies and consulates change frequently, too. One month the Vientiane Embassy might be dishing out multiple-entry tourist visas; the next, the best you can hope for is a double-entry. As a result, it isn't possible to give a comprehensive and up-to-date guide to the visa situation here. For the latest information, complete with field reports from (un)satisfied consular customers, check the aforementioned web forum.

Thailand offers a visa exemption scheme for tourists arriving from the United States, Australia, New Zealand and most European countries by air. The scheme offers travellers a free stay of up to 30 days. For longer stays, a 60-day tourist visa can be obtained from Thai embassies and consulates. Stays can also be extended in Bangkok itself at the immigration office on Soi Suan Phlu, Sathorn Tai Road (0-2287-3101). A 60-day visa can be extended for a further 30 days, while a 30-day stay can be lengthened by 7–10 days.

If you wish to work, study or retire in Thailand, you'll need a 'non-immigrant' visa, which can give you up to a year in the kingdom at a time. Depending on your job and the status of your employer, you may have to leave the country every 90 days, however, giving rise to the need for the dreaded 'visa run'. A few companies will take care of the whole trip for about THB2,000, including transport, visa fees and a meal. A Google search for 'visa run bangkok' will turn up several.

Many foreigners looking to stay in Thailand for extended periods without working choose to get an education 'ED' visa, which can be secured by students enrolled in educational institutions of various kinds, including language, diving, massage and *muay Thai* schools, not to mention universities. If you're going the language-school route, you'll need to sign up for a minimum of four Thai lessons per week for a minimum of 90 days. Most language schools offer information on how to apply for the education visa, which will need to be done at an embassy or consulate outside the country.

Overstaying your visa – that is, remaining in Thailand after your visa has expired without permission from Immigration – should be avoided. If your visa has expired when you leave the country, you'll be fined THB500 for every day of overstay up to a maximum of THB20,000. However, if you're caught by the police without a valid visa inside the kingdom, you can be sent to an immigration detention centre (not pleasant places by any means) and deported.

WORK PERMITS

Unless you're employed by an embassy or certain international organisations like the UN, technically you need a permit to do any sort of work in Thailand. Even volunteering for free counts as 'work', though in such cases the law rarely seems to be enforced. Once you have

Visa runs

The 'visa run' is a curious aspect of the Bangkok expat experience, and one that only the most fortunate of exiles – the diplomats, the UN staffers – will not experience at least once. The objective of the visa run is merely to cross one of Thailand's borders, only to re-enter and thus renew your permission to stay in the kingdom. Alas, the visa run eats into your spare time, costs you money and seems to send a dispiriting message, courtesy of the Thai state: 'Don't get too comfortable'.

The well-funded expat uses the visa run as an excuse to fly to a nearby capital and enjoy a weekend away in a swanky hotel. For less fortunate souls, the visa run entails spending an entire day stuck in a minivan or tour bus with a bunch of bleary-eyed strangers. The destination is inevitably a shady Cambodian border town that nobody in their right mind would otherwise want to visit, while the highlight of the trip is likely to be a grim meal obtained with a voucher in a Chinese casino, and the opportunity to purchase some knock-off cigarettes that taste like chemically treated tree bark.

a work visa, your employer should prepare the requisite documents for you and send you to the Labour Department to apply for a work permit. They may be able to take care of everything themselves.

There are strict rules about how many work permits a company can issue to foreigners, which depends on various factors including the number of Thai staff the company employs. This leads some companies to try to employ foreigners without work permits. Bear in mind that this is illegal. Being caught working without a permit can result in your prosecution, imprisonment and deportation.

ACCOMMODATION

For a major world city, Bangkok has some of the best value accommodation on the planet. Unlike some cities, it's remarkably easy to find a new home and move straight in. Having said that, it's worth dedicating some time to finding somewhere to live: if you're signing a contract for a year or more, a few extra days of house hunting could result in big savings. Rents vary significantly depending on the same kind of factors affecting any real-estate market: location, transport links, local amenities and the quality of the property itself. There are bargains to be had – and rip-offs to be wary of.

Temporary

Unless your employer is taking care of your accommodation for you, you'll need somewhere to stay while you look for something more permanent. If you don't have friends with a spare room or sofa, a hotel is the obvious option. This is one area in which Bangkok is blessed, offering what may be the best-value hotels on the planet, and lots of them. With scores of websites devoted to hotel ratings and reservations, finding one is a task I'll leave you to figure out for yourself.

But this being the 2010s, there are other options. The Airbnb website (www.airbnb.com/s/Thailand) and smartphone app allows owners of vacant apartments, condos and houses to let their properties on a short-term basis. Rentals can be as brief as a single night, or months at a time. The longer you commit to renting a place the better value it becomes. In May 2013 a New York City court ruled the site illegal in the Big Apple – reasoning that you can't run your apartment as an unlicensed 'hotel' – but in the freewheeling Big Mango, it's still going strong, with hundreds of listings.

If cash is an issue and you don't have too much luggage, there's always Couchsurfing (www.couchsurfing.com). The site offers a similar service to Airbnb, though spare rooms, camp beds and couches take the place of whole properties. Needless to say, the sacrifice in privacy is reflected in the savings you make: it's free. Perhaps more importantly, if you're lucky you'll stay with a host who's willing to do more than just provide a bed – as a local, they'll be able to give you advice and maybe even play tour guide. A 'vouching' and 'testimonial' system helps to ensure you don't end up staying with a serial killer.

Where to live

If 'location, location, location' describes the essentials of a desirable property, then that's even more true in a city with traffic as bad as Bangkok's. At rush hour, a 20-minute journey on clear roads can turn into a 90-minute nightmare. Unless you want to spend a fifth of your waking hours in traffic, you'll want to make sure your journeys are manageable. With a family to consider, finding the right place to live becomes more complex still, with journeys to schools to consider, too. The BTS Skytrain, MRT and BRT systems (*see pages 189–192*) have improved commutes for people living in large swathes of the city, though rents have increased in those areas to reflect that.

Before you dive into housing websites or make calls to estate agents, then, your first step should be to choose a neighbourhood of the city to base yourself in. Its character can have a considerable bearing on your experience here. The Sukhumvit strip from Phloenchit to Ekkamai is quite different from the rest of Bangkok. Only in this area – and, to a lesser extent, Silom, Sathorn, Banglamphu, Ari and Pratunam – will you find foreigners in large numbers. You'll also find other things that are less readily available: quality Western food, for example.

The further away from the city centre you move, the more life will resemble life in the rest of Thailand. And there are plenty of benefits to living in a more 'Thai' neighbourhood. You'll be getting a more culturally eye-opening experience and have more chance of making Thai friends. You probably won't get invited to join a *wong lao* (drinking circle) in Thonglor, but out in the suburbs of Bang Na you just might. Food prices and rents fall in such places and they're almost certainly where a lot of the city's best street grub is to be found – on Sukhumvit, not so much.

What to think about

When looking for a home, you may want to consider the following:

- How long will it take me to get to work?
- How long will it take the children to get to school?
- Is there a long walk to the BTS or main road?
- Will I have to use motorcycle taxis and am I comfortable with that?
- Does the area flood during the rainy season?
- Is the local area served by shops and restaurants?
- How noisy is the place? Can you hear traffic?
- How well ventilated is it?
- Will I need to use the air-conditioning constantly?
- Are the air-conditioning machines old, and thus expensive to run and noisy?
- What are the water and electricity charges?
- What is the water pressure like? If it's no good, can it be fixed?
- If I leave before the contract expires, will I lose my deposit?
- Can I keep a pet?

Finding a home

Once you've settled on an area, how you find a place to live will depend entirely on how lazy you are. The energetic method is to pound the streets, which has the advantage of giving you a feel for the prospective neighbourhood. Vacant houses for rent will often have a sign outside saying so, with a telephone number to call. Sometimes such signs can be found on lampposts all over a neighbourhood, and aren't necessarily hanging anywhere near the property. In apartments and condominiums, ask at reception to see any rooms available. In the case of condominiums, the owner may have to be notified to show you around, but frequently reception will have a spare key and be able to take you up themselves. It goes without saying that this process will be much easier with a Thai speaker in tow.

More sedentary house hunters may choose to look for a property on the Internet. I've listed some prominent property sites below. Alternatively, you can enlist the services of an estate agent, who will select properties for you and arrange viewings; you need only meet the agent somewhere and follow them around for however many hours it takes. Many firms employ foreigners for this job. They are paid on commission, though this money will come from the landlord, not you. Nevertheless, some agents may try to exert pressure on you to make a quick decision, knowing that once you're out of their reach, you might not call them back.

Properties come furnished and unfurnished and for rental periods of anything from a month to years at a time. However, a minimum contract of one year is standard, particularly when it comes to houses. Always bargain. If you tell your agent you aren't willing to pay over a certain price, they will do the negotiating for you. You might ask for furniture or appliances to be thrown in, or for certain modifications to be made to the property. Nothing is off the table in the Land of the Deal. The deposit will usually be two months' rent, so when you move in you'll need to be ready to pay three months' rent up front. The value of breakages will be deducted from the deposit when you leave. You'll generally lose it all if you leave before the contract is up.

Useful websites
The following websites have searchable databases of properties to rent:
- www.thaiapartment.com
- www.bangkokfinder.com
- www.bangkokapartment.org
- www.mrroomfinder.com
- en.9apartment.com

Electricity
Thailand's electricity supply is 220V. Sockets used to be two-prong only but three prongs are becoming the norm in new properties. They usually accommodate both flat and round prongs. If you have a three-prong device but only two-prong sockets, buy an adaptor rather than snapping off the third prong. Adaptors cost relatively little and can be found at any

hardware store, supermarket or, failing that, department store. If you come from a country that uses 110V supply such as the United States, check the power rating on any devices you wish to bring with you. If it gives a range such as '100~240V', it can be used in Thailand.

Electricity is relatively expensive. If you use a lot of air-conditioning, you will notice the size of your bills, particularly if the machines are old. You'll notice the noise, too. Power cuts are not unheard of but rarely last for more than an hour or two. Surges can also be a problem in older properties. Uninterruptible power supplies (UPS), which keep your computer running during cuts and protect the motherboard from getting fried, are available at hardware and department stores.

Water

Tap water is cheap, but don't drink it. Bangkok's Metropolitan Water Authority says the quality of its water surpasses international standards, and at the point of production, it likely does. However, the World Health Organisation recommends avoiding drinking tap water in Thailand, which it says is 'still questionable' in some places because it may have been contaminated in the piping. You may wish to buy a water boiler or have a filter installed on your tap, though the simplest policy – and the one nearly all expats follow – is to drink only bottled water. Tap water is safe enough for brushing your teeth and washing dishes.

Bottled water can be bought in stores, though there are better options. Many apartments, for example, have water dispensing machines on the ground floor. They usually charge one or two baht per litre. Once you've

Should I drink that?

Street-food establishments nearly always provide metal jugs of free water on their tables. They are usually filled from large bottles in the back of the restaurant. Alternatively, they may contain boiled tap water. If the water is slightly yellow, it is weak tea and will definitely have been boiled. Regardless, the water at these establishments is generally safe to drink, though bottles can be ordered if you're unconvinced. The WHO recommends that you 'avoid ice cubes and crushed ice'. I don't know anyone who avoids ice cubes. I've consumed melted ice almost every day that I've lived here, and it's difficult to see how you'd get by avoiding it.

emptied a few bottles of store-bought water, refill them at the machine and store them in the fridge. Alternatively, there are water delivery services such as Sprinkle (0-2712-7272) which sell water in 18.9-litre bottles. Buying in bulk like this will save you time and money.

Staff

You may not be used to employing domestic help in your home country, but you'll probably want to do so in Bangkok, even if you just need someone to come in and clean a couple of times a week. Maids can also buy groceries, do laundry, pay bills, help with childcare and cook. English-speaking maids, who command a higher wage, can also serve as translators and interpreters.

Finding maids and nannies isn't difficult. There are plenty of agencies that provide domestic workers based in the city. A quick Google search should turn up several. The advantage of using an agency is that they will take care of the contract and any other paperwork. If you need to make a complaint or give instructions to your non-English-speaking maid, you can tell the agency, who can relay your instructions. The agency has an incentive to ensure its staff don't steal from you or help burglars to do so; it has a reputation to protect. Agency maids tend to be more expensive, however.

You might also find staff through word-of-mouth. A maid who has worked for someone you know is the best option. Your landlord may also be able to provide a recommendation. If you live in a condominium or apartment building there will be maids already working for other residents. Staff at reception should be able to give you their contact details. Maids also advertise their services on classifieds sites such as Craigslist, though be warned: you'll have to sift through some unseemly stuff, like 'naked maid with special services' ads. If you employ a maid without going through an agency, make sure to check their references and get a copy of their ID card and a recent photograph.

It's essential that you make sure your maid understands exactly what tasks you expect her to perform from the outset. Expect to pay a full-time maid THB 7,000–10,000 per month.

She should have at least one day off a week as well as Thai national holidays. If she's living in, she will need a bedroom, bathroom as well as allowance for her own food. Be prepared to pay her a bonus of about one month's wages at New Year or Songkran (Thai New Year).

Phone

Landlines are increasingly quaint furnishings and with mobile networks offering attractive rates on international calls, there's less and less reason to have one these days. Still, if you do need one, it's easy to have one installed: TOT (tel: 110), TT&T (tel: 1103) and True (tel: 1686) can set up a landline in your new home. Bills arrive monthly.

Otherwise, you'll need a mobile, most easily found at a shopping mall. If you're looking to save money, there's a thriving market in second-hand devices. IT malls such as Pantip Plaza and Fortune are good bets, though almost all malls have an electronics floor featuring grids of small mobile-phone stalls.

The three mobile networks are AIS/One-Two-Call, D-TAC and True. All three offer mobile broadband Internet services, which are nominally '3G' but frequently fall short of the speeds you'd expect. At the time of writing, True's mobile Internet service is the fastest in Bangkok, though the situation could change.

There are two ways of paying for phone calls and Internet services in Thailand: pre-pay and post-pay. The former means you top-up your account with credit whenever you need it. If your credit runs out, your service will be cut. You can arrange monthly mobile Internet packages with pre-pay. You will have to ensure you have enough credit in your account on the day the package starts each month. If not, your service will be cut, but you can always top-up and then ask the call-centre to restart it. You can pick up a pre-pay SIM card at any phone shop or stall, though they're on sale in convenience stores and supermarkets, too..

Monthly or 'post-pay' contracts, on the other hand, allow you to pay a fixed or variable fee at the end of each month. The bill will be sent to your home and can be paid in a number of ways, most easily by visiting your nearest convenience store. This type of contract will save you significant amounts of money, though you need a work permit to set one up. Post-pay contracts can be set up at the networks' respective stores, which can be found in all major shopping malls.

Internet

Mobile connections aside, there are several Internet service providers (ISPs) in Thailand, and I've listed the major ones opposite. At the risk of invoking a Catch 22, I'd suggest you do some Internet research before settling on one. (Nearly all modern cafes offer Wi-Fi these days, while every neighbourhood has at least one Internet cafe.) Speeds and reliability seem to vary considerably between networks. Since so many expats in Bangkok work in IT – the city tends to attract contractors who can base themselves anywhere – there are plenty of reports on network performance on the usual expat forums. Connections are billed monthly, and bills can usually be paid in convenience stores.

Internet service providers

The following companies provide Internet services in Bangkok:

- True Internet (tel: 1686)
- 3BB (tel: 1530)
- TOT (tel: 0-2240-0701)
- CAT [tel: 1322]

Television

There are six free analogue terrestrial television channels in Thailand: Channel 3, Channel 5, Channel 7, Modernine (Channel 9), NBT and ThaiPBS. Channels 5 and 7 are owned by the Royal Thai Army, which, incidentally, turns out to have a remarkable range of business interests. Nearly all shows are in the Thai language. A television licence is not required.

If you want to watch English-language programming or international channels, you'll need to subscribe to a pay TV service, either by having a satellite installed or a cable connection. TrueVisions offers the best range of international channels, including Fox and Star Sports, news channels like CNN, BBC World and Bloomberg, kids' channels such as Nickelodeon and the Cartoon Network, as well as HBO and other movie providers. Its full package is also the most expensive service out there in terms of monthly fees, though there are more affordable options. Competitors such as CTH offer cheaper packages in terms of monthly rate, while others can be installed for a one-off fee.

MONEY

The Thai currency is the baht. The baht is denominated in 0.25, 0.5, 1, 2, 5 and 10 baht coins and 20, 50, 100, 500 and 1,000 baht notes. Conventional wisdom has it that you should never stamp on a coin, since it has HM the King's head on it; doing so would supposedly invite patriotic passersby to teach you a violent lesson for disrespecting the monarch. Whether this is true or not is open to debate, but why put it to the test?

One baht is divided into 100 satang, which is where the Thai word '*tang*' comes from, as in the phrases '*mai mi tang*' ('I have no money') and '*kep tang*' ('collect the money'), used to ask for the bill at street stalls and cheap restaurants. Satang aren't worth much these days, though tiny bronze 25 and 50 satang coins remain in circulation. Supermarkets and grocers still give items prices like THB8.50, so these coins *will* find their way into your purse or wallet, annoying as they are. Some stores will refuse to take them as payment, making them hard to get rid of. Save them and donate them to charity or see the back of them using what I like to call the 'handful of change' tipping manoeuvre.

Finding ATMs in Bangkok is never a problem. They're everywhere, and there's usually at least one in front of every 7-Eleven. If you're withdrawing money from a foreign account, you will be charged THB150 for the pleasure. It's therefore worth making relatively large withdrawals and using a debit card where you can.

Don't be surprised if your card mysteriously stops working. If you forgot to inform your local bank that you were going to Thailand, they will often put a freeze on the card to prevent fraud – the kingdom is regarded as a hotspot for credit card crime. Don't panic: a phone call to your bank should get your account unlocked within minutes.

There are no black-market money changers in Thailand, as in neighbouring countries. Foreign exchanges are easy to find – just look for banks. It's worth changing your money in Thailand rather than abroad as you'll get much better rates.

Banking

If you intend to stay in Thailand for a lengthy period of time, it's worth setting up a Thai bank account. It may be essential, since some employers will only pay your wages by cheque or transfer into a local account. Even if you don't strictly need a Thai account, those THB150 foreign withdrawal ATM charges can quickly add up. Thus, opening a local account and making a large transfer from abroad will probably save you money.

There are seven or eight large Thai commercial banks. They are handily colour-coded. Kasikornbank (green) and Bangkok Bank (navy) are the most popular with foreigners. Both have English-language websites and offer the full range of modern banking services, including mobile, telephone and Internet banking, as well as international money transfers.

Rather anachronistically, the Thai banking system is still branch-based. You will be charged extra for withdrawing money from branches or ATMs other than your own branch. It's therefore worth choosing a branch near your home or place of work.

Officially, you need a work permit to set up an account. In reality, it's possible to set one up without one. Whether or not you can do this at a particular branch is up to the manager. Check the usual web forums for reports from other foreigners on which branches are currently offering bank accounts without work permits. The minimum deposit can be anything from THB100 to THB500.

You should be offered a VISA debit card with your account, which can be used abroad. You will also be given a bank book, though there is little you can't do with a card and online banking service these days. When using an ATM, getting your PIN code wrong three times will result in your card being irretrievably eaten. If this happens – or you lose your card – you will need to go to a branch to get a new one, which will set you back another THB100 to THB500.

Many large foreign banks also have branches in Bangkok, though they're not the best choice for the casual customer. Still, Thai banks will give you pitiful interest rates. For savings purposes, you'll want to use a foreign savings account or fund.

VAT

There is a 7 per cent value-added tax (VAT) on most goods and services. If you haven't spent more than 180 days in Thailand over the previous year, you can get a refund on the VAT when leaving the country by air. When you make a large purchase – such as electronic goods or handbags, for example – tell the shop you will be applying for a VAT refund. You will need to present your passport. They should provide you with a tax invoice and VAT refund form to complete. Bring these to the airport and go to the VAT refund kiosk to reclaim your money.

TOILETS

If you spent your life in Bangkok swanning from luxury hotel to high-class restaurant to gleaming shopping mall, there'd be nothing worth telling you about the toilets. In such places they're usually the same as those you're used to. But since you're probably more adventurous and less fortunate than that, sooner or later you can expect to encounter a squat toilet – essentially a hole in the ground dignified by a porcelain frame. Even if you operate a 'no squats' policy, you will likely be forced to use one at some point. If you embrace spicy food, expect the odd 'emergency'.

Here's how to use one. First, facing the door, stand with your feet on the porcelain foot stands. Pull your undergarments down, but not too far – pulling them to your ankles will expose them to the risk of becoming collateral damage. Squat down so that your feet are flat on the floor, in front of your bottom. Go for it.

In most squat toilets there won't be any toilet paper. Instead, expect to see a large bucket or porcelain tank filled with water, with a small plastic bowl or pan floating on the surface. Using your right hand, scoop up some water with the bowl and use your left hand to clean yourself with your fingers, dipping them into the bowl to clean them off. (Because of this, you are not supposed to try to shake a Thai person's left hand. In Bangkok they likely don't still wipe themselves the old-fashioned way, but a taboo against shaking left hands persists.)

Still, you may be relieved to hear that the squat toilet is in the process of going down the pan. The Public Health Ministry has drawn up a masterplan to ensure that all public places are serviced by at least one Western-style toilet, so it seems likely the squatter won't last forever. This is no bad thing, since squat toilets aren't much fun for the elderly and disabled. But despite the rise of the seated toilet, some Thais, particularly those from rural areas, still aren't comfortable with the practice.

The meaning of squat

The philosopher Slavoj Žižek has an amusingly silly theory that a civilisation's ideology is reflected in the design of its toilets. Explains the Slovenian thinker: The French design, in which the waste immediately vanishes down a hole at the back of the bowl, reflects a revolutionary ethos, one in which 'undesirables' should 'quickly be liquidated, like a guillotine'. The old-fashioned German toilet, in which waste lands on a platform and may be inspected before its removal, denotes a conservative, reflective mindset. Meanwhile, Anglo Saxon toilets, in which waste floats in water before being flushed away, reflect a more pragmatic ethos that avoids the extremes of the Continental designs. The academic provocateur admits this 'may be madness', but it's nevertheless fun to consider the meaning of traditional Thai toilets. Would it be pushing things too far to suggest that the Thai desire to keep the undesirable aspects of life hidden beneath the surface – in this case the literal surface of Thailand itself – is reflected in the Thai squatter? Or perhaps the truth is more mundane: a hole in the ground is simply the easiest way to build a toilet.

Thus, many Western-style seated toilets feature signs banning people from standing on the rim and squatting over the bowl. Old habits die hard, especially when it comes to procedures as fundamental as vacating the bowels.

The bum gun

Even where Western-style seated toilets are concerned, you can expect some differences to what you're used to at home. People from parts of the world in which toilet hygiene is particularly advanced, such as the United States or Japan, may be disappointed by the lack of paper seat-cover dispensers. To protect your precious cheeks, you will either have to do something time-consuming using toilet roll, or learn to deal with the disquieting sensation of bum-on-public-porcelain.

And then there's the hose-like object to the side of the toilet, known variously as the 'bidet hose', 'bum spray' or, most poetically of all, 'bum gun'. The bum gun is little more than a hose with a valve and trigger on the business end. For the device to work its magic, the water pressure must be in the 'Goldilocks zone': too weak and the jet doesn't clean you; too strong and it delivers an involuntary enema. There will be a handle or metal dial at the base of the spray that you can use to control the intensity of the jet, though often the underlying pressure won't be strong enough, in which case the bum gun is useless. Once you've sprayed yourself, use toilet roll to dry yourself off, if it's available.

In many cases the plumbing needed to process toilet paper isn't in place. Expect to see signs telling you not to flush paper down the toilet, in which case there will be a bin for you to throw away waste tissue. The idea of filling a bin with used toilet paper may disgust you, but if there's enough water pressure, use of the bum gun should ensure the paper is fairly clean.

In some of Bangkok's snazzier shopping malls – the Paragon, Emporium and Central World, for example – the gun is absent. This seems to be an ill-considered attempt to conform to the cultural norms of the West. Most expats eventually come to agree that in this area, Thai culture is vastly superior to their own. The bum gun is, quite simply, a more civilised way to 'toilet'.

GETTING AROUND

When traffic's as bad as Bangkok's, getting around becomes a major concern. Rush hour – oh, for a single 60-minute rush hour – supposedly lasts from around 6am to 9am and 4pm to 7pm. But some sections of road can be choked with traffic until the wee hours. And traffic also follows other rhythms.

There's no nice way to put it: Bangkok's traffic is a nightmare.

Friday nights are not a good time to be braving the roads, while the snarls seem to get worse at the end of the month, after pay day, when fun-loving residents are flush.

There are now more than 7.5 million cars registered in a city with just 8,000km of road. In 2013, a Bangkok Metropolitan Administration spokesman told the *Bangkok Post* this was 'less than a quarter' of what was needed. The current government's 'first car' scheme, which has offered a THB100,000 tax rebate for first-time car buyers, has – surprise, surprise – done nothing to improve the situation. In 2012, 470,000 new cars were registered in the capital. The Bangkok Metropolitan Administration recognises the need for more roads but says it lacks the cash it would need to expropriate the necessary land. The situation, it seems, will get worse before it gets better.

Walking
Some writers have claimed that Bangkok rewards the flâneur – the intrepid explorer of the city streets immortalised by French writers like Baudelaire. This may be true. But it certainly doesn't reward the commuter, the traveller, the

pram-pusher or anyone with an aversion to exhaust fumes, noise and heat. With seemingly devilish intent, lampposts and trees are planted in the middle of narrow pavements. Vendors bring colour to the streets, but take up vital space and cause bottlenecks. Semi-open drains leave long stretches of pavement reeking of sewage. And motorcycle riders aren't afraid to save time and money by riding on the pavements, pedestrians be damned.

Still, the streets of Bangkok are generally safe at any time of day or night, though there are areas to be wary of. Muggings are not unheard of, albeit much rarer than in Western cities. Being very drunk and alone in the area around Khao San Road late at night is not recommended. Take care at crowded markets, tourist areas and transport facilities as pickpockets can be operating. At pedestrian crossings, and particularly those on junctions, be careful. Some drivers assume they can always turn left, and don't spare the gas.

Buses

There are only two reasons you'd ever want to ride a Thai public bus: you're broke, or you want 'an authentic experience'. Otherwise there's little to recommend these often-hot and always-slow soot-belchers. Nevertheless, they are generally clean, safe and cheap as chips. Air-con bus fares start at THB10, fan buses at a piddling THB7. Buses in Thailand still feature conductors, so expect one to come round after you sit down.

Buses can be a nuisance for other road users, since their size means they can bully other vehicles. Drivers often ignore their own regulations with brazen manoeuvres like stopping in the wrong lane. Still, without the bus system much of Bangkok's working class couldn't afford to go to work or school. And if more of Bangkok's population dumped their cars and took buses to work, the traffic situation would get immeasurably better. So praise the buses, the buses be damned.

Taxis

There are three types of taxi in Bangkok. In descending order of comfort and safety – and ascending 'rock'n'roll' factor – they are the air-conditioned sedan taxi, the iconic tuk-tuk and the motorcycle taxi.

Sedans

Besides the temples and their saffron clergy, Bangkok's huge taxi fleet lends it colour. Sky blue, shocking pink, two-tone combinations – the city's cabs come in all sorts of hues, though the vast majority are the same model: the Toyota Corolla. Green-yellow cars are owned by their drivers. Red-blue ones are owned by a garage, which might own a fleet of 20 cabs. The other colours are owned by large firms with hundreds of cars to their name.

An illuminated red light – the Thai word 'ว่าง' meaning 'vacant' – on the corner of the windscreen indicates the vehicle is, you guessed it, vacant. To hail a taxi, hold out your arm with your palm facing down, then wave your fingers backwards and forwards in a beckoning motion.

Bangkok taxis are remarkably cheap – perhaps too cheap. Fares start at THB35 for the first 2km, rising THB4.5 for each of the next 10km, then THB5 for each subsequent kilometre to 20km and THB5.5 per km after that. They also rise THB1.25 per metre in traffic jams. That makes sedan taxis a bargain, especially when compared to tuk-tuks.

This generous regime might seem good for passengers on paper, but the growing number of taxi drivers either illegally demanding flat fees or refusing to take passengers at all suggests they aren't making enough from the regulation rates to make a living. Drivers who rent their cars can pay anything from THB700 to THB1200 to the owner per 12-hour shift, and have to make that back, plus petrol fees, before they start making money. So it clearly isn't easy being a driver, though being aware of that does little to alleviate the frustration of being refused by cab after cab after cab. If you get into a taxi and the driver doesn't switch the meter on, say '*pert meter ka/khrap*'. If he refuses to do so, get out.

Why does a driver agree to some journeys and not others? He may be worried about getting stuck in traffic, since he'll make less if the cab doesn't move. He may think he won't be able to get another fare from your destination and have to drive all the way back into the city, using twice the fuel. His rental may be about to expire and your destination might be too far from where he needs to return his car. Or he may even be looking for tourists to rip off with a grossly inflated flat fare.

The Metropolitan Police Bureau is supposed to impose a fine of THB1,000 on drivers who are caught refusing fares despite having a lit 'vacant' sign. You can complain about any taxi driver who does this by photographing the licence plate number and dialling the Land Transport's special hotline at 1584. Some taxi drivers have been known to react angrily to people doing this.

So how can you improve your 'hit rate', so to speak? Some Bangkokians claim you should get in the taxi and shut the door before stating your destination, which they say makes the driver less inclined to refuse, since doing so would require the more confrontational move of making you get out of his cab. But many drivers have little compunction about doing this. One thing's for certain: taxi drivers will be more likely to want to take you if you agree to use the tollway. You'll have to pay the fee, of course, but you'll reach your destination quicker and the taxi driver will make a better profit. You can tell the driver you want to use the tollway by saying '*chai toh-way kha/khrap*'.

Never open a taxi door onto incoming traffic. Always alight on the pavement side, and even then, make sure you look before opening the door. It's easy to forget about motorcycles, though hard to do so once when one slams into your car door.

To call a cab

For a THB20 surcharge, the following companies will send a cab to your location 24 hours a day:

- Taxi Radio (1681)
- Siam Taxi Cooperative (1661)
- VMS Communication (1545)

Tuk-tuks

All Thailand newbies love tuk-tuks, most veterans loathe them. The tuk-tuk ride's initial charms – amusing engine noise, exposure to the elements, element of danger ('surely these things aren't safe?') – rapidly turn into reasons to avoid these iconic irritants. Surely they *aren't* safe: imagine being caught in a ~~tuk-tuk in a spin~~ human mincing machine. Sooner or later, the truth becomes clear: sedan taxis are safer, more comfortable, and cheaper too.

Some tuk-tuk drivers – generally those in tourist areas – are among the city's most prolific rip-off merchants. They have been known to try to charge unwitting tourists outrageous prices. One tried to stick some friends-of-friends with a THB4,000 bill for a 15-minute ride from Pratunam to Soi Ari. Make sure you agree the fare before you go anywhere.

Other tuk-tuks offer to take you where you want to go 'for free' or a tiny sum such as THB10. In exchange, you are expected to consent to being taken on a route that happens to include stops at stores offering 'very cheap' prices on suits and gemstones. The drivers are paid by these establishments to bring them customers. Avoid these rouses. If you want a suit, do some research and find a tailor with good testimonials. Don't let a tuk-tuk driver choose one for you. Needless to say, the same applies to dropping hundreds of dollars on gemstones.

So why bother with the tuk-tuk? Well, on short rides tuk-tuks are often faster than cars. They can fit through gaps a Toyota Corolla can't. And it's rare to get turned down for a journey by a tuk-tuk driver – if only because he'll choose a price that suits him. Tuk-tuk fares can be haggled and you can generally get THB10–20 off the initial price. But if the fare seems reasonable, why bother?

Motorcycle taxis

If you really need to make time, there's always the motorcycle taxi, known in Thai simply as the *motosai*. Motorcycle taxi drivers are easy to spot, since they congregate in groups, known in Thai as '*win*', and wear coloured bibs marked with the name of their area. The vast majority are men from the poor Northeast, though the occasional woman also takes up this dangerous profession.

Taking a *motosai* can be a hair-raising experience. Some drivers ride like maniacs and it really is a lottery as to what sort of driver you get. To catch a *motosai*, simply catch one of the drivers' eyes by raising your hand. The driver whose turn it is for the fare will be alerted and get his bike started. You may dislike the driving style, bike or personality of a particular driver, but asking for another one will likely cause offence. If a driver appears to be drunk, walk away and find another way to get where you want to go.

You will usually not be offered a helmet when you get on the bike, so make sure you ask for one before you set off. If the drivers don't understand the word 'helmet', tapping your own head should get the message across. Any helmet they give you is likely to be a fairly flimsy plastic affair, but better than nothing. It will also, of course, have had hundreds of heads in it, but that's a price you should be willing to pay if you value the integrity of your skull.

At most *motosai* stands there will be a sign listing prices to common destinations, albeit usually in Thai. Fares generally

Motosai drivers congregating in a *win*. Motorcycle taxis are the quickest way to get around – though not necessarily the safest.

start at THB10, though they vary depending on the area. They rise precipitously in areas that throng with tourists, such as Pratunam. If you appear to know what you're doing, motorcycle drivers won't usually try to rip you off. Otherwise, you might be charged a little extra for being a foreigner. The best thing to do is to ask someone you know about the standard price for your journey, and to give the driver that amount before he has a chance to ask for more.

Rapid transit

Bangkok is served by two rail-based mass transit systems: the Bangkok Mass Transit System (BTS), often referred to as the 'Skytrain', and the underground Metropolitan Rapid Transit (MRT). When you're trying to get somewhere, the lazy option is usually to dive into the nearest taxi – if it'll take you. But most of the time going to the effort of climbing the BTS stairs – or descending to the depths of the MRT – is the smart manoeuvre, given the time and money it saves. Trains on both systems are air-conditioned, quick and frequent.

The BTS isn't the relaxing, spacious ride it used to be – sardines are often the order of the day – but it remains a godsend nevertheless.

BTS

The BTS opened in 1999, despite opposition from people living along its routes. The complaints are mostly forgotten now, though the network has undoubtedly helped to give many of Bangkok's most important streets an oppressive, almost subterranean feel. Still, the BTS has improved the traffic situation in many parts of the city – and property values along its lines have soared. At first, the system was less popular than hoped, but today it has almost been a victim of its own success: a recent extension of the Sukhumvit line out to Bang Na means crowding at rush hour is approaching London Tube levels.

Tickets for individual journeys have to be bought at ticket vending machines. At the time of writing, most still didn't accept notes, forcing commuters to queue at counters to get coinage before queuing again to get their ticket. To buy the correct ticket, look at the map to the left of the buttons, which shows the price to each station. Then press the appropriate button, insert the money and receive your ticket. If you accidentally travel too far on a ticket of insufficient value, you will be alerted at the exit gate and will have to ask a member of staff in the ticket booth to top-up your ticket.

If you plan on using the BTS regularly, buying a Rabbit Card is recommended as it will save you time and money. They can be purchased at the ticket counters, and staff know enough English to sell you what you need. There are two types of pass. The 'Stored Value SmartPass' costs THB30 and allows you to top up any amount from THB100 to THB4,000. The other type is the 30-Day SmartPass, where you buy a fixed number of journeys for a fixed amount, though all must be taken within 30 days or they expire. The Rabbit Card can also be used on the BRT (Bus Rapid Transit) and plans are afoot to allow travellers to use it on the MRT, though at the time of writing this much-needed facility had yet to be implemented.

MRT

The MRT started operating in 2004 and has yet to reach BTS levels of crowding. There is just one line, the Blue Line, stretching between Bang Sue in the north of Bangkok and Hualamphong, the city's main train station. The MRT and BTS intersect in three locations: Asok Intersection (BTS

Asok, MRT Sukhumvit), Chatuchak Park (BTS Mo Chit, MRT Chatuchak Park) and on Silom Road (BTS Sala Daeng, MRT Si Lom). A second line is under construction, the Purple Line, from Bang Yai to Rat Burana, as are extensions to the Blue Line.

BRT

The Rama III area in southern Bangkok is served by the Bus Rapid Transit (BRT) system, an unusual network that falls somewhere between a traditional bus route and a train line. The BRT connects with the BTS in two places: Chong Nonsri and Talat Phlu on the Silom line. Served by the same kind of ticketing system as the BTS and MRT lines, the BRT has barriered platforms, and its buses drive on dedicated lanes on the roads. Naturally, they move a lot faster than the traffic on neighbouring lanes.

Boats

In a sense, the most truly Bangkokian way to get around the city is to take a boat. On the Chao Phraya River, an express-boat service plies a 21km route from Krung Thep Bridge in the south to Nonthaburi in the north. Along the way the

Boats used to be the only form of transport in Bangkok. Now they're one of many, but they still have their uses.

boat stops near many of the tourism attractions in the old city, Chinatown, the famous hotels on Charoen Krung Road like the Oriental and the Shangri-La, and the Skytrain at Saphan Taksin station. (At the time of writing the Bangkok Metropolitan Administration was planning on demolishing Saphan Taksin and installing a 710m moving walkway from Surasak, the next BTS station.) For more information on the service visit www.chaophrayaexpressboat.com.

There are also river taxis that run along Khlong Saen Saeb. The canal parallels Sukhumvit Road, and the service makes it possible to live in Bangkok's old town and commute to work in the Sukhumvit area. The service begins in Panfa Leelard, close to the Golden Mount in Pom Prap Sattru Phai District, and runs 18km to Wat Sriboonrueng in Bang Kapi District in Eastern Bangkok. There's a compulsory change from one line to another at the stop in Pratunam. For more information on the service visit www.khlongsaensaep.com.

BUYING A VEHICLE

If you don't have children to worry about, it's difficult to imagine why you'd want to join the city's status-conscious middle classes in driving your own car. Traffic is hellish, but even if you have no option but to use the roads, taxis are cheap and plentiful. And if you need a car for a weekend or holiday, you can always rent one. Still, things are different for families, of course. And there are a few reasons why you might think about investing in a motorbike.

Motorcycle emptiness

Bored of life in one of the world's most exciting cities? Then why not buy your own motorcycle? The excitement of daily near-death experiences is bound to bring back your *joie de vivre*. And if it doesn't do that, at least it puts your life back into your own hands – instead of those of meth-addled *motosai* riders and taxi drivers who believe road safety is a function not of careful driving, but of the number of amulets they have hanging from their rearview mirror.

Riding a bike is one of the best ways to get to know the city. Without actually controlling your own vehicle, it's hard to learn how this chaotic city of flyovers and byzantine shortcuts through networks of small *sois* fits together. While Bangkok traffic can be frustratingly sclerotic for the car driver, motorbike traffic can get through gaps other vehicles cannot.

The city certainly isn't the best place to learn to ride a bike. But if you're already confident on one, there are good reasons to use one in the city. If you're truly committed to the art of Making Time, it's the only way to travel.

There are no restrictions on foreigners buying vehicles in Thailand. When you buy one it will need to be registered with the local Department of Land Transport office. Most vehicle dealerships should be able to deal with the registration and ownership transfer process for you. The DLT will want to see your passport and visa and, if you're buying a car, work permit or letter of residence.

The process should take about a week. Until it's complete your vehicle will have a red 'dealer' licence plate. Vehicles with dealer plates can only be legally driven between 6am and 6pm. Once registration is complete you will receive a permanent white plate as well as a registration book known as the 'blue book' (for cars) or 'green book' (for motorcycles) that records your ownership of the vehicle.

You will have to take out compulsory motor insurance (CMI), which must be renewed yearly. It's available in three classes: 1st, 2nd and 3rd, with 1st being fully comprehensive. Vehicles are also taxed annually and must display a sticker showing the tax has been paid, which can be obtained at a DLT office. If you buy a second-hand vehicle, make sure the tax has been paid. Horror stories abound of people buying cars, then being stuck with the bill for several years of unpaid tax.

Getting a driving licence

Foreign licences are not supposed to be used in Thailand, although you can usually get away with using them. If you want to be fully legal, you will need either a valid International Drivers Licence or a Thai licence to drive here. If you're resident in the country you should obtain a Thai licence. Some insurance companies specify that this is necessary for coverage. To obtain a Thai licence you'll need to go to a Department of Land Transport office (0-2271-8888) with:

1. Passport and Non-Immigrant Visa, with photocopies of main page and visa page
2. Certified proof of address from your Embassy or the Immigration Bureau
3. Medical report (obtained at a hospital or clinic)
4. Valid International Drivers Licence or one from your home state or country
5. Two recent 1" passport photographs
6. Fee: THB105 (car) or THB55 (motorcycle)

HEALTH AND HOSPITALS

Bangkok is an excellent place to get sick – if such a thing exists, that is. Even the most expensive private hospitals like Bamrungrad, Samitivej, BNH and Bangkok Hospital offer great value for money compared with healthcare in most other parts of the world. Receiving care in one of these hospitals can be a revelation for foreigners used to the cold, sterile state facilities common in Europe; the affordability of care similarly impresses those from the United States. With bright, warm furnishings and a focus on guiding the patient through each step of the care process, hospitals here seem to have learned much from Thailand's hospitality industry.

A simple consultation and prescription at these private hospitals might cost THB2,000–3,000, giving rise to a temptation, especially among younger expats, to avoid getting health insurance completely. But while the hospitals are good value, costs can quickly run into hundreds of thousands of baht if you need surgery or are admitted for a few days. Taking out health insurance is therefore advised. Assuming you're insured it's always worth checking into one of the better hospitals mentioned above, rather than whichever one happens to be nearest.

If you're paying your own way and come down with something that clearly isn't serious, a less expensive hospital is probably the best option. For more serious ailments, it's sensible to 'splash out' if you can. While the treatment at the good private hospitals is generally excellent, tales of poor treatment at government hospitals abound. If you're at all in doubt about a doctor's diagnosis, seek a second opinion at a different institution.

If anything, the problem with Thai hospitals is often more one of over-prescription than under-prescription. Doctors seem reluctant to send patients away without a bag of goodies – a prescription with several medicines designed to treat each one of the symptoms seems to be the norm.

Unless you're vegetarian, get ready for fresh, cheap fish becoming a regular part of your diet.

FOOD SHOPPING

Many expats forgo food shopping entirely, since delicious street food is so cheap. For those who want to cook, there are plenty of options for buying ingredients. If you're planning on cooking Thai food, you're probably best off going to one of the city's wet markets. The prices are rock bottom, and you get a much more colourful experience. The massive Khlong Toei market (BTS Khlong Toei) and Or Tor Kor market near Chatuchak are both excellent options.

Otherwise, the easier, less stressful option is to buy your food at supermarkets such as Big-C and Tesco Lotus, which are found all over the city. The produce at such places often isn't all that different from what the fresh markets sell, and they're cheap, too. On the other hand, if it's imported Western products you're after, the upmarket malls all have good supermarkets. Chains such as Villa Market and Tops will also do the job, though you will, of course, pay for the pleasure.

STAYING INFORMED

Thailand is served by several daily newspapers that run the gamut from scurrilous tabloids to staid business papers. There are two national English-language newspapers: the

Thai sunshine makes for some fabulously sweet fruits.

Bangkok Post and *The Nation*. The *Bangkok Post* is probably the better of the two. *The Nation*, which uses the not-entirely cogent slogan 'Insightful, In Trend, Independent', has seen better days. It fell into debt in the late 2000s and was forced to downsize significantly. (Full disclosure: I worked as a sub-editor at the newspaper.) Both papers are conservative in outlook and lean towards the yellow side in Thailand's red-yellow political divide.

The hard copies of both papers are widely available, though newsagents in overwhelmingly Thai neighbourhoods rarely stock them. Both papers have subscription services that offer large discounts on their cover prices, and both have popular websites. The *Bangkok Post*'s latest news stories are free to read, but subscription is required to view articles that are over 60 days old. *The Nation* allows users to view a certain number of free articles per month; to view more you have to pay. Prachatai (www.prachatai.com) is a free online newspaper that focuses on social issues and takes a much more progressive line than its competitors. Coconuts Bangkok (bangkok.coconuts.co) is also free and covers Bangkok-related news with more of an irreverent twist.

For international news, you will of course be able to access your preferred news source online. But if you really do prefer a hard copy, there are options. An edition of the *International Herald Tribune* (at the time of writing set to rebrand itself as the *International New York Times*) is printed in Bangkok and available in the larger malls and newsagents in tourist and business areas. Meanwhile, Newspaper Direct allows you to subscribe to locally printed copies of more than 1,700 newspapers from 94 countries in 44 languages (*see* www.newspaperdirect-asia.com/thailand). So if you really can't live without your daily copy of *The Moose Jaw Times Herald*, fear not, there is a way.

Journalism

In my days as a sub-editor at the *Phuket Gazette*, we used to read the local Thai rag each morning to look for stories we'd missed. One day the paper had a picture of what looked like a dead *farang* on a hospital bed on its front page, together with a caption saying he was a tourist who'd died of a heart attack.

Dead *farangs* being our editorial bread and butter, we sent a reporter to check out the story. At the hospital, she asked one of the nurses what had happened to the dead foreigner. 'Oh, he discharged himself yesterday,' the nurse said. It turned out the Thai paper's photographer had gone into the hospital, spotted the man lying still on a bed, snapped a picture and told his editor it was that of a dead man, without even bothering to ask the nurses what had happened to him.

This isn't to claim that this is typical Thai journalism practice. But it goes to show that you shouldn't believe everything you read in the papers in Thailand. Or anywhere, for that matter.

Here, it's all too common to see news stories in which the writer has simply reported – unchallenged – a single bureaucrat's comments on a particular issue. 'Speaking truth to power' is not the *raison d'etre* of most newspapers here. Journalism is considered a rather lowly trade and reporters aren't held in particularly high esteem. This, combined with the Thai tendency to defer to authority, means it's rare to see reporters aggressively challenging the great and the (not-so) good.

What's more, the media often self-censors on stories concerning the rich and powerful. According to Thai law, a libel plaintiff merely needs to prove that the defendant's accusation damaged his or her reputation, regardless of whether the accusation is true or not. So it's not uncommon for a rich suspect's identity to be protected from the usual publicity.

But while the rich often get an easy ride, others aren't so lucky. In February 2013 one paper published a photograph on its website of the ID card of a Scottish girl who was gang-raped in Nakhon Si Thammarat. After an outcry, it removed the image. Almost as outrageous is the ritual of the reenactment, where police force suspects to show a scrum of photographers how they committed a crime – even crimes they deny committing.

If all this gets you down, fear not: there is an antidote. The 'Not The Nation' website has been satirising the media, Thai politics and expat life since 2007, and doing so hilariously. In the world of this anonymously written Onion-like journal, the World Pizza Council has revoked the Pizza Company's right to use the word 'pizza', Thai Airways runs daily flights between Bangkok's two airports, and crowds gather at the last spot in the whole of Bangkok that could be described as quiet: 'The spot was discovered after one passerby was transfixed by what he could only describe as an "eerie absence", but later realised was best defined by the phenomenon his grandfather had called "silence".' If the media's a joke, why not read news that doesn't pretend to be otherwise?

SCHOOLS

There are three types of schools to choose from in Bangkok: government schools, Thai private schools and international schools. It is highly unlikely you would want to send your child to a government school, where the language of instruction is Thai and students still learn by rote. Schools retain a military flavour, with corporal punishment still employed in many schools and male students required to keep their hair cut short (*see page 103*). Students are expected to obey teachers without question and are taught traditional Thai values of deference and obedience to authority.

The fees at low-end Thai private schools are modest but buy a noticeable improvement in teaching standards and equipment. Many offer English programmes, meaning that the language of instruction for most subjects (though not necessarily all) is English. The teachers may not necessarily be native speakers, however, with Filipino teachers commonly employed alongside Thais. There is a reason many of the Thai elite send their children to international schools or to boarding schools abroad; most Thai schools continue to focus on learning by rote and are unlikely to teach your child much in the way of critical-thinking skills. Some Thai schools have more progressive educational philosophies and it is worth putting time into seeking these schools out.

International schools charge fees ranging from THB200,000 to THB1 million per year, putting them out of reach of some expats. Most international schools follow either an American curriculum, a British curriculum or the International Baccalaureate. A small number teach in other languages such as Japanese, German or French. All Thai students registered as Thai nationals are required to study Thai language or culture, though this requirement is waved for foreigners. For a list of schools, see the Resource Guide on pages 319–322.

What to think about when choosing a school
- What is the ratio of foreign children to Thai children at the school?
- What is the ratio of foreign teachers to Thai teachers at the school?
- What are the class sizes?
- Are the teachers native English speakers?
- Does the school provide transport for students?
- Are there any hidden costs such as registration fees or facility fees?
- What qualifications does the school offer?
- Which organisation is it accredited by?

BIRTHS, MARRIAGES AND DEATHS

Having a baby
With some excellent quality hospitals (*see page 195*), Bangkok is a safe place to have a baby. Once the baby is born, the hospital will issue a birth certificate, which will

state the nationality of the parents. The hospital will usually be able to arrange to have it translated into English, which may take a few days. Otherwise, you should have a licensed translation company translate the certificate for you.

You will then need to have your embassy certify the birth of the baby and apply for its citizenship and passport. Procedures vary, so contact them before the birth to find out what's required. For the birth to be legally recognised under Thai law, you will also need to register the birth and baby's name at the local District Office. If neither of the parents are Thai, the baby won't automatically receive Thai citizenship. If at least one parent is Thai, it will.

For more information about childbirth and childcare in Bangkok, contact Bangkok Mothers & Babies International (BAMBI), a non-profit organisation dedicated to helping pregnant women and parents of young children of all nationalities in Bangkok. For more about BAMBI, see www.bambiweb.org.

Getting married

The legal and ceremonial procedures for getting married are two different things – we'll consider only the legal aspects here. (The issue of paying a 'bride price' is discussed on page 153.)

A certificate of marriage can be obtained at the local District Office. As a foreigner, you first need to get an affidavit of marital status from your embassy and have it translated into Thai. Bring that along with any divorce certificates and your passport to the District Office, which will issue the marriage certificate. Once it is translated into English by an official translator, it will be recognised around the world.

Death and other legal issues

If someone you know dies, contact your consulate, who will be able to advise you on the local procedure and help in case you wish to ship a body out of Thailand. In case of other legal issues, you should also contact the consulate, which will provide you with a list of reliable lawyers.

The bureaucrat

In her account of her time as a teacher to the wives, concubines and children of King Mongkut, *The English Governess at the Siamese Court*, Anna Leonowens described arriving in Siam aboard a steamboat in 1862: 'The Custom-House is an open sala, or shed, where interpreters, inspectors and tidewaiters lounge away the day on cool mats, chewing areca, betel and tobacco, and extorting money, goods and provisions from the unhappy proprietors of native trading craft, large or small; but Europeans are protected from their rascally and insolent exactions by the intelligence and energy of their respective consuls...'

While the general attitude of Thailand's public servants has improved hugely since that time, going to any sort of Thai government office is not an experience many people – whether Thai or foreign – look forward to. While the younger generation of *kha ratchakan* (civil servant) is usually polite and sometimes even eager to help, most expats will have at least one tale about running into a bureaucrat of the 'old school'.

The roots of this 'lack of public service zeal', shall we say, stretch back hundreds of years to the traditional *sakdina* system of government (*see page 95*). Back in those days, officials appointed to work for a higher authority such as the king would not be paid directly for what they did. Instead, they'd be allowed and expected to extract fees from the people for services rendered, or to retain a portion of the taxes they collected before forwarding the rest to the crown. It goes without saying that this was not a system that led to an ethos of devoted public service.

It's only been in the last couple of decades that Thailand has made serious efforts to tackle this kind of attitude in its public servants. The ideal that officials should be glad to perform services for the public – and without any financial 'encouragement' whatsoever – is relatively new. The desired ethos is usually promoted in English under the rather wonky phrase 'service mind', which can be seen on signs in most government offices these days. But changing the old mentality is not an easy task, and one which won't happen overnight.

FOOD

BANGKOKIANS MAY GAZE LOVINGLY at their iPhones, but don't let that fool you: *food* is the dearest thing to their hearts. Until 1943, when the dictator Plaek Phibunsongkhram decreed that the artificial, Sanskrit-derived '*sawatdi*' would be the nation's official word for 'hello', the Siamese usually hailed each other by asking if they'd eaten rice yet ('*kin khao rue yang*?'). Old habits die hard, especially when it comes to food: the phrase is still in common use today.

In Thailand, rice and food are synonymous. The grain is a sacred thing, used in rituals marking everything from birth, to marriage, to death. Complain about the rain, and a Thai from the provinces may scold you: without the deluge, there would be no rice. Traditionally, a mouthful of rice is eaten first during a Thai meal, acknowledging the grain's singular importance. (But good luck finding someone who actually observes this custom in today's Bangkok – they're more likely to be a foreigner trying to learn 'Thai culture' than a Thai.)

Some Thais consider it bad etiquette to leave rice uneaten. I was once having lunch with a Thai friend – a rather outspoken one, it must be said – and after running out of *phat kraphrao mu*, I left half a plate of jasmine rice uneaten. 'You don't respect our farmers,' she told me, half joking, half not. 'I respect them, I just can't eat this much rice,' I attempted, but she was unmoved. I cleared the plate.

A traditional Thai meal – shared, of course – will generally consist of the following: a *nam phrik* (spicy dip), a curry, a soup, a stir-fry, a salad and some grilled meat or fish. The *nam phrik*, an often dangerously fiery blend of spices and aromatics, similar to the *sambal* of Indonesia and Malaysia, is served with fresh or boiled vegetables, or grilled meat or fish, such as the street staple *pla thu* (Thai mackerel). Many of the curries, such as *kaeng khiao wan* (green curry) and the Islamic-flavoured *massaman*, will be well known to foreigners. Some Thai soups are spicy – *tom yam kung* or *kaeng som*, for example. Such dishes start fires. Others, soothing and aromatic, are there to put them out.

If two words define Thai cuisine, they are 'balance' and 'complexity'. Each ingredient in a curry paste, for example, should have enough presence to influence the flavour, but without overwhelming the others. Zooming out the meal as a whole should also be balanced. Five flavour elements should be present: sweet, sour, bitter, spicy and salty. Balance might not be the first thing that comes to mind when you're dripping with sweat over *nam phrik kung siap*, but even if one dish is heavily sour or spicy, it should be complemented by others that cool the palate.

The four main regions of Thailand (Central, Northeast, North, South) each have their own styles of cuisine, and all can be found in Bangkok. As with most capitals, the city attracts a constant flow of migrants from other parts of the country. They bring their own culinary tastes and customs with them. At the same time, the city acts as a magnet for Thailand's most ambitious and talented cooks – or those whose ancestors left them the best recipes. Restaurants that succeed in the provinces often set up shop in the capital, trying their hand at impressing Bangkok's pickier – and more affluent – eaters.

Central Thai cuisine covers most of the best-known Thai dishes. Of the other regional cuisines, the Northeast is best represented at the tables of the capital. The relative poverty of Isarn ensures that in Bangkok you're never far from a good bowl of *som tam*. Fiery Southern food is also everywhere, particularly ready-cooked *khao kaeng* (rice and curry) and deep-fried chicken. (The affluent South seems better at retaining its best cooks than other regions, and the general

Charcoal stoves are the weapon of choice for many of the city's street vendors.

standard of Thai cooking seems to be higher there.) The milder, Burmese-influenced cuisine of the North is hardest to find in Bangkok. You have to hunt hard to find a good bowl of *khao soi*, a curried noodle dish that tends to beguile most foreigners who try it. Some say there *is* no good *khao soi* in Bangkok; I'm still looking.

As with most cuisines, Thai food is evolving. There are ingredients you might call classically Thai: shallots, chillies, lemongrass, galangal, lime, fish sauce, garlic, coconut milk. Their flavours help define the cuisine. But be wary of those who are adamant about what constitutes 'authentic' Thai food; there is rarely a single way to cook a particular dish, and rules change. A dish like *lap*, the Northeastern herbal meat salad, has traditionally been made with chicken, beef, pork or catfish. These days it's not unusual to see it made with salmon. *Phad khi mao*, a fiery stir-fry of chillies, garlic and holy basil, is made with spaghetti as often as noodles. Do *lap sa-mon* and *sapaketthi phad khi mao* constitute 'authentic' Thai food?

As David Thompson writes in his treatise on the cuisine, *Thai Food*, 'The true genius of Thai cuisine is its ability to incorporate the unfamiliar, whether it be ingredient or technique, and absorb it so completely that it becomes an integral component; to "Siam-ise" it to a degree that it becomes indistinguishable from the indigenous.' The ultimate example: the humble capsicum. Until around 500 years ago, no Thai had ever seen a chilli pepper. Now you couldn't imagine Thai food without it.

How is *khao klong* like lobster?

White rice is the staple carbohydrate in Thailand, referred to admiringly as *khao suai*, literally meaning 'beautiful rice.' Less popular is its rougher, unrefined sibling, *khao klong*, or cargo rice. *Khao klong* has a purple, brown or maroon hue. It's more nutritious than white rice because it retains the bran and germ, where the nutrients lie. So here's a question: How is *khao klong* like lobster?

In the northeastern United States in the 17th and 18th century, lobster was so common it was considered 'poor man's food' and fed to servants and convicts, even being used as fertiliser. Massachusetts passed a law making it illegal to serve prisoners lobster more than twice a week. A daily dinner of the crustacean was thought to constitute cruel and unusual punishment. (Oh, the inhumanity!)

In Thailand, *khao klong* has undergone a similar journey. Before the introduction of refining processes that removed the bran and germ, *khao klong* was all anybody ate. Then, over the course of the 20th century, white rice became the norm. Still, for many years, *khao klong* continued to be fed to prisoners because it was cheaper. Prisoners and their advocates weren't happy with this state of affairs. They complained that being denied white rice like the rest of Thai society was 'inhumane'. The Department of Corrections eventually caved and took *khao klong* off the menu.

Today, prisoners continue to eat white rice, but *khao klong* is enjoying a renaissance. Made newly trendy by its proven health benefits, *khao klong* is finding its way onto the menus of upscale Thai restaurants. It is no longer thought of as poor people's food. Thus, *khao klong* is the lobster of the rice world.

EATING WITH THAI PEOPLE

While you will see plenty of Thai people eating on their own in Bangkok, they're far less inclined to do so than Westerners. Here, food is a thing to be shared, and in doing so to form and solidify social bonds. If you make Bangkok your home, you'll need to learn to share your food, too. This can be difficult

Typical dishes

Tom yam kung (ต้มยำกุ้ง)

A sour and spicy soup made from an energising mix of stock, lemongrass, galangal, kaffir lime leaves, lime, fish sauce and chillies, not to mention shrimp, *tom yam kung* is quintessentially Thai; it even lent its name to the 1997 'Tom Yam Kung' economic crisis. There are sour, spicy soups in Korean and Chinese cuisines but none offer the distinct blend of flavours found in *tom yam*. The soup can be made with a clear broth ('*nam sai*') or thickened with coconut milk ('*nam khon*'). You could call *tom yam* the 'chicken soup' of Thailand, since Thais believe it's good to eat when you have a cold. (It's also great for hangovers.)

Chicken and coconut milk soup (ต้มข่าไก่)

Tom kha kai is the soothing, ambrosial cousin of *tom yam*. Present are most of the same herbs and aromatic flavours of the latter, though instead of a stock base, here it's coconut milk, and shrimp is replaced by chicken. When this creamy soup is spooned onto rice it takes on the feel of a wonderful savoury rice pudding. Adding the right quantities of fish sauce and lime lifts *tom kha kai* into the realms of the sublime.

Papaya salad (ส้มตำ)

Som tam, a refreshing salad of unripe papaya, is the best-known dish of the Northeast (Isarn). The first syllable, '*som*', means 'orange' or 'sour', while the second, '*tam*', means 'to pound', referring to the preparation of the salad in a pestle and mortar. (The sound of this pounding is described by the Thai onomatopoeic word '*pok-pok*', which is where the famous chain of restaurants in the United States gets its name.) There are many variations on *som tam*, the standard one in Bangkok being *tam Thai*, which generally contains shredded papaya, tomatoes, yardlong beans, peanuts, chillies, palm sugar, garlic, lime, fish sauce and dried shrimp. A more potent variation is *som tam pu pla ra*, a pungent dish seasoned with fermented fish paste and small pickled blue crabs. That's one for the pros.

Green curry (แกงเขียวหวาน)

The name of this well-known dish translates to 'sweet green curry'. The word 'sweet' refers not to the flavour, as is often supposed, but to the gentle green hue of the curry, called *khiao wan* ('sweet green') in Thai. That colour derives from the green chillies in the curry paste, the pigment of which leaks into the coconut milk base. The meat in the dish can be pork, beef, chicken, shrimp or fish balls, usually accompanied by mini eggplants, though sometimes sweetcorn or carrots are used (to the dismay of purists). The dish may contain lumps of what looks like a deep-purple mousse – actually coagulated chicken blood, known as 'chicken blood tofu'.

Phad Thai (ผัดไทย)

This dish of Vietnamese-style noodles, stir-fried with eggs, fish sauce, tamarind juice and chillies, has become famous the world over. Despite its name, *phad Thai* is arguably one of the least 'Thai' dishes described here, not least because noodles are ultimately a Chinese import. Some sources believe the dish was invented in the 1940s in the household of dictator Phibunsongkhram. The strongman promoted *phad Thai* as Thailand's national dish during a period of 'modernisation' influenced by the fascist states of Europe, leading Thai writer Pitchaya Sudbanthad to waggishly dub the dish the 'Volksnoodle'. It's also, for better or worse, the 'tourist's favourite', perhaps due to its name and relative mildness.

Massaman curry (แกงมัสมั่น)

This complex curry is believed to have been brought to Thailand by the first Persian envoy to Ayutthaya, Sheik Amed, who established the aristocratic Bunnag family. The ingredients in a *massaman* paste are too numerous to list here, and it's probably its complexity, together with the motherly combination of coconut milk, meat and potatoes, that make this dish so beloved. Beef and chicken are the most common meats used, though variations exist. (Pork seems sacrilegious, but is not unheard of.) In 2011, CNNGo declared the dish the most delicious in the world. I'm not sure I'd go that far, but when it's done well, it is indeed a marvel.

Sour orange soup (แกงส้ม)

Kaeng som is often thought of as a Southern dish, probably because that's where a lot of the best fish comes from, but variations on this sour, spicy soup exist all over Thailand. The dish gets its pigment – not to mention sweet and sour flavour – from the liberal use of tamarind water. A meaty, fatty fish is used since it provides a soothing contrast with the tart liquid. *Kaeng som* can also contain vegetables, including bamboo shoots, coconut meat, Siamese watercress or cabbage. The fish is usually sliced and cooked on the bone, a practice that foreigners generally dislike. As David Thompson notes in *Thai Food*, however, Thais believe this makes the fish taste better.

Phanaeng curry (แกงพะแนง)

This Malaysian curry comes from the island of Penang, hence the name. Milder and drier than most Thai curries, *phanaeng* is traditionally made with beef. The flavours of Thai basil, coconut milk and peanut shine through, and the dish is usually finished with a topping of shredded kaffir lime lives. This is another dish popular with foreigners, perhaps owing to its relative mildness.

Nam phrik kapi (น้ำพริกกะปิ)

There are countless types of *nam phrik* (relishes) in the Thai cooking canon but *nam phrik kapi* is the best known. It's also the most fundamental, since it serves as the basis of many others. The key ingredients are pungent shrimp paste (*kapi*), garlic and chillies. The dish is always served with accompaniments, frequently mixed raw or boiled vegetables or grilled meat or fish. The pungency and spiciness of *nam phrik kapi* make it a challenging one for an inexperienced palate to appreciate. But once you acquire the taste for it, everything else just seems a little… bland. An interesting variation is *nam phrik maeng da*, which contains flakes of mashed up water beetle that impart an almost menthol-like flavour to the relish.

Phat kraphrao (ผัดกระเพราว)

For many Thais, *phad kraphrao* (fried with Thai basil) is the dish you order when you can't be bothered to think. The best-known variation is made with pork, though pretty much any protein can be prepared *phat kraphrao*, which involves frying it up with oil, fish sauce, soy, garlic, pepper and – of course – Thai holy basil. Thai holy basil has a different flavour from its European cousin, and to use the latter in preparing the dish would be something of a travesty (though probably not unpleasant). The dish is best topped with a fried egg (*khai dao*), creating a very Thai alternative to the sausage and egg sandwich.

Fish steamed with lemon (ปลานึ่งมะนาว)

Few Thai dishes – indeed few dishes, period – are as delicious as *pla nueng manao*. In Bangkok it's most commonly made with sea bass, which is served whole in a fish-shaped metal dish. The fish should be half-submerged in a bubbling broth, heated from below and rich with fish sauce, garlic, chilli and lime and topped with coriander. The broth has the energising medicinal quality of *tom yam* and can be ladled into small bowls and sipped like soup.

for some foreigners, though most get used to eating the Thai way eventually. Many, myself included, come to prefer it. Having lived in Thailand for years, the way Westerners eat now seems strange, each person territorially hoarding their own dish. Why put all your eggs in one basket?

Eating with Thais is generally an informal business and there are few rules to remember. Thais eat with a fork and spoon, not chopsticks, unless they're eating Chinese or other East Asian food. The spoon is held in the right hand and used to scoop food from the plate. The fork is an auxiliary tool to help load food onto the spoon. Thais don't put forks in their mouths if they have a spoon, though in Western restaurants where knives and forks are the norm, this rule is waived.

Northeastern food, which is served with sticky rice, can be eaten by hand, or a combination of hand, spoon and fork. The rice will be served either on a plate, packed into a plastic bag, or in a basket. Small chunks are pulled off and rolled into balls about half the size of a golf ball. They can then be dipped into the ruby-red dressing that collects on a plate of *som tam*, and eaten by hand, or placed on the plate before being loaded onto a spoon with accompaniments. (Tip: when eating sticky rice from a basket, replace the lid every time you take out a handful. This will prevent the rice from drying and going hard.)

When a Thai meal is served, each dish should have its own spoon, called the *chon klang* ('the middle spoon'). For reasons of politeness and, ultimately, hygiene, make sure you use the *chon klang* to scoop food from the central dishes. Here's what *not* to do: calculate the fraction of a given dish that 'belongs' to you and scoop that portion of the dish onto your plate. The way Thais eat is to take one spoonful of a dish at a time, place it on their plate and then scoop a mixture of the rice and accompaniment onto a spoon.

In general, let common decency be your guide: don't devour more than your fair share of any particular dish. And make sure you compliment the cook or host on the quality of the food with an '*aroi*' ('delicious') or even '*aroi mak*' ('very delicious'). If you're eating Isarn food, saying '*saep*' ('delicious') or '*saep lai*' ('very delicious') will delight

Northeastern friends. Don't go too far with the praise, however, or you risk looking insincere or sarcastic.

When eating noodle soup, Thais use a combination of chopsticks and a short, wide metal spoon. The chopsticks are used to pluck out the noodles, which are then coiled onto the spoon. The broth itself is eaten with the spoon, never drunk. Slurping noodles in the Japanese style will get you funny looks; as with most areas of life, Thais eat gracefully. In a custom borrowed from the Chinese, chopsticks should be placed flat on the rim of the bowl once the dish is finished. (Leaving them sticking out is considered a harbinger of death, since they resemble the incense sticks burned at funerals.)

Another Chinese custom often – but not always – observed in Thailand: Having eaten one-half of a whole fish, the spine and ribs should be pulled carefully off the remaining flesh to expose the other flank. To 'flip the fish' is considered unlucky because it resembles the capsizing of a boat. This superstition originated on Chinese fishing vessels, though it later spread onto dry land: to flip the fish in someone's restaurant could be taken to mean you wish their business would 'capsize' too. Needless to say, in 21st-century Bangkok there are plenty of Thais who don't buy such superstitions.

Eat with your mouth closed – but then, you do that anyway. Toothpicks will usually be supplied on tables, either in a plastic jar or a compartment of the napkin holder. The polite way to use one is to use one hand to pick, holding the other over your mouth to block views of the rather ungraceful process you're engaged in. If you happen to get bones in your mouth, don't stick your fingers in your mouth; turn away from the table and gently drop the troublesome bone into a napkin.

When Thai people go out drinking, food is inevitably involved. Usually, they will order a special category of dish called '*kap klaem*', essentially meaning 'accompanying snacks'. These will often be salty and fatty: deep-fried sausages, pork crackling, nuts or *daet diao* meat: succulent, salty jerky that has spent a day drying out in the sun. Conversely, many Thais – certainly nowhere near all – don't drink alcohol while eating meals. Don't be surprised if Thai

people remark on the strangeness of *farang* drinking beer with dinner, but doing so isn't exactly rude.

And at the end of the meal, who picks up the tab? If someone is hosting you, even if you know you are wealthier than they are, give them the honour of paying. If it's not clear who the 'host' is, then the social superior pays. On the other hand, in the case of a group of friends of roughly equal social status going out together, it's common to share the bill. When on a date, whoever made the invitation should pay. Many, perhaps most, women still expect men to pay for their meals. However, some financially independent Thais will be keen to show themselves as such, and will insist on paying. 'Going Dutch' is not unheard of in such cases either.

THAI SERVICE
Thai service has an excellent reputation, though there's some debate among expats over whether it's entirely

deserved. To be sure, Thai waiting staff are almost always polite, as well as suitably deferent (if you appreciate that sort of thing). Having said that, they can lack initiative and be unreceptive to complaints. The fact that there isn't really a tipping culture in Thailand means there isn't the same incentive that staff have in places like the United States to 'go the extra mile'.

What's more, the Thai concern with saving face brings its own challenges. Complaining is frequently fruitless, your concerns generally met with embarrassed shrugs by staff who aren't trained to deal with such scenarios. If you merely think something doesn't taste very good, complaining will probably get you nowhere. Getting angry with the lack of receptiveness or making a scene will only make things worse. If the restaurant has made a serious mistake, by all means point out the error, but do so discreetly. As always in Thailand, it's best to face problems with a smile, not a scowl.

Another point to bear in mind: most serving staff you're likely to come across won't speak English very well. They will be able to take orders, and they will probably know the names of the dishes on their menu (though they may need to check the Thai by looking at the menu). You should make allowances for this – asking waiters to tell you what is in each dish will often be beyond their abilities. You'll only embarrass them.

In other respects, the tolerant regimes at most Thai restaurants are refreshing. Cheap places don't charge corkage (though in more upscale joints, it's the norm). You can wander into an establishment carrying not only alcohol, but sometimes even food too. So long as you're spending *some* money in the restaurant, staff rarely care if you bring in 'extras' (or are too polite to make a fuss). If you're drinking a bottle of whisky, for example, the restaurant will happily make its money off the mixers. Frequently, a member of staff will take on the duty of ensuring your glasses never run empty. Even better, if you ask for a drink that's not in stock, a staff member may be willing to go to the nearest 7-Eleven or supermarket to buy it. Make sure you tip in such cases.

Even monks need to stay in touch.

Durian, the legendary Southeast Asian stinky fruit, is banned from many hotels. That's hardly surprising, given its stench. Don't let that stop you from giving it a try: a good durian can be a joyously creamy experience.

Most of the city's canals were filled in long ago, but some remain. Hiring a longtail boat for a tour of the Thonburi waterways is thoroughly recommended.

Take your pick: *khao kaeng* (literally, 'rice, curry') is cheap, delicious and ready to eat in seconds.

When the going gets hot, Bangkok's air-conditioned shopping malls provide welcome respite.

The views from the city's many rooftop
bars can be spectacular.

TIPPING

To tip or not to tip? It's a question that can cause headaches for foreigners in Bangkok, particularly those with neurotic tendencies. The difficulty stems from the lack of any hard and fast rules. In the United States, a diner knows she has to leave a tip of 15–20 per cent or her lack of generosity will be met with angry glares or worse. There's no such formula in Bangkok.

There are really two questions to be answered here, related but distinct: how do Thai people tip, and how should *you* tip? The first thing to bear in mind is that Thailand doesn't really have an indigenous tipping culture. Tips are not considered an essential part of the waiting staff's wages, as in parts of the West. At a street stall or cheap restaurant, it's perfectly acceptable to leave nothing at all, or at a push, the shrapnel. As you head upscale, one or two THB20 notes can be left as a token of appreciation. In Western restaurants, something around 5 per cent seems to be the norm. A THB5,000 meal might attract a THB200 tip.

As a foreigner, you will have to decide if you want to tip as the locals do, or be more generous. To do so won't cost you much. And it would be naive to imagine that the vast numbers of tipping tourists that pass through the country haven't raised waiters' expectations of a little extra. Having said all that, an increasing number of upmarket restaurants – perhaps most of them – now add an automatic service charge of 10 per cent to the bill. In that case, there's no need to tip. So the question – to the relief of the neurotics out there – is increasingly moot.

FINDING PLACES TO EAT

You'll see hundreds of restaurants as you move around the city. How can you judge which ones are worth trying? When it comes to Thai restaurants, the simple rule of thumb is 'the crowd test': Does the place look popular? You might also pay attention to the balance of foreigners and Thais at the tables. If it's full of foreigners, expect the cuisine to be less spicy and less intensely flavoured. This might be what you want, but if it's so-called 'authenticity' you're after, follow the locals.

Another axiom worth remembering is that the best Thai restaurants don't tend to look like much. The tastiest cuisine is found in places that are clean, functional but without much ostentation. Expect simple metal or wooden tables and metal or even plastic chairs. I don't trust Thai restaurants that are too luxurious. Neither do I trust those that have the best views – the restaurants on the riverbanks or perched on top of skyscrapers. Such places rely heavily on the *panyakat* – atmosphere – to attract customers and don't need to try so hard in the taste department. You may be happy to make this sacrifice, of course, but if you're simply after the best food available, the humblest venue with the biggest crowds is where you'll find it.

Food reviews

Bernard Trink's name is less well-known than it used to be, though this old New Yorker used to be the most famous expat in Thailand. For 40 years, Trink wrote a column for the *Bangkok Post* called 'Nite Owl', a scurrilous weekly round-up of the city's nightlife – bargirls, brothels and all. It was canned eventually, deemed too politically incorrect by the paper's editors.

Trink also reviewed restaurants under the name 'Friar Tuck'. One day Trink dined at a new restaurant opened by a Thai lady with a famous surname (a Thai euphemism for 'an aristocrat'). Trink thought the food was 'piss poor' and said so in his *Post* column. The owner, to use Trink's words, 'went ballistic'. She reportedly told the paper that Trink had made her lose face in front of her family and that her powerful uncle would destroy the *Bangkok Post* unless Trink was sacked. The paper caved, and Friar Tuck was no more.

As this story illustrates, public criticism isn't welcome in Thailand. As a result, most publications that cover the restaurant scene tend to confine themselves to gushing praise. The review procedure usually works like this: the writer calls the venue and announces he would like to come for a meal. The venue under 'scrutiny' provides him with a free dinner. In turn, the writer says nice things about the place – regardless of its actual merits. (The nice things, nevertheless, must not be lies. The less appealing aspects of the experience are mostly brushed under the food-spattered rug, though a criticism or two may be permitted in order to provide a semblance of objectivity.)

So how to tell the wheat from the chaff? Fortunately, there are some publications that do try to provide the reader with honest restaurant assessments. Local lifestyle mag *BK Magazine* is one: the weekly free magazine and website does an admirably thorough job of covering the newest openings around the city, and when a place doesn't make the grade, it isn't afraid to say so. *Coconuts Bangkok*, a local news and reviews website, operates the same policy: its writers don't accept free meals for review purposes, and say exactly what they think (full disclosure: I've written reviews for Coconuts).

But today there is a growing number of websites and smartphone apps that circumvent the need for professional reviewers entirely, pooling user reviews written by the general public instead. Not all of these writers are skilful, discerning or concerned with being fair, but taken en masse they can certainly help you make a decision. The best known of these is *TripAdvisor*, which at the time of writing featured more than 35,000 reviews of at least 7,000 Bangkok restaurants. *Zodio*, another reviews app with more of a location-based focus, can generate a map of your area showing all the restaurants its users have reviewed, not to mention hotels, shops and facilities of all kinds.

Some apps focus more closely on food. In Bangkok, the most popular of these is *Wongnai,* the name of which means 'inner circle'. While the site probably has the most reviews on it, the vast majority are in Thai. Two English-language apps that

Tough crowd

When you're impressed by a Thai restaurant, it's natural to want to know what your Thai friends make of it. Don't get your hopes up; they're unlikely to be as excited by the place as you are. Most Thai people are fantastically difficult to impress when it comes to their cuisine. They have, after all, been eating this stuff their whole lives. A former Thai teacher of mine in Mae Sot employed a brutally simple taxonomy of the restaurants in the town. A place was either *'mai aroi'* ('not delicious'), *'chai dai'* ('usable', 'serviceable') or *'aroi'* ('delicious'). There were no other categories. To my disappointment, I never found a single restaurant he was willing to reward with a better rating than *'chai dai'*.

already have a good number of users in Bangkok are *Foodspotting* and *Burpple*. Both offer social-network-like functionality and location-based search. Best of all, both can display sliding arrays of food photos taken by users in restaurants near your current location. If you see something that looks appealing, you can bring up a map that shows you exactly where it's being served. The rich and powerful might have silenced Trink, but they can't silence 14 million Bangkokians.

SPLASHING OUT, THAI-STYLE

While you can eat like a king on the street or in any number of humble Thai restaurants, there are ways to throw more money at Thai food. Gourmet Thai restaurants are nothing new. They're often set in old colonial-style mansions and suburban villas. Lavish decor and a Ye Olde Siam aesthetic are the norm, as are waiters dressed in traditional garb, such as *jongkraben* wraparound trousers and silk shirts. Many

are international chains with branches in places like Geneva, London and Paris.

Higher-quality ingredients are the order of the day, as are fusion dishes using European ingredients regarded as *hi-so* by the *hi-so*: foie gras, imported steak, game. Truth be told, the food at these places isn't always tastier than the grub you get on the streets for a twentieth of the price.

Many of these restaurants claim to serve something called 'Royal Thai Cuisine', which naturally brings to mind refinement, lavishness and antiquity. Nevertheless, some critics believe Royal Thai Cuisine is little more than a marketing scheme. That's certainly the argument of one of Thailand's most famous chefs, Chef McDang. McDang, whose name means 'red squid' in Thai, is of royal extraction and grew up in a Bangkok palace – so he should know. McDang says many of the dishes served in the palaces are the same as the famous Central Thai favourites we all enjoy: green curries, *tom yam* and the like.

Some like it hot

Thai food is among the spiciest cuisines in the world. If you're from a Western country, you're unlikely to be used to food this hot, even if you've eaten lots of Thai food before. Thai restaurants abroad usually reduce the spiciness to levels the locals can tolerate. In Bangkok, restaurants in tourist areas also tend to turn down the heat. But at most other tables, don't expect culinary kid gloves. The widespread use of fresh chillies – the small ones are the most dangerous – can generate an explosive spiciness you just don't get from chilli powder.

Sometimes a restaurant will considerately reduce the heat. '*Tom yam kung*! It's for a *farang*!' At others, the server will ask you if you can handle spicy food – possibly in English. If they do so in Thai, it's '*than phet dai mai?*' (To say 'yes', say '*dai*'. Otherwise, say '*mai dai*'.) If no enquiries are forthcoming, take the initiative. To ask for a mild dish, say '*mai phet*'. To ask for 'a little bit spicy' say '*phet nit noi*'. 'Spicy' is '*phet phet*', while 'very spicy' is '*phet mak*'. Alas, no matter what you say, some restaurants just won't believe that when you say 'very spicy', you really mean it!

The main difference is that palace food is prepared with an added level of meticulousness only possible with a large staff. Thus, a grilled fish might be cooked, then completely de-boned, then resealed as if it never had any bones in the first place. Perhaps the royal family still eat like this, but you couldn't find a Bangkok restaurant showing that kind of dedication.

Recommended Thai restaurants

These Thai restaurants are consistently excellent:

- **Thon Krueng**; 239 Soi Thonglor 13, Sukhumvit 55; www. thonkrueng.com; 0-2185-2873. The confusing layout of this restaurant is a testament to its success. Thon Krueng is made up of several indoor and outdoor areas that have been added one-by-one over its 30 years in business. The decor is nothing fancy and the chatter can be deafening, but the food makes it all worthwhile, as suggested by the crowds that fill the place every night of the week. The baked pomfret with black soy beans may be more Chinese than Thai, but it's still one of my favourite dishes in the city.
- **Soul Food Mahanakorn**; 56/10, Sukhumvit Soi 55; www. soulfoodmahanakorn.com; 0-2714-7708. American food writer and restaurateur Jarrett Wrisley's Soul Food Mahanakorn is in all the guidebooks, and deservedly so. Wrisley travelled the country, picking up recipes for the best regional dishes Thailand has to offer: *khao soi* (Northern-style curried noodles), *kaeng hang le* (Northern ginger and pork belly curry) and *nam tok* (Northeastern-style meat salad), among them. Then he put them all on one simple menu and served them up with strong and delicious cocktails in a cosy shophouse venue. What's not to like?
- **nahm**; Metropolitan Hotel, Sathon Tai; www.comohotels. com/metropolitanbangkok; 0-2625-3388. Australian chef David Thompson probably knows more about Thai food than anyone who isn't Thai in the world. While his restaurant certainly deserves the title 'fine dining', the cuisine is resolutely Thai and informed by Thompson's encyclopaedic knowledge of the cuisine. The restaurant recently made No. 32 in The World's 50 Best Restaurants list, so expect great things.
- **Ban Phuengchom**; 38/1 Soi Chua Chit, Soi Ari; 0-2279-4204. Secreted at the end of a quiet *soi* coming off Soi Ari, Ban Pheungchom has a devoted local following. If you don't make a reservation, you'll probably be sitting in the

garden, but that's no bad thing. Very reasonably priced, the restaurant boasts some unusual dishes that aren't even on the menu. Ask your waiter for recommendations. The *wun sen phat sam men*, 'glass noodles with three smells', boasts a pungent combination of shrimp, stink beans and acacia leaves – fantastic, though it won't do your breath any favours.

Pretty Thai for a white guy

Recent years have seen the launch of a few Thai restaurants boasting something many Thai diners aren't entirely comfortable with: *farang* chefs. In 2009, husband-and-wife cooking duo Dylan Jones and Duangporn 'Bo' Songvisava opened Bo.lan, a fine diner taking a similar approach to Thai cuisine as David Thompson's acclaimed London restaurant nahm, where both had previously worked. The following year saw the launches of a Bangkok branch of nahm, Jarrett Wrisley's bar-eatery Soul Food Mahanakorn, and a Bangkok outpost of Sra Bua, a Michelin-starred Copenhagen restaurant that applies molecular gastronomy techniques to Thai cuisine.

While all four restaurants have been embraced by Western customers, the reception from Thais has been mixed. The reaction from Chef McDang, the outspoken Thai celebrity chef, to the cuisine at Sra Bua might be instructive. McDang wrote scathingly on his blog of the Copenhagen restaurant's experimental Thai food, focusing his ire on one dish that consisted of a carrot served with a mayonnaise-based red curry emulsion. 'Thai food doesn't have emulsions,' he fumed. 'What the hell *is* this… This is a restaurant with a Michelin Guide background yet they've forgotten that carrots don't even originate from Thailand.'

Then David Thompson threw fuel on the fire. Opening his Bangkok outpost, Thompson told *The New York Times* that Thai cooking was 'decaying', that the food was becoming less complex and varied, and that he was on a mission to 'revive' it. For many Thais, proud of their cuisine and sensitive to foreign criticism, this was too much. Suthon Sukphisit, a food writer and authority on Thai food, was unimpressed. 'He is slapping the faces of Thai people!' he said. 'If you start telling Thais how to cook real Thai food, that's unacceptable.'

In an op-ed for *The Nation*, ML Saksiri Kridakorn took aim at the whole Michelin ratings system. 'Thai cuisine does just fine without Michelin multi-star foreign cooks trying to further promote the Western rating of his "Thai culinary skill". Just to make a simple point: how many Thais are on the Michelin panel of judges? And how many of the Michelin judges really know what authentic Thai cuisine tastes like?' On his own blog, McDang agreed, suggesting Thais should take the Japanese line on the Michelin guide: 'This is a bunch of bunk!'

- **Supanniga Eating Room**; 160/11 Sukhumvit Soi 55; 0-2714-7508. Serving unusual Thai dishes in a crisp, modern setting, there's something of Soul Food Mahanakorn in the curiously named Supanniga. (Stop sniggering at the back; a *supanniga* is a type of Thai flower). The crowd is more Thai, though, and the flavours more intense. Some of the dishes are hard or impossible to find elsewhere in Bangkok, since the recipes are Trat specialities handed down from the proprietor's grandma. The pork curry with *cha muang* leaves is worth the trip alone.

- **Polo Fried Chicken**; 137/1-2 Soi Polo, Wireless Road; 0-2655-8489. This budget restaurant combines two wonderful things: deep-fried chicken and Isarn food. That should be all you need to know. The fried chicken is fat, juicy and sprinkled with deep-fried shallots, while the *som tam* holds its own against the best the city has to offer. A binge at Polo provides the perfect end to a day spent lazing in nearby Lumphini Park.

- **Taling Pling**; 25 Sukhumvit 34; 0-2258-5308-9. Taling Pling is a well-established chain, but don't let that put you off. I can't vouch for all the branches (most are in malls) but the flagship branch on Sukhumvit 34 is a treat. The striking dining room, with its chequered floor and vibrant colours, is an obvious draw but the cuisine is reliably tasty. An extensive menu combines Central, Southern and Isarn dishes, while some Western desserts round things off in refreshingly undogmatic fashion.

- **Bo.lan;** 42 Soi Pichai Ronnarong Songkram, Sukhumvit 26; 0-2260-2962; www.bolan.co.th. Run by alumni of nahm's London outlet, Dylan Jones and Duangporn 'Bo' Songvisava, Bo.lan was the first restaurant to bring what might be termed the 'nahm' approach to Thai cuisine to the city, beating Thompson's place by a year. The restaurant combines the service and setting expected at fine-diners with recipes plucked from the cookery books of the palace kitchens of yesteryear. Uncompromising in their commitment to authenticity, expect big flavours and serious spiciness.

- **Kua Kling Pak Sod**; Phahonyothin Soi 8; 081-811-5458. With another branch on Thong Lor Soi 5, this Southern restaurant run by a Thai-Chinese family from Chumphon consistently serves up some of the tastiest food in town. The flavours are unapologetically intense and the produce wonderfully fresh. The *sator phad kapi kung*, stink beans fried in shrimp paste, is an explosively delicious dish, bursting with umami flavour and served with large, meaty prawns. The *kaeng lueang pla*, sour, spicy soup with fish, is equally deserving of a mention.
- **The Local**; 32 Sukhumvit 23; 0-2664-0664. The Local may play up to the 'localism' trend in a clunkingly shameless way, but that's a minor quibble, because the cuisine served in this elegant restaurant is excellent. Like Bo.lan and Nahm, many of the restaurant's recipes have been resurrected from old recipe books, and the restaurant has that 'Ye Olde Thailand' feel of many of the city's upmarket Thai restaurants. The Thai mackerel with coconut milk and lotus stem is a creamy, aromatic highlight.

STREET FOOD

Fancy restaurants are all well and good, but it's street food that makes Bangkok a magnet for food lovers. A first foray into one of Bangkok's street-food neighbourhoods can be a thrilling experience. Huge platters of fried insects, skewered baby squid roasting over glowing embers, gory piles of braised pork trotters – there are some strange and wonderful things to be seen – and eaten – amid the fumes.

While prices are rising, street food remains gloriously cheap – at least from an expat perspective. Cooking yourself often ends up costing you more than having someone do it for you. And it's hard to compete with those masters and mistresses of the flash-fry, out there on the streets

Collect the money or check the bill?

There are two phrases used to ask for the bill in Thai eateries: '*kep tang*' and '*chek bin*'. The former means 'collect the money', while the latter is derived from English: 'check the bill'. At street stalls and cheap Thai restaurants, use '*kep tang*'. At upmarket places, say '*chek bin*'. Both would produce the desired effect in any establishment, but saying '*kep tang*' in the Oriental Hotel will probably bring a smirk to your waiter's face.

Along with coconut milk, taro, beans and fruits, ginkgo nuts are a common ingredient in Thai desserts.

doing culinary push-ups, getting ready to kick your ass in the kitchen stakes. The easy availability of cheap, delicious and fast food means many exiles forgo cooking in Bangkok entirely, and eating out becomes their vocation.

What is it that makes street food taste so good? First, a woman who spends her whole working day doing nothing but cooking noodles will become very good at cooking noodles. Second, a street vendor does not have the luxury of a pretty venue to attract customers, and thus lives and dies by the quality and value-for-money of the food. So there's a strong incentive for vendors to make it as downright delicious as possible (this can entail liberal use of the dreaded monosodium glutamate, of course).

A third reason is competition: street food stalls tend to cluster together, and areas become known for their street cuisine. Any vendor competing in one of these areas needs to offer a quality product or they will find that customers will vote with their feet, and spend their baht elsewhere.

That's not to suggest that all of Bangkok's street food is good. It isn't. And it's tempting to over-romanticise street cuisine. Some writers will tell you the exhaust fumes make the food taste better, and that the street rats lend atmosphere. Let's not get carried away. But the best street stalls offer the most bang for your baht, the best flavours for the smallest outlay.

Eating at a street stall

It's not always obvious what to order at a street stall, or even how to do it. Many of them don't have menus. Of those that do, most will be in Thai. Until you learn to speak and/or read Thai, your finger will be your friend. Point at what you want (it's rude to point at people, but not at curry). Most street vendors will at least understand basic English numerals, so you should be able to order multiple portions without difficulty.

When ordering at a stall, be bold. Many vendors won't acknowledge you until you say something to them. You'll probably see Thai customers going straight to the vendor

---

Street gurus

Some Bangkok writers have dedicated themselves to seeking out the best street food in the capital. These English-language blogs provide handy shortcuts to the tastiest budget meals out there.

www.eatingthaifood.com This food blog run by US food obsessives Mark Wiens and Dwight Turner is a great place to start, with regular posts on unusual dishes and their latest street-food finds.

www.austinbushphotography.com Lonely Planet writer and food photographer Austin Bush blogs on the best food he unearths on his travels around Thailand. His site's Google map of Bangkok street food is a godsend, perfect for smartphone-guided wanders into the unknown.

www.bangkokglutton.com Thai-American writer Chawadee 'Chow' Nualkhair has an infectious passion for Bangkok's street bites. Her blog sees her muse on the nature of gluttony, all the while alerting the reader to some of the best street food in the city. (She's also the author of *Bangkok's Top 50 Street Food Stalls*, a useful and handily compact guidebook with maps of many of the city's best street food neighbourhoods.)

and shouting their order, regardless of who was there before them. This doesn't necessarily mean they've jumped the 'queue', just that the vendor will know what they want when their turn comes.

You'll see a few condiments at street stalls that you may not recognise. At an *ahan tam sang* (single-dish stir-fry) joint, expect to find a pot of fish sauce mixed with finely chopped chillies. Fish sauce is used instead of salt in Thailand, though it's given a spicy kick, Thai-style. Confusingly, the mixture can be referred to as either *nam pla phrik* (chilli fish sauce) or *phrik nam pla* (fish sauce chillies). Although the first seems grammatically logical, the latter is just as common. Perhaps it depends on whether your main interest is saltiness or spice.

At noodle joints, condiments come in plastic holders, with four chambers for the essentials: sugar, dried chilli, vinegar (with sliced chilli) and fish sauce. To the Western palate, a soup may taste fine without seasoning. For Thais, however, it's part of the ritual to *prung* ('flavour') the dish to perfection. This will often mean adding large amounts of everything – very sweet, very salty, very sour and very, very spicy being the ideal.

An instinct to prung

Thais like to *prung* (season) their food, especially when they feel flavours are lacking. I remember being amused, even a little shocked, when I went to eat pizza for the first time with two Thai friends. When our order arrived, they immediately began squeezing the contents of ketchup sachets over the top of their pies. Perhaps I shouldn't have been so horrified: this was at a Pizza Company, whose products probably don't deserve too much reverence.

Tabletops will usually be furnished with a branded holder of thin pink napkins, which seem to have very little absorbent capacity whatsoever. In fact, their primary purpose is to clean the cutlery, which many Thais don't trust to be spotless. Why pink? As Philip Cornwel-Smith explains in *Very Thai*: 'The dye indicates recycled paper costing just 16.50 baht: every half-baht counts. It's pink because extracts of tomato and cinnabar annatto score best at disguising the speckly blemishes from recycling... And pink proves more appetising with food than, say, blue, brown or green.'

Perhaps the suggestion of dirty cutlery has set alarm bells ringing. Is street food safe? Mostly yes, sometimes not. If you eat a lot of street food, expect to be stricken with a bad belly now and again. It comes with the territory. A good rule of thumb is that a busy restaurant is generally a safe restaurant. You don't get popular by poisoning people.

A GUIDE TO BANGKOK STREET STALLS

With tens of thousands of street food stalls in Bangkok, recommending specific places risks absurdity. Instead, I offer two things: a list of some of the best street-food neighbourhoods in the city, and a guide to the types of stalls you can expect to encounter and how to recognise them. I've added the names of these in Thai, to help you decode the squiggles.

'Food to order' (อาหารตามสั่ง)

Whether in shophouse or street corner, *ahan tam sang* ('food to order') outlets are the places to go for quick, delicious stir-fried dishes. They offer pork, chicken, crispy pork, shrimp and mixed seafood prepared in a few standard ways. These include *khao phad* (fried rice), *phad kraphrao* (fried with holy basil leaves), *phad phrik kaeng* (fried with curry paste) and *tot krathiam* (fried with garlic). You can always order these dishes with a *khai jiao* (omelette) or *khai dao* (fried egg) on top, a simple culinary custom so effective that you begin to wonder why it isn't more common in other cuisines – fried egg on spaghetti bolognese, anyone? To request an egg with

Street food Meccas

The following areas are packed with street food and well worth exploring:
- Yaowarat Road
- Victory Monument
- Sukhumvit Soi 38
- Soi Ari
- Banglamphu
- Soi Convent
- Ramkhamhaeng Road
- Tha Phra Chan
- Charoen Krung
- Huai Khwang Market

a runny yoke, say '*khai dao mai suk*', though be warned: this often has no effect whatsoever on what comes out of the kitchen (or worse, results in an undercooked egg).

Rice and curry (ข้าวแกง)

A lunchtime favourite, *khao kaeng* joints serve pre-cooked food and are thus the fastest way to get full. While it's easy to disparage these places for serving 'food that's been left out all day', good *khao kaeng* can be delicious. Vendors cook the dishes in the morning, then keep them in metal display trays or pots, frequently behind a translucent plastic screen. Common dishes include green curries, chicken fried with ginger and mushrooms, pickled cabbage fried with egg and slices of catfish fried in spicy sauce. The server will load up a plate of rice before asking you to select your accompaniments. You can choose up to three or four dishes; just point at whatever takes your fancy. It's best to come to these places as early as possible. The food will be at its freshest and you'll beat the crowds. They'll still happily serve you at a lunchtime *khao kaeng* place at 2pm, but don't expect the food to be at its best.

Hainanese chicken rice stalls are a common sight on the streets. Yellowish birds hanging from hooks mark the spot.

Hainanese chicken rice (ข้าวมันไก่)

Known in Thai as *khao man kai* (literally, 'chicken-fat rice'), Hainanese chicken rice is almost as popular in Bangkok as it is in its more established bastions of Singapore, Malaysia and – you guessed it – Hainan Island in the South China Sea. There are variations, but the basic formula is the same: boiled chicken served on rice cooked in chicken stock, accompanied by a spicy sauce. In Bangkok, a golden chicken carcass suspended from a hook marks the spot for this popular dish, which is easy to fall in love with (though just as easy to tire of). The key to a champion *khao man kai* stall is a superlative sauce. As Thais often say, be careful with this dish: eating rice cooked in chicken fat is a great way to put on the pounds.

Stewed pork and rice (ข้าวขาหมู)

Khao kha mu is a wonderfully unhealthy dish that fits the bill when all you want is a big plate of fat and carbohydrates, cunningly disguised as food. Pork trotters are braised in soy sauce and cinnamon five-spice for a couple of hours, then sliced on top of rice and served with kale, pickled greens and a boiled egg. You can opt out of the gelatinous skin/fat that accompanies the dish by saying '*mai ao nang*'. Recognise these places by the huge metal pots and pans piled high with maroon-coloured trotters: a gruesome sight for vegetarians, a mouthwatering one for carnivores.

Red pork and rice (ข้าวหมูแดง)

Khao mu daeng, 'red-pork rice', is another street staple of Chinese ancestry. Expect a scoop of rice topped with slices of barbecued red pork, roasted pork belly, *kun chiang* (a type of Chinese pork sausage, ruby red and very sweet) and a boiled egg. The dish is brought together with a dousing of sweet pork gravy, and finished with a sprig of coriander. Recognise a *khao mu daeng* outlet by the golden pork bellies, slabs of red pork and long, thin *kun chiang* hanging from hooks in glass cabinets.

Rice porridge (โจ๊ก)

Almost every Asian country from India to Indonesia has its own congee. In Thailand it's known as *jok*. (The word comes

from Cantonese; pronounce it with a long vowel as in the English word 'joke'.) Commonly eaten at breakfast (though not always), *jok* is, at its best, hypnotic comfort food. It also serves as a gentle stomach-filler for the sick. Short-grain rice is boiled down into a creamy rice porridge, which usually contains balls of minced pork. Intestines and liver are often in there too. If you're not so crazy about offal, say '*mai sai khrueang nai*'. Chopped scallions and sliced ginger add zing, but you can liven things up even more by adding pepper, fish sauce, soy sauce or pickled chillies in vinegar. Sometimes *pa thong ko*, deep-fried dough fritters, are provided on the side and can be added to the soup. Last but not least, another essential component of a bowl of *jok* is a chicken's egg, poured raw into the hot porridge. To order one, say '*sai khai*'.

Rice soup (ข้าวต้ม)

While it lacks the flavour pyrotechnics of most Thai cuisine, *khao tom* is a gentle way to ease your digestive system into the day. This rice soup is thinner than *jok*, and the long-grain rice used retains its granularity in the stock. The dish comes in two forms. The first is mostly eaten at breakfast and will contain pieces of meat – chicken, pork, shrimp, mixed seafood or fish. The second is *khao tom kui*, which is plain rice porridge eaten with side dishes, which are spooned into the soup. Common accompaniments include stir-fried morning glory, chicken fried with ginger, and salty minced pork with Chinese olives.

Make it special

The most important word you need to know when ordering street food is this one: '*phiset*'. Literally, the word means 'special', but in the context of the Bangkok roadside eatery, it means 'give me an extra large portion'. This will usually cost you THB5–10 more than normal. In some places, with some dishes, you can order specific components of your dish '*phiset*'. For example, at a *bami kiao* joint you might ask for '*phiset kiao*' ('extra dumplings') or '*phiset mu*' ('extra pork').

Rat na noodles (ราดหน้า)

Another Thai-Chinese dish, *rat na* consists of flat rice noodles, meat (usually pork) and greens such as kale or Chinese broccoli, doused in a gravy. Sometimes, crispy egg noodles are added for texture. The gravy is thickened with tapioca flour; it can often have a gelatinous, almost mucus-like texture which may not hold much appeal to the foreigner. The flavours are muted, making this dish another prime target for the usual Thai seasonings – sugar, fish sauce, dried chilli flakes and chillies in vinegar.

Fried chicken (ไก่ทอด)

It's a wonder KFC does any business in Thailand. In this writer's opinion, Thai-style fried chicken is some of the best in the world – and it certainly beats the Colonel's product. The oil may look like it's been reused a thousand times – and it probably has. But that just might be what makes the chicken taste so good. The chicken is marinated in a blend of aromatics and spices before it's dipped into the rice-flour batter. This ensures the meat is infused with flavour and encased in a thin, crispy coating. Thais serve fried chicken with sticky rice, a perfect accompaniment that soaks up the grease. Tip: look for Muslim fried chicken stalls, often marked with Arabic-like script. They're often the best of the bunch, not least because they serve their product with a sprinkling of deep-fried shallots, a touch that lifts the dish from good to great.

Noodle soup (ก๋วยเตี๋ยว)

There are enough variations on noodle soup to fill a chapter, but I'll try to keep things brief. You can categorise noodle soups by the type of meat used to make the broth: generally beef, pork, chicken or duck. There'll usually be a choice of noodle: *sen lek* (thin rice noodles), *sen yai* (wide rice noodles), *sen mi* (super-thin rice noodles), *bami* (egg and wheat noodles), and instant noodles, usually referred to by the most common brand name, '*mama*' (as in 'hoover', 'band-aid' and 'jacuzzi'. Floating in the soup will be some combination of meat, intestines and offal, as well as processed meatballs, which come in pork, beef and fish varieties. Greens are usually present, in the form of morning glory, cabbage or kale.

There are some common variations. *Kuaitiao ruea* or 'boat noodles' originated in the floating markets of Ayutthaya. The dish may now be served by land-lubbers, but it can still be a dark, sensual joy, the broth thickened with a dash of pig's blood. Another popular dish is *kuaitiao tom yam*, which brings Thai and Chinese together in one bowl (complete with

Thai street stalls let you have it all: cheap and delicious.

Thai cooks do things with pork that will convert all but the most stubborn beef lovers.

fishballs, squid and tofu). Often sold at the same stalls is *yen ta fo*, another popular noodle dish. The latter is an unusual blend of various types of fish balls, tofu, squid, pork crackling, greens and deep-fried dumplings. The dish has a distinctive bright pink hue, which comes from the sweet-sour fermented tofu paste that characterises *yen ta fo*.

One final variation is *bami kiao*, a soup of egg noodles and wontons with slices of red pork, duck or crab meat. A common brand is Chai Si, the logo for which is a bowl with a number '4' in it. Chai Si stalls are bright yellow, with red lettering. There are better *bami kiao* outlets but Chai Si provides an easily recognisable introduction to the dish.

Isarn food (อาหารอีสาน)

Isarn or Northeastern Thai food is hugely popular, and not just with Northeastern migrants. The most famous dish is *som tam*, described on page 208. Other favourites include grilled meats, particularly chicken (*kai yang*) and pork neck (*kho mu yang*); grilled catfish, which are caught in the rice fields; and spicy meat salads such as *lap* and *nam tok*, heavy on herbs and the flavour of toasted rice powder. Isarn food is eaten with sticky rice; to eat it with jasmine rice just isn't the same.

FOOD COURTS

It's easy to dismiss food courts, which are often housed inside sterile, corporate settings like shopping malls, department stores, transport hubs and office complexes. The romance of the street is decidedly absent. But hold the judgements. Food courts, essentially gatherings of street stalls in a single indoor space, actually have a lot going for them. Hygiene standards tend to be higher, they're cheap and, most importantly, they're air-conditioned – sometimes you just need to get out of the heat.

The food, while never spectacular, is generally of a decent standard; the competition effect described above applies as much to food courts as it does to street food. Since the staff generally cook, serve food and process payments, food courts use a coupon or card system. Look for the coupon counter first, then go and exchange your money – THB100 per person is a safe amount, and you'll probably use only half of it. Don't forget to get your change on your way out – cards usually expire after the day you purchase them.

- **MBK**, Phayathai Road; BTS National Stadium;0-2620-9000. MBK's vast 6th-floor food court has a range of stalls to match its size. If it's Thai and it's edible, it's probably here.
- **Terminal 21**, Asok Intersection, Sukhumvit Road; BTS Asok; 0-9038-4554-7. This relatively new 'around the world'-themed mall features an impressive food court in the top-floor 'San Francisco' zone. Prices are a little steeper than in some of the older malls but the food is of a high quality.
- **Siam Paragon**, Rama I Road; BTS Siam; tel: 0-2610-7911. The food court on the ground floor of this most fancy of malls is one of the swankiest in the city. Expect gourmet versions of Thai classics, as well as Japanese and Korean street fare.

FOREIGN CUISINE

Thais are fairly conservative when it comes to food, particularly in the provinces. Many eat Thai food as a rule and have it fixed in their minds that they don't like foreign cuisine, much of which is considered bland (Western) or even smelly (Indian). A friend's Northeastern mother-in-law, for example, refuses to travel abroad without her rice cooker.

You may think yourself more open-minded than that, but after a few days, weeks or months in Bangkok, there will come a time when you crave the flavours of home. More than that, you'll probably find yourself hankering after something, *anything,* that is neither fried, nor spicy, nor – dare I say it – bursting with flavour. Worry not: there is a vast range of international cuisine on offer in Bangkok. If you crave it, you can probably find it.

You will have to pay for the privilege, of course. Imported ingredients are expensive, as are waiting staff who can speak English and provide service in the style Westerners are used to. What's more, the quality of foreign cuisine is patchy. If you find yourself in an unknown Thai-run restaurant that serves both Thai and Western cuisine, the best move is usually to order Thai. It will certainly be cheaper and probably far better.

There are a few reasons for this. Thais abhor blandness and their intensely flavoured cuisine reflects that. But they

Riverside restaurants are some of the most pleasant places to eat in the city, though not necessarily the tastiest.

often want foreign cuisine to reflect that, too. Large quantities of salt and sugar can find their way into dishes most expats might think they have no business being. Be vigilant: you probably won't enjoy your first encounter with sickly sweet tuna mayonnaise.

Many of the ingredients needed for foreign cuisine can't be grown in Thailand, and the local equivalents just aren't the same. Quality potatoes and tomatoes, for example, are very difficult to grow in this climate. Thus, imports become necessary, which don't come cheap and can mean the food has been frozen, robbing it of its freshness and flavour. Or, to keep things affordable for Thai diners, there are substitutions – Thai basil for Mediterranean basil, for example, which just doesn't taste right in a *caprese* salad.

There has also been a tendency for inexperienced foreigners to set up restaurants. Opening a restaurant serving your homeland's cuisine is a tempting option for expats the world over, and this has long been true in Thailand. Unfortunately, some of the people who do so aren't the best cooks. (I can, for example, think of one *farang*-run restaurant in Thailand that substitutes melted Kraft cheese slices for hollandaise in its eggs benedict.) This is not to say that there aren't some good restaurants run by non-professional cooks. But there are duds.

Fortunately, in the last five years or so, things have vastly improved. A growing cohort of young Thais have studied abroad and returned to Bangkok to open restaurants. This new generation know what the cuisine is supposed to taste like and are broad-minded when it comes to food. And while being a chef used to be thought of as a fairly lowly profession, the rise of celebrity chefs like McDang and Ian Kittichai, as well as shows like the Thai edition of Iron Chef, mean young Thais increasingly aspire to join the restaurant industry.

What's more, as Western economies flounder and the economic centre of gravity moves East, skilled foreign chefs and restaurateurs are increasingly moving to Bangkok. They bring skills and recipes with them, but also ideas: localism, organic, slow food, nose-to-tail and even molecular gastronomy. The fine-dining scene certainly has a long way to go, and Michelin is yet to produce a guide to the city, but top chefs are stopping off in Bangkok to do residencies here. Pasta sauces with the sugar content of *crème brûlée* may still be out there – but they're becoming mercifully rare.

Best of the West

- **Appia**; 20/4 Sukhumvit 31; www.appia-bangkok.com; 0-2261-2057. Having rethought the Thai restaurant with Soul Food Mahanakorn, US restaurateur Jarrett Wrisley launched Appia with Roman chef Paulo Vitaletti in 2013. Bucking the 'eat local' trend, Vitaletti imports most of his ingredients from his homeland – yes, even the eggs. The results are phenomenal. The menu focuses on substantial fresh pastas in bold sauces and succulent rotisserie meats such as *porchetta*, organic pork rolled up and stuffed with pork liver and herbs. Carefully chosen Mediterranean wines make things even more interesting.

- **Le Beaulieu**; Athénée Tower, 63 Wireless Road; www.le-beaulieu.com; 0-2168 8220. If you're in the mood to splash out, this superb French restaurant is a reliable bet. Chef Hervé Frerard's traditional cuisine weds quality French ingredients with the Thai produce. Frerard serves as a consultant to the Royal Projects, which gives him first dibs on the best produce the farms have to offer. The lunch, in particular, is great value, offering three perfectly executed courses for THB695++ .

- **Water Library**; The Grass, Thonglor 12; www.mywaterlibrary.com; 0-2714-9292. The name and concept of this restaurant, which has two Bangkok branches, might verge on the absurd; the Water Library boasts an enormous collection of imported, bottled waters. But the Thonglor outlet, which spurns a la carte in favour of a 12-course tasting menu that changes with the seasons, serves the most exciting cuisine in Bangkok. There are just 10 seats, which are arranged along a sushi-style bar facing the chefs. Part theatre, part gastronomic extravaganza, the Water Library is bloody expensive but, if you can afford it, worth the damage.

- **Chu**; Exchange Tower, Sukhumvit Road (BTS Asoke); 0-2663-4554. Chu does a mean line in desserts (churros, brownies, pancakes) and full plates (fried breakfast, eggs benedict, Norwegian scrambled eggs 'n' smoked salmon). Accompanying the food is a nice selection of what you might call 'comfort drinks' like hot chocolates and cream sodas. The coffee's good too, but the ice-cream sandwich – homemade ice cream sandwiched between two perfectly chewy cookies – is the best reason to make the pilgrimage.

- **La Monita**; 888/26 Mahatun Plaza, Phloenchit; www. lamonita.com; 0-2650-9581. This little, unpretentious Mexican restaurant is easy to love. The highlights of the menu are the San Francisco-style burritos, which in true Frisco style are wrapped in foil and filled with the good stuff: guacamole, sour cream, rice and plenty of meat. Combine those with a jug of margarita and you have the ingredients for the perfect boozy lunch.

- **Pala Pizza Romana**; BTS Asok, Sukhumvit; palapizzabangkok.com; 0-2259-1228-9. Pala specialises in rectangular Roman-style pizza, served by the slice or half-metre. The bases are thick, light and bread-like and the toppings delightfully fresh. Unlike most of the cheese-heavy pizzas that are the norm in Bangkok, you can have Pala for lunch without falling into a food coma, which scores this small-but-perfectly formed restaurant a lot of bonus points. It's tough walking past the restaurant without succumbing to the temptation to grab a slice.

- **Opposite Mess Hall**; Sukhumvit 51; oppositebangkok. com; 0-2662-6330. After building Quince into one of Bangkok's best restaurants in 2012, Australian chef Jess Barnes joined forces with the owners of trendy drinking hole WTF to launch Opposite Mess Hall. With a moody, masculine vibe, the joint is as much about drinking as eating, and Barnes's menu focuses on the kind of thing you'd want to eat while getting a skinful, his triumphant pork buns and tortillas being prime examples.

- **Tapas Cafe**; Sukhumvit 11; tapasiarestaurants.com; 0-2651-2947. I've never had a bad time at this bright tapas bar in the busy little backstreet behind Sukhumvit 11's legendary Cheap Charlie's. Where a lot of Mediterranean cuisine in Bangkok can err on the lacklustre side, given the difficult in sourcing the right produce, Tapas Cafe's offerings always taste pretty damn fresh. The fun, informal atmosphere – and the *gambas al ajillo* – make it a favourite.

VEGAN/VEGETARIAN

In culinary terms, Thailand is not the best place for vegetarians. Pescetarians seem to do fine, but take the seafood and fish sauce off the Thai menu and you're left with a bunch of samey stir-fried vegetable dishes. Your average *ahan tam sang* joint, for example, won't offer much to anyone who doesn't eat meat – don't expect tofu. Many dishes that sound vegetarian contain fish sauce or oyster sauce. You'll need to ask the shop to use soy instead.

Vegans have it even worse. Take eggs out of the picture and even fried rice is a no-no. Having said that, veganism isn't an entirely alien creed in Thailand. Some Thais, particularly Sino-Thais, follow a vegan diet, called '*jay*'. *Jay* restaurants are marked with big yellow signs featuring the word 'เจ' in red. These places specialise in soy-based mock meats – faux red pork, faux meatballs, faux chicken, you name it. Be warned: *jay* also forbids strong-tasting vegetables like garlic, chives and onions, so don't expect too much in the way of flavour. If you want to avoid the fate of a vegetarian colleague of mine, who ate vegetable fried rice almost every lunchtime for two years in Bangkok, you'll probably need a kitchen.

HAVING FUN

SAYING YOU CAN'T ENJOY YOURSELF in Bangkok is a little like saying you can't relax in the Maldives, or find New York City a bit on the quiet side. The glib point to make here is that if you can't have fun in this city, you probably need stronger medication. But in reality, things are a bit more complicated than that. How much you get out of Bangkok depends on what kind of person you are. The entertainment available is certainly weighted towards the visceral, at the cerebral's expense. Those of a more arty or intellectual bent have to work harder to keep themselves entertained here than they might in many other cities. But they usually find a way – or give up and move to Paris.

NIGHTLIFE

It's often claimed that Bangkok has some of the world's best nightlife. While that's debatable, the city certainly has a lot going for it. It boasts a huge variety of nightspots catering to every budget, taste and peccadillo, including the Volkswagen van bars that line Soi 11, the *hi-so* Thai clubs of Thonglor-Ekkamai, stodgy British and Irish pubs, Ashley Sutton's whimsical fantasy venues, old Vietnam-era dive bars and 'indie' hangouts like WTF and Bar 23. The crowds are friendly and unpretentious, you often end the night with more friends than you started with, and there's always somewhere to go next, if staying out all night's your thing.

Bangkok is also blessed with a phenomenon referred to as the 'beer garden', which bear little resemblance to pub beer gardens and are a tad less picturesque than their name suggests. They're mostly set up outside shopping malls during the 'winter' months of November–January, when it can be relied on neither to rain nor be brain-meltingly hot. Expanses of pavement are covered in tables and chairs and stages are erected, from which covers bands can belt out the latest – and not so latest – hits. Surrounding the seating areas are stalls selling *kap klaem* – beer snacks. When Thais drink, they eat.

You can buy beer by the glass, the jug, or, for the full Bangkok beer garden experience, the 'tower', a tall plastic tube filled with lager, cooled by a central shaft of ice. A server will often man it for you, ensuring no one's glass ever gets empty. Is this beer heaven? Craft beer lovers would no doubt disagree, but it certainly makes boozing easy.

Bangkok is a city of music lovers, though it's a little short of paradise for the expat aficionado. Those who develop a liking for Thai rock and indie music tend to get on fine. For those who are fussier about what's invading their ears during a night out, the nightlife can leave a little to be desired. There are places to hear good Western music, and sometimes big-name musicians and DJs come to town, but there isn't usually a wealth of options.

Real Thai-style clubs are quite different from Western-style ones. Firstly, a house band is almost *de rigueur*. The band will generally play covers of famous rock and indie hits that every Thai in the club will know the words to. Spend a few nights in these places and you'll probably start to learn the 'classics' too, or at least recognise them. The band usually alternates with a DJ playing commercial hip-hop and dance music. Dancefloors, however, have tables on them, which groups of revellers stand and dance around. Things get pretty crowded in the popular clubs, so there's little space to 'throw shapes'.

Drinking is relatively expensive. You can easily find yourself racking up tallies of thousands of baht in a night. Having said that, in a Thai nightclub you can buy whole bottles of spirits for not much more than they cost in the liquor stores. Thais tend to share bottles of whisky, which they heavily dilute with soda water. There's a certain aspect of conspicuous consumption in whisky drinking: the brand of bottle you're drinking is clear for all to see. Whiskies like Johnny Walker cunningly colour-code their bottles for this reason. Whether you're drinking 'red', 'black', 'gold' or 'blue' is read as a message by the city's status-conscious denizens.

The city does have a few Western-style nightclubs with clear dancefloors, playing 'serious' dance music, whether techno, house, electro, trance, dubstep, hip-hop, drum and bass and disco. And then there are the late-night clubs, places like Bossy and Spicy. Almost everyone ends up in one of them sooner or later, since they pay taxi and tuk-tuk drivers commission to bring them 'bodies'. The crowd in these places tends to be an assortment of mangled male revellers from every corner of the world, and prostitutes.

Nightlife hubs

Lower Sukhumvit

The last few years have seen the entire northern flank of Sukhumvit, from Nana to Asok, turn into one big debauch after dark. As soon as the sun goes down, clothes stalls are replaced with makeshift bars. The party, fuelled by booze, meth, and the potent energy drinks stocked in every 7-Eleven, lasts all night. As late as 8am drunken stragglers can still be seen staggering through the streets, or holding court on stoops in front of boggle-eyed ladyboy prostitutes, always the last of all to go to bed. Welcome to hell – or heaven, if you like that sort of thing.

But there's more to the area than sleaze. Sukhumvit Soi 11 has turned into a *farang*-oriented nightlife hub in recent years, and the crowd is classier than down the road – at least a tad, anyway. There's cheap boozing to be done here: Volkswagen beer bars now line the road, perfect for alcoholic pitstops. It's also the home of quirky street bar Cheap Charlie's, something of a Bangkok institution. Occupying a small *soi* off the main drag, it's as cheap as its name suggests and was – surprise, surprise – founded by a guy called Charlie about 30 years ago.

New bars and clubs seem to open on Soi 11 every month. In recent years, longstanding nightspots like Bed Supperclub

The infamous Soi Cowboy, where the rich exploit the poor, the desirable exploit the undesired, and you won't find many actual cowboys.

and Q-Bar have been joined by a flood of newer propositions, including bar-restaurant Oskar and rooftop hangout Above Eleven, with its – I kid you not – Peruvian-Japanese dinner menu. Newer clubs include the popular Levels and Bash.

Bed, the big white pod on the right-hand side of the *soi*, closed in 2013. The club wasn't for everyone – the crowd tended to the posey, the prices to the extortionate – but it did try to bring some of the world's biggest DJs and musicians to Bangkok. After the announcement of its demise, club owner Sanya Souvanna Phouma told *BK Magazine* that the area had gone downhill. 'You have to walk past guys drinking at vans to get here. When we moved in, the *soi* was all houses with gardens.' Yes, drinking while sitting round a Volkswagen isn't for everyone.

Close to Asok Intersection is the infamous Soi Cowboy, a lane of some 40 girly bars dating from the Vietnam era. The road was reputedly given its name by *Bangkok Post* nightlife columnist Bernard Trink, who named it after T.G. 'Cowboy' Edwards, an American airman who opened one of its first bars in 1977. Edwards, a tall African-American, liked to wear a cowboy hat. Some of the dive bars along the street look no different from the way they did in the 1970s, and provide a window into 'old expat Bangkok'. At least, that's one way to look at them.

Not too far from Soi Cowboy on a lane running off Sukhumvit Soi 23 is Glow nightclub, a three-storey shophouse space that's been turned into a club. It's probably my favourite club in Bangkok, though it might be a little bit grungy for some. Glow is one of the few places where you can confidently say the crowd is there for the music, and not to show off or hook up. It doesn't see much in the way of 'big names' but seems to have found plenty of local DJs who can do just as good a job with the crowds.

Upper Sukhumvit

In the Phrom Phong area are a number of British pubs. Soi 33/1, in particular, boasts The Robin Hood, The Dubliner and The Royal Oak, as well as a few Japanese restaurants and ramen shops. Soi 33, meanwhile, is nicknamed 'Soi Dead Artists'. The girly bars that line the road, for some reason lost to time, have names like Goya, Monet and Degas.

Further east along Sukhumvit are Thonglor and Ekkamai, Sukhumvit Soi 55 and 63 respectively. They're where the rich folk go to party – not that you need to be rich to afford a night out there. But there is an awful lot of wealth on display: revellers at some of the trendier clubs arrive in European sports cars. Clubs such as Funky Villa and Demo throng with the beautiful people. On Ekkamai, newer club Sonic has a more 'indie' crowd, and plays host to an eclectic mix of styles of music.

On Sukhumvit Soi 51, meanwhile, is WTF bar, which is hidden on a small alley that seems to have become the centre of operations for Bangkok's media-hipster-art set.

Urinal massages

Bathroom attendants are the bane of right-thinking folk the world over, but in Thailand they take on an unusual local form: the urinal masseur. Yes, many Thai clubs employ men to massage their patrons after and sometimes even while they pee. It's a little disconcerting to be approached from behind by a strange man at a urinal, but don't worry – all they're there to do is give your tired back a stretch. If you don't want a massage, just say 'mai ao khrap' and they should get the message. Otherwise, raise your arms, let them place a hot towel on your neck, and let them do their stuff. You can pay them whatever you feel like – 20 or 40 baht is usually enough.

Bangkok has a large Japanese community, and a good bowl of ramen isn't hard to find.

WTF doubles as an art gallery, and when it holds an event, the crowd makes you feel like you never left Hackney. The Sazerac is a Bangkok must-drink. On the opposite side of the alley is bar-eatery Opposite Mess Hall, owned by some of the same folk and serving up the delightful home-style cuisine of chef Jess Barnes. You don't need army fatigues to get in.

Back over on Ekkamai is quirky drinking hole Tuba, which looks like the living room of someone with an extreme retro fetish and little concern for things like 'taste' and 'colour coordination'. On a small lane close to Thonglor Soi 18 is Shades of Retro, a relatively quiet bar with a – you guessed it – retro theme and vintage furniture for sale. Their mojitos are excellent and the free salted popcorn they ply you with ensures you'll be thirsty for several.

Silom
Silom's most famous *soi*, Patpong, has become a by-word for Bangkok's sex industry. The Patpongpanit family, immigrants

from Hainan, bought the area in 1946 and built the road now known as Patpong 1. At first lined by shophouses, during the Vietnam War nightclubs began to open there and by the 1970s Patpong became famous for what it's still famous for: go-go bars and sex shows.

The shows, sometimes featuring props like razor blades and live birds – not to mention ping-pong balls – tend to the profoundly depressing. Still, it remains standard practice for some expats to shock visitors with a visit to at least one of them, as well as to one of the go-go bars to proudly show-off the beauty of the local transsexuals.

There is, on the other hand, a diamond in the rough. Madrid, around 100 metres down on the left of the street from Silom, is a quiet haven amid the sea of sleaze. It still has the feel of an old-school Bangkok dive bar, and many of the staff and customers look like they've been there since Vietnam. The American menu is worth exploring – after all, they've had more than enough time to perfect the recipes.

Close to Patpong is Soi Thaniya, a Japanese street lined with hostess bars aimed strictly at Japanese tourists. Things take a different turn on Silom Soi 2 and 4, which host Bangkok's gay scene. The venues generally operate a mixed door policy, and whether you're gay or not, clubs like DJ Station tend to offer a great night out.

RCA

'RCA, a government designated Entertainment Zone, is frequently visited by young people,' reports Wikipedia, a sentence that sounds like it might have been cut-and-pasted from a guidebook aimed at

Hillary's bars

Sukhumvit Soi 4, at least up to its intersection with Soi 6, is lined with beer bars, several of which are named 'Hillary Bar'. The name dates from the late 90s, when the Clintons lived in the White House, the Monica Lewinski scandal was making political waves and Bill was playing semantics with the term 'sexual relations'. By the end of 1999, Bangkok boasted a complex of go-go bars inspired by the presidential libido: Clinton Entertainment Plaza, which stood between Sukhumvit Soi 13 and 15 and also featured an establishment called The White House. Clinton Plaza is gone now, a casualty of Thaksin Shinawatra's 'social order' campaign, but the Hillary Bar empire lives on. Whether Secretary of State Clinton was informed of the existence of so many 'fine' establishments bearing her name during her visit to Thailand in 2012 is unknown.

Right or Wong?

It's probably fair to call Wong's Place a Bangkok institution, though the crowds are divided over its actual merits. This diviest of dive bars, almost hidden on Sathorn Soi 1, has been going for 30 years. The original owner Wong – now dead – gave his name to the bar before it was later taken on by his brother, Sam Wong, who can usually be found standing on a chair in the bar, coordinating drinks sales by barking at his staff and customers through a megaphone.

The crowd is a mixed gay-straight Thai-*farang* crowd of journalists, NGOs, teachers and assorted ne'er-do-wells. The place gets so crowded you can't help but find yourself talking to a variety of strangers, some interesting, some just plain weird. It doesn't even get going until 2am or so and stays open until the last person leaves. Needless to say, 'things get weird' in there pretty often.

North Korean pensioners. Still, it's basically true. RCA, which stands for Royal City Avenue, is where many of Bangkok's energetic young things go to party. A new road built on a large swathe of mostly empty land between Phetchaburi Road and Rama 9 Road, you'll need to take a taxi or tuk-tuk to get there. The drivers all know it.

The crowd is mostly Thai, and younger than that in the more exclusive venues of Thonglor-Ekkamai. Plenty of *farang* go there too – mostly men hoping to meet one of the gorgeous young Thai women who flock there. Many of the clubs charge foreigners to get in, but not Thais, though the fee will usually include a couple of 'free' drinks.

The most famous of RCA's venues are Slim and Route 66, both enormous places with several bars and rooms to them. Route 66 has expanded to occupy not only its cavernous dancefloors but the whole of the road outside. Cosmic Café offers a more bohemian vibe, while LED Club – formerly Astra and 808 – is the place to go to hear 'proper' dance music – underground house, techno, dubstep, jungle and all the rest. The RCA outlier, meanwhile, is Old Leng, a Thai bar done out like an antiquated Chinese-style tea house.

Banglamphu

Banglamphu is the 'gateway drug' that hooks many young foreigners on Bangkok. Those that have spent more time in the city tend to gravitate towards Sukhumvit Road, both as an area to live and party. But a trip down memory lane to Khao San Road is often called for. The bars on the road itself make excellent vantage points for people-watching while drinking the devilish concoction of backpacker choice: the 'bucket', a proudly revolting super-sweet melange of whisky, red bull, coke and ice.

There are other options, too. Soi Rambuttri, parallel to Khao San and snaking road Wat Chana Songkhram, boasts a ton of guesthouse bars. On Chakraphong Road, perpendicular to Khao San, is Middle East-themed rooftop bar Gazebo. On Ratchadamnoen Klang is Club Culture, one of the city's better nightclubs, hosting well-known parties like Dudesweet and Trasher. And there's a very different vibe at Adhere the 13th on Samsen Road, a down-and-dirty blues bar.

Tawan Daeng

I can't resist pointing you in the direction of one outstanding night out: the Tawan Daeng German Brewery. This enormous beer hall on Rama III Road produces its own brews under the supervision of a Bavarian beermaster. There's an extensive menu of tasty Thai cuisine, combined with a few German specialities – the pork knuckle is worth the trip alone. Aside from that, though, the crowds are drawn to the place for its spectacular variety show, which features more than 50 short performances that pay kitsch tribute to a host of styles and singers, both Thai and Western. The singing and dancing only seems to get better as the night goes on. Whether this is due to the acts improving or the towers of German lager you inevitably get through isn't clear.

While Khao San will probably always be known for its backpacker denizens, in recent years more and more Thais have been drawn there. At first, they came simply to walk the street and look at the bizarrely dressed, unkempt Westerners it attracted. But these young locals ended up opening more Thai-oriented bars and clubs. The always-packed Brick Bar, a ska club at the back of the Buddy Lodge mini-mall, is a personal favourite.

Beers of Bangkok

Chang

Ah, Chang. Its logo is tattooed on the skin of a thousand ill-informed backpackers, and strange rumours surround it: 'It contains formaldehyde', say some. 'They can't control how strong it is', say others, who claim the beer can contain anything up to 9 per cent alcohol. There might be some truth to this, as

(continued overleaf)

there seems to be some variability in the flavour of the beer, which varies from pleasant to highly chemical. I once opened one that tasted strongly of TCP. What's not debatable is this: Chang *is* powerful stuff. The 'drunk' you get from the beer is unlike any other. It's energetic, and silly things can happen under its influence – hence why some expats call it the 'tequila of beers'. This may also explain why it's possibly the only beer in the world to have a particularly unpleasant strain of hangover named after it: the Changover.

Singha

'Singha beer don't ask no questions, Singha beer don't tell no lies.' So goes the refrain from The Pogues' 'House of the Gods', a song about a man relaxing on Pattaya beach with a bottle of Singha. Not that Shane McGowan cares, but he – like many foreigners – pronounces the name wrong. Thais say 'Sing', without the 'ha'. It's the only Thai beer to display the Garuda on the bottle, the symbol indicating royal approval. Whether King Bhumibol enjoys a tipple isn't known, but it is the most popular beer in Thailand.

Heineken

Brewed in Thailand and widely available, Heineken is much maligned by newcomers to Bangkok, who wonder why anyone would want to drink a Dutch beer in Thailand when there are local alternatives. Once those newcomers become more familiar with the kind of hangovers that come with drinking those local alternatives, many jump ship to the 'cold greens'. To be sure, Heineken is a divisive beer. Some dislike its taste, which is strangely redolent of 'skunk' marijuana. Others love it, perhaps for the same reason.

Leo

Leo is the cheaper, younger sibling of Singha. And it really is cheap, coming in at a good 30-baht-a-large-bottle less than a Heineken. Leo has rapidly established itself as the beer of choice for many working class Thais and some of the expat community. So it has its proponents, though I've always found its flavour faintly reminiscent of drains. It's also likely to leave you feeling like you've had some sort of minor cranial trauma the next day.

MUSIC

Luk thung and mor lam

Luk thung, which literally means 'children of the fields' but is often translated as 'Thai country', is the sound of rural Thailand, the lyrics expressing the hard lives led by the country's farmers and rural migrants to Bangkok. Luk thung singers employ plenty of vibrato, which gives the music its haunting quality and leads to comparisons with American country and western. The excellent Pen-Ek Ratanaruang movie 'Monrak Transistor', a bittersweet love story, concerns a man from the country who becomes a Bangkok luk thung singer, and touches on many of the themes of the genre.

Also commonly heard in Thailand is mor lam, an ancient form of rural music from Laos, recognisable by the distinctive sound of the khaen, a type of mouth organ made from bamboo pipes. A faster, more modern variant is mor lam sing, 'sing' deriving from the English word 'racing'. Where luk thung is usually mournful and slow, mor lam sing is fast, bawdy dance music often heavily laced with humour. Singers employ a conversational style reminiscent of rapping. If you get the chance to see a live mor lam sing band in Bangkok, take it. The Paradise Bangkok night, organised by Zudrangma Records (www.zudrangmarecords.com), has been known to bring them to the capital, always resulting in a great party.

Phleng Phuea Chiwit (Songs for Life)

It's not hard to recognise an old fan of phleng phuea chiwit – a genre of Thai folk-rock dating back to the protest days of the 1970s. Long hair, bandanas and facial hair give them away – think Carlos Santana, if he'd been born on the banks of the Chao Phraya. Songs for Life has its origins in Art for Life, an artistic movement founded by the Marxist intellectual Chit Phumisak back in 1957 that aimed to challenge the stifling strictures of military rule. In the 1970s, as protests against the generals finally started to erode their grip on power, phuea chiwit began to take shape as a music of rebellion and biting social commentary.

Caravan, formed in the wake of the 1973 student massacre (*see page 31*), are generally considered to be the originating *phuea chiwit* band, though it was the later Carabao that were to really popularise the genre. The latter, whose name means 'buffalo' in Tagalog, were formed in 1976 by three Thai students who had fled to the Philippines following that year's crackdown. Today, the band's leader, Add Carabao, is one of the most famous people in Thailand. The band's sound takes in a variety of styles, including Thai styles like *mor lam* and *luk thung*, as well as Western rock, folk, reggae and Latin beats. The band's 1984 album 'Made In Thailand' is its biggest seller, managing to shift five million copies. Add also found time to launch a successful energy drink, Carabao Daeng.

No booze for you!

Alcohol sales are banned in Thailand between 2pm and 5pm and 12am and 11am. Sales times were restricted to 10 hours per day in late 2004 as part of Thaksin Shinawatra and his deputy Purachai Piumsomboon's 'social order' campaign. The rules were ostensibly intended to cut alcohol consumption by school children, though it's not entirely clear how or why.

Having said that, if you buy in bulk – 10 litres or more – the restrictions no longer apply, a get-out clause seemingly favouring drinkers of excess. Apparently, it's actually intended to allow stores to buy extra stock if they unexpectedly run out.

Don't tell the 'boys in brown', but it's rare to find an independent 'mom and pop' store that won't sell a bottle of beer at 3pm. Indeed, it's tempting to wonder if this wasn't the plan all along: to give Thai mom and pop a competitive edge against the likes of 7-Eleven and Tesco, who are under more scrutiny and can't get away with flouting the law. But perhaps that's over-thinking things.

Thai pop and rock

Thai pop and rock music has been heavily influenced by Western styles, though artists have also drawn from more other parts of Asia and indigenous sources to create their sound. Thai pop music could be said to have first emerged in the 1960s. The first Thai popsters started off imitating bands like The Shadows, creating a genre called '*wong shadow*'. Chinese and Hong Kong music later began to influence Thai pop, driven by young Sino-Thais, and by the mid-80s a genre of Thai pop had emerged called '*string*'. In the 90s, this type of bubblegum pop took over the airways and *luk khrueng* popstars like Tata Young and Bird Thongchai McIntyre become hugely famous in Thailand.

Violinists are rare as far as the city's street musicians go. Blind *luk thung* singers probably outnumber them 1,000 to 1.

In the late 1990s a wave of Britpop influenced artists such as Moderndog, Loso and Crub emerged. In the next decade, though, it was the corporate nu-metal sounds of bands like Linkin Park that seemed to become most influential in Thai rock, and bands like Big Ass, Bodyslam and Silly Fools became the biggest names around. Whether or not you like Thai rock music, it's everywhere, and if you go to Thai clubs at all regularly you'll get to know many of the songs. The acoustic-guitar-toting troubadour is a common feature of Bangkok bars, always playing folksy soft-rock covers of well known songs, and showing little sign of going away.

Thai indie/hipster culture

The urge to stand out and be different contradicts old conceptions of Thai culture. In a hierarchical society defined by deference to elders and respect for status, the young did not traditionally rebel or dissent with cultural norms through dress and standards of behaviour. It certainly wouldn't have been tolerated under the military regimes that ran the country for much of the previous century.

Over the last couple of decades, things have changed. Thailand has an 'indie' subculture, with influence on dress, commerce and the arts. Thai indie culture draws from movements both within Thai society and without. The Songs for Life and Art for Life movements, with their rejection of authoritarianism and conformity, played a role. The aesthetic, though, has been strongly influenced by Western indie culture and, more recently, 'hipster'.

Unlike in the West, in which youth subcultures have often paired the same desire to identify with a tribe with certain ideological tendencies, Thai indie culture is more about standing out and looking different, without necessarily making any demands on your politics or worldview. You can be a Thai indie kid, or even a punk, and still profess a conservative worldview. You can still love the king, though your image of Bhumibol might be a Warholesque pop-art portrait, rather than a framed photograph. A Thai Sex Pistols, an Anarchy in Thailand, is still unthinkable. And when you see where Western rockers tend to end up – accepting knighthoods, appearing on trashy reality TV shows – perhaps that's not such a bad thing.

The advent of 'hipster' in the West, a subculture that doesn't really stand for anything but the accumulation of cultural capital through the 'curation' of styles and cultural references, is perfect for appropriation by the Bangkokian youth. No 'punk rock' attitude is necessary – just the right look.

CINEMA AND FILM

Is Bangkok a good place to be for the movie lover? Many of them take advantage of the abundance of knock-off DVDs, which can be found in any of the tourist areas or IT malls. But I couldn't possibly condone that kind of behaviour. It's illegal, don't you know.

So to the silver screen. When it comes to film in Bangkok, I'd have to say: great cinemas, shame about the cinema. By which I mean that many of the cinemas in the capital, particularly those in the poshest malls, are excellent: comfortable seats, brand new fittings, and all for less than half the price you'd pay to see a movie in much of the West.

The problem, from the film enthusiast's perspective, is the films themselves. Let's leave Thai cinema aside for a moment and just consider foreign movies – or more accurately,

American movies. The reality is that the vast majority of Thais don't speak English well enough to get much out of dialogue-driven films. And their taste for movies, in general, is informed by their preference for the *sanuk* over the serious, when it comes to entertainment, anyway. Thus the unfortunate reality is that it

Movieseer

If you want to know what movies are on in Bangkok, the website www.movieseer.com makes things easy. The site features the showtimes for every cinema in the city. You can also browse lists of every movie currently showing in Bangkok, then see which cinemas are showing whatever takes your fancy.

is mostly the biggest, 'dumbest' products of Hollywood that make it to the multiplexes. 'The Fast and the Furious' is so popular its Thai fans refer to its many sequels as '*fae(s)t*'.

More 'difficult' films and 'indie' movies tend not to make it to the multiplexes, though there are a small number of cinemas that specialise in indie films, notably the Lido and Scala, both of which are in Siam Square, and House at RCA.

You might be the kind of person who usually cocks a snook at shopping malls. But in sweltering Bangkok, you could well learn to love them – or their air-conditioned climates, at least.

GREEN SPACES

Bangkok isn't blessed with an abundance of green space. The days when the likes of Silom and Sukhumvit still had orchards and rice fields by their sides are long gone. Nevertheless the city does have a number of parks, some of which also feature sports and exercise facilities. The most famous of all of them, perhaps Bangkok's equivalent of New York's Central Park, is Lumphini, one of Bangkok's highlights. Built in 1925 by King Vajiravudh, the park features an artificial lake, pathways and playgrounds. In the morning it throngs with joggers and tai chi classes; in the evenings the aerobics crowd get their turn. There's a swimming pool on site, as well as an outdoor gym.

Lumphini is named after the birthplace of the Buddha, and that's fitting: the park is a much-needed space for quiet reflection in this city of endless chaos. In its own way Lumphini has served as a source for its own brand of turmoil. In 2005–6, it was where PAD leader Sondhi Limthongkul first started whipping up his yellow storm of protest against Thaksin Shinawatra. It's remained the yellow shirts' protest ground of choice ever since.

North Bangkok, meanwhile, is served by Chatuchak Park and its two adjoining siblings, Queen Sirikit Park and Wachirabenchathat Park, still known to most people by its old name, Suan Rot Fai ('Railway Park'). As the latter name suggests, all three parks were built on land owned by the State Railway of Thailand. Chatuchak, a long, thin strip of land running alongside Phahonyothin Road, was the first to open, in 1980; to the park's south is its more famous namesake, Chatuchak Weekend Market. The huge Suan Rot Fai is the highlight of the three. The park has dedicated bike tracks, and is hugely popular with cyclists, many of whom fly round the course at an almost terrifying speed. It also features tennis and basketball courts, a swimming pool and you can even take kayaks out on its artificial lake.

In eastern Bangkok is Rama IX Park, which is visited by few foreigners, despite being the largest park in Bangkok. Perhaps it's the suburban location – the park is a 15-minute taxi ride from Udom Suk BTS station. The park was opened in 1987 in honour of King Bhumibol's 60th birthday. As well as featuring a museum devoted to the king's work – set in a retro-futuristic building that looks like it might one day take off to the stars – it includes botanical gardens and a water park. Various countries have gardens devoted to them: England, Japan, China, the US and Italy among them. The real must-see, though, is the gorgeous royal pavilion set in the middle of a lotus pond.

In the Old Town area is Romaneenart Park, close to Wat Suthat and the Giant Swing. A non-ceremonial park featuring sports and exercise facilities, it was built on the site of the old Bangkok jail. Remnants of the old facility, including sections of wall and guard towers have been preserved. The site also hosts the Corrections Museum (*see page 268*).

There is a number of smaller parks dotted here and there. By the side of the Emporium shopping mall on Sukhumvit is Benjasiri Park, which opened in honour of the Queen's 60th birthday in 1992 and features a central lake surrounded by gardens. It's worth exploring, though, particularly to seek out the sculptures that pepper the greenery. In Banglamphu, where Phra Athit Road turns into Phra Sumen Road, is Santichaiprakan Park. Its main feature is Phra Sumen Fort, which dates back to the 18th century. The park usually buzzes with a mix of the Phra Sumen Road crowd: backpackers and bohemian Thai student types.

But the highlight of Bangkok's green spaces isn't technically in Bangkok at all. To the south of the Chao Phraya River, opposite the Khlong Toey Port, is the peninsula of Phra Pradaeng, in Samut Prakan province. This huge swathe of greenery is in remarkable contrast to the city that surrounds it. Where Bangkok is chaotic and frantic, its 'green lung', as Phra Pradaeng is often called, is unhurried and peaceful. The area has a huge network of cycle paths and quiet country roads, making it ideal for exploration by bicycle. The area was settled by Mon people, and the people retain a distinct identity, notable in the traditional skirts that many older women wear.

FESTIVALS

Most of these events take place according to the Thai or Chinese lunar calendars, so their exact dates vary each year.

Songkran (April 13, 14 and 15)

If there's a purer expression of the Thai love of *sanuk* than Songkran, I'd like to hear about it. The Thai New Year festival, taking place in April at the hottest time of the year, is a remarkable spectacle. All over Thailand, for anything from one to 10 days, the Thai people drop everything to get out on the streets and soak each other in enormous city-wide water fights.

In Bangkok, Khao San Road and Silom are where things get craziest. But the city most famous for its Songkran celebrations is Chiang Mai, where the festival goes on for as long as 10 days. For much of the celebrations the city centre is a watery warzone. Pickup trucks drive endlessly around the moat, carrying kids – big and small – brandishing water guns, who dump huge blocks of ice into water barrels to make their liquid ammunition as effective as possible. Unsurprisingly, Songkran can be dangerous: drink driving is rife and people aren't afraid to toss icy buckets of water on people on motorbikes. There is a considerable death toll on the roads every year.

Needless to say, the festival, celebrated in similar fashion in Laos, Cambodia and Myanmar, started rather differently. It's traditionally the time when Thais go home to be with their families; Songkran was originally about paying respects to one's elders. The water element derives from the custom of cleansing Buddha images, New Year being a time of renewal. The water that ran off the images, now holy, would then be poured gently on the shoulders of the elders. This gradually evolved into the practice of splashing water, and then into the rowdy water fight it is today.

Not everyone is pleased with these developments. Critics complain the true spirit of the festival has been lost. 'Can Thais learn to respect the spirit and meaning of the festival, or is it too late to save it from drunkenness, lewd behaviour, violence and road carnage?' asked *The Nation* in a pre-

Songkran editorial in 2013. The answer? Some can, some can't.

It would take a cold soul indeed not to enjoy his first Songkran. Nevertheless, it can become tiresome – once a year starts to seem like a lot – and many foreigners use the Songkran holidays as an opportunity to get out of Thailand. According to the unwritten rules of the festival, you can't get angry with someone who splashes you. Those unfortunate souls who still have to work during the period have a hard time staying dry.

Loi Krathong (November)

It may lack the excitement of Songkran, but Loi Krathong is many visitors' favourite Thai festival. More in tune with the spirit of Buddhism, it takes place on the evening of the full moon of 12th month in the traditional Thai lunar calendar, in November. It's said to be a romantic festival, a time for couples to wish for success in love.

'*Loi*' means 'to float', while a '*krathong*' is a kind of decorative float traditionally made from a slice of the trunk of a banana tree. (They can also be made from styrofoam, though styrofoam floats are often banned for polluting the river.) On the day of the festival, participants decorate their *krathong* with flowers, banana leaves and candles, often with a coin placed inside as an offering to the river spirits. At night, people flock to riversides, lakes and the ocean to light their *krathong* candles, place it in the water and push it off into the darkness. The cumulative effect of hundreds of these bright lights drifting slowly away is undeniably beautiful.

The origins of the festival aren't known for sure, though King Mongkut once wrote that it was a Brahmanic festival that was adopted by Thai Buddhists. The candle light is supposed to honour Buddha, and the floating of the *krathong* symbolises letting go of hatred, anger and sins. There's also an animist element to the festival: many Thais see it as thanking the Goddess of Water, Phra Mae Khongkha.

In Bangkok, Loi Krathong is celebrated wherever there's water. Popular locations include the Chao Phraya Riverside in Banglamphu (Phra Sumen Road) and parks such as Lumphini and the Queen's Park next to the Emporium on Sukhumvit Road.

Alternatively, many people choose to go to Chiang Mai to celebrate the festival, where it coincides with a Lanna (Northern Thai) festival called 'Yi Peng'. In Yi Peng, people release thousands of lanterns into the night sky, resembling a shoal of bright jellyfish slowly floating into space. Thus, in Chiang Mai at Loi Krathong, both sky and water are filled with light.

Chinese New Year (January or February)

Once you start hearing firecrackers, you know it's coming. Chinese New Year is a massive occasion for Bangkok, given that a good 10 per cent of the population identify as Sino-Thai and at least half have some Chinese ancestry. The centre of the celebrations is, unsurprisingly, Chinatown. Yaowarat Road, busy at the quietest of times, goes into overdrive. Expect huge crowds, dragon dances and lots and lots of noise: revellers set off firecrackers in the belief that they scare off evil spirits.

For Sino-Thais, it's a family occasion. On New Year's Eve parents give red envelopes containing money – called *ang pao* – to their children. They enjoy a large banquet, pray to the gods and pay respect to their ancestors. Most will take New Year's Day off work, since the day is supposed to be reserved for doing little except enjoying time with family.

Phuket Vegetarian Festival (October)

The words 'vegetarian festival' might conjure images of nut cutlets and circles of bearded folk singing Kumbaya. Not so in Thailand. The annual Vegetarian Festival takes place across the country but reaches an apogee of bizarreness on Phuket. A trip to the Andaman island to witness the spectacle is well recommended, though be warned: it's not for the squeamish.

Although the festival doesn't exist in China, it's become a kind of national celebration for Sino-Thais. Like Chinese New Year, the Vegetarian Festival has grown in popularity over the past decade or so as Sino-Thai pride has risen along with China's stature. Participants in the festival are expected to eat a special diet called *jay* for 10 days, which is actually more vegan than vegetarian. All meat and animal products are forbidden, as well as certain strong-tasting foods like garlic and onion.

Devotees are also expected to refrain from consuming intoxicants and having sex. In Phuket, where most of the local population has some Chinese ancestry, the whole business is taken pretty seriously. Most of the population of Phuket Town wears white clothes for the duration, making it look a little like you've stumbled onto the grounds of some sort of cult.

But what really draws visitors to the island are the parades of *ma song* (spirit mediums) and the bizarre feats of self-mutilation they perform. In the early hours of the morning at Chinese temples across the island, local men and women carry out special ceremonies that are supposed to induce a trance-like state. They believe they become possessed by the spirits of their warrior ancestors.

Then comes the gory part: their cheeks are pierced with knives and needles, then they insert large objects through the holes. It's almost become a competition to see who can insert the largest, weirdest object through their cheeks. The *ma song* then parade through the city, gibbering as if possessed by demons. Some carry axes, slicing their tongues as they walk.

The last night of the festival is particularly memorable. What seems like half the population of the island gathers in Phuket Town to let off firecrackers, turning the town into what feels like a warzone – in a good way.

Yasothon Rocket Festival (May)

Every culture has fertility ceremonies, which frequently involve phallic symbolism. Whereas my own countrymen, the English, tie ropes to their phallic symbols and dance around them in lederhosen, the Isarn Thai fire theirs into the sky while getting shitfaced on moonshine. I have no desire to return to the United Kingdom.

Rocket festivals – '*prapheni bun bangfai*' – are a Lao tradition. They take place all over Northeast Thailand at the beginning of the rainy season. The biggest and most famous of all is the Yasothon Rocket Festival, which is held for three days each May. One of the objectives of the event is to fire huge rockets into the sky in order to ensure a healthy season of rains.

What tends to take place is more like a huge, three-day party that takes over most of Yasothon city centre. It's a bawdy event, rife with cross-dressing and powered by vast quantities of Leo beer and *lao khao*, the local rice wine spirit.

On the Friday, there are performances of *mor lam sing* (*see page 251*), which go on all night. On Saturday comes a procession of huge rockets, parades of dancers and musicians. Giant toads are also a common sight. Local legend has it that the Buddha, during his incarnation as the Toad King, defeated the King of the Sky to end a drought that had lasted seven years, seven months and seven days.

On Sunday is the main event: the rocket competition. Traditionally, *bang fai* are gunpowder-filled bamboo bottle rockets. Newer ones are made with PVC pipes. They come in various sizes, from small *bang fai noi* to larger ones named *muen* ('ten-thousand'), *saen* ('one hundred thousand') and *lan* ('one million'), the largest of all. The latter are nine metres long and can be stuffed with 120kg of gunpowder. They can reach an altitude of several kilometres. The rockets are judged on how high they go, the straightness of their flightpath and the 'beauty' of the trails they leave behind.

With huge quantities of alcohol and gunpowder involved, the festival can be dangerous, with rockets occasionally flying into the crowd or exploding prematurely. In 2009, a man had his head blown off by a stray rocket, while in 1999, five people were killed when a 120kg rocket exploded after takeoff. Nobody ever said *sanuk* was safe.

Naga Fireball Festival (October)

Known as *bangfai phayanak* in Thai, the Naga Fireball Festival takes place around *wan ok phansa*, the last day of Buddhist Lent, in October. On that day, mysterious balls of light are supposed to arise from the waters of the Mekong River in Nongkhai Province. The lights vary in size from eggs, to basketballs and rise to a height of around 100 metres before vanishing. While they have been reported from Nongkhai

Town, the best places to see them are the towns of Phon Phisai and Rattanawapi.

Local people believe the fireballs are made by the Naga, a mythical serpent-like beast believed to live in the river, and which exists in various forms in indigenous belief across Asia. But if you don't buy that, the phenomenon hasn't been adequately explained. Some suggest the balls are caused by trapped methane gas being released from the riverbed, with the conditions being perfect at that time of year. But it seems unlikely that such conditions would happen to align with *wan ok pansa* so perfectly.

It's a sensitive topic. In 2002 a Thai TV programme supposedly showed that the balls were produced by tracer fire in Laos, on the other bank of the river. This provoked furious protests from local people, who remain convinced the lights come from the Naga. And, let's face it, it's much more fun to believe that – if you can.

THE WEEKEND GETAWAY

As all residents of this city know, the secret to a happy life in Bangkok is getting the hell out of Bangkok. As entertaining and exhilarating as it can be, the city can start to feel stifling after a few continuous weeks in its sweltering embrace. Fortunately, it happens to be surrounded by its own antidote: the rest of Thailand, a country as effective at relieving stress as the capital is at causing it. What's more, Bangkok is a regional transport hub, served by several low-cost airlines that can take you all over Southeast Asia within one or two hours. I can only scrape the surface of the possibilities here, but here are some ideas for weekend getaways within Thailand.

Koh Samet

Koh Samet is around 200km from the city, so you can set off from the office on a Friday evening and be sitting on one of its white-sand beaches that very same night. It takes around 2.5 hours to drive to the port of Ban Phe in Rayong province, from where you can get a ferry to the island, which takes 30–45 minutes. It's a national park, so there's an entrance fee – THB200 for foreign adults and THB100 for foreign children (Thais pay less). The island has a wide range of accommodation, from cheap backpacker bungalows to classy resorts. In July 2013 there was an oil spill in the Gulf of Thailand that washed up on Ao Phrao beach, which was subsequently closed to visitors. Check the Internet for the current situation.

Pattaya

Hear me out. There are obvious reasons to take a trip to Thailand's very own Sodom-and-Gomorrah-on-Sea, but there's actually a bit more to Pattaya than hookers, Russian mobsters and Tim Sharky. The town attracts more families than you might expect, and as such has plenty of entertainment for kids and adults alike. You're not going to get high culture here and the beaches are nothing special, but it's only two hours drive from Bangkok and there's a lot to do, including golf courses, aquariums, water parks and all the rest. It also features plenty of good resorts and hotels, which tend to be cheaper than those in the more picturesque coastal areas of the South.

Phuket

Phuket is highly developed these days, though it retains parts that are worth visiting, especially in the north (Mai Khao and Nai Yang) and southeast (Cape Panwa). There are plenty of excellent resorts on the island, so even if you don't fancy braving the tourist-packed environs of Patong and Kata-Karon, you don't need to leave your hotel. Phuket Town is well worth a visit, with its iconic rows of Sino-Portuguese shophouses, as well as outstanding Thai and Sino-Thai cuisine. Visiting Phuket during low season is a gamble: accommodation is cheaper, and you might luck out with beautiful weather. Alternatively, it could easily be a wash-out.

Phang Nga and Krabi

For a more relaxed vibe than Phuket, try the nearby Andaman provinces of Phang Nga and Krabi. Khao Lak in Phang Nga is an hour's drive to the north of the island and features plenty of beachfront resorts nestled in the jungle hillside facing the sea. During the low season it's still possible to get a real bargain at these places, if you just show up and negotiate a discount. Krabi, which has its own airport, also features some wonderful scenery. Rai Lay Beach, in particular, is famous for the beautiful limestone cliffs that surround it, which also draw climbers from around the world.

Khao Yai

If you want to see the abundance of Thailand's natural environment in all its glory, skip the beach and head to one of the country's many national parks. One of the most impressive is Khao Yai, around four hours' drive away. It's mostly located in Nakhon Ratchasima province on the mountainous terrain that leads up to the Khorat Plateau. The park features incredible scenery and a remarkable variety of flora and fauna, including wild elephants, Asiatic black bears, gibbons and 320 species of birds. There are plenty of resorts and hotels in the area, though many travellers choose to camp in the park itself.

Kanchanaburi

Kanchanaburi is a province of great natural beauty, featuring several national parks that include some of Thailand's most spectacular scenery. But it's the building of the so-called Death Railway by foreign POWs during the Second World War that draws in most foreigners, who flock to see the so-called Bridge on the River Kwai (pronounced to rhyme with 'air', not 'why') made famous by the Alec Guinness movie. Thing is, the original bridge that was built by the Allied prisoners was destroyed during the war. The current bridge was built by the Japanese as reparations after it ended (albeit using some of the original materials). Thus the bridge in question is a, not the, Bridge on the River Kwai. But that doesn't stop the crowds. That aside, the area also features a war cemetery and museum. Perhaps the best way to go to the area is to take a train from Hualamphong Station and travel down the 'Death Railway' itself.

Chiang Mai

Chiang Mai, the capital of the former Lanna kingdom and the biggest city in Thailand's North, retains a charm that captures the heart of many a foreign visitor. It's a pretty busy city these days, with bad traffic and trouble with smog, but the city retains a feeling of antiquity that Bangkok has mostly lost. The Old Town is fun to explore, while the newer Niman Hemin area hums with a more bohemian vibe provided by the students at nearby Chiang Mai University. Chiang Mai is surrounded by mountains and spectacular jungle scenery, which many visitors choose to explore in trekking tours.

LITERATURE AND ILLITERATURE

Much has been written by foreigners about the Thai capital. The large 'Thailand Interest' sections of the city's bookstores are proof of that. Unfortunately, exaggerated memoirs about stints in Thai prisons, tracts about the joys of sleeping with bargirls and horror stories about being ruined by Thai wives are not for everyone.

In terms of fiction, or at least serious fiction, Bangkok remains curiously undocumented, given its size and importance. It has, of course, provided inspiration for a lot of crime fiction. Some of the authors, like John Burdett and Christopher Moore, have produced well-crafted crime novels that demonstrate a level of insight into Thai society few other outsiders have reached. Others haven't fared so well.

The city's crime writers have formed a scene of sorts, the so-called 'Bangkok Noir', which crystallised in 2011 in the form of the book *Bangkok Noir*, a collection of 12 short stories by Thai and Western writers edited by Moore himself. Chris Coles, a painter specialising in Expressionist portraits of the denizens of the city's libidinous nightlife, is also involved, and has published a book of his work, *Navigating the Bangkok Noir*.

Bangkok Noir is unusual as a scene in that it appears to have been driven by the artists themselves, rather than critics and journalists. Local author and critic Tim Footman says he 'doesn't blame the writers for that at all'. Bangkok lacks the kind of critical apparatus that exists in many parts of the world that might identify such a scene from the outside. 'I can understand why they're doing it. No one else was going to do it for them,' he says.

Outside of the crime fiction genre, relatively little fiction of note has surfaced about Bangkok in the English language. Why? Is there something about the city and its inhabitants that defies the foreign writer? At least part of the reason must lie with the difficulty foreigners have in penetrating and understanding Thai society itself. As novelist Lawrence Osborne says, 'Obviously, foreigners are not going to be writing delicate comedies of manners about Thais, because they don't really move easily in such a hermetic culture.'

Perhaps the city's wilder side hypnotises foreign writers – the lights of this city are so bright that that's all they see. Footman tells of writing a novel set during the 2010 red-shirt protests. Not setting out to write about the city's seedier elements, he eventually came to a plotting cul-de-sac. 'Suddenly, and I have no idea how it happened, there was a hooker in there.' He later abandoned the book.

Naturally, more has been said about the city by Thais themselves, but few foreigners get good enough at Thai to be able to access it. There's also the reality that Thailand doesn't have a particularly literary culture. It's a shame: many visitors to the country would appreciate access to the kind of insight into ways of life and thinking that only fiction can really provide.

MORE IDEAS

If you want comprehensive listings of what's on in Bangkok, try one of the many other guidebooks likely standing on the same shelves as this one. But here are some Bangkok highlights:

- **Thonburi canal tour**; Thonburi's network of canals mean it still retains the charm that the big bad city on the other side of the river has long lost. Longtail boats can be hired at Tha Chang, Tha Thien and Sathorn piers, and will take you on a tour of the canals for as long as you're willing to pay. Alternatively, found a tour company who'll take you and throw in a guide, lunch and a warmer experience.

- **Bangkok Poetry and Bombyx Stories**; www.facebook. com/bangkokpoetry. Bangkok Poetry, an evening of readings – whether poetry, fiction or anything else you can read – takes place at WTF bar (*see page 245*) every six weeks. Its sister night, Bombyx Stories, has seen plucky folk with stories to tell regale the audience with tales on themes like 'I wish I never...' and 'Things get messy'. For some reason such material is easy to come by in this city.
- **Bangkok Corrections Museum**; 0-2226-1706. If you think Thai prisons sound bad now, Bangkok's answer to the London Dungeon proves how much things have improved, with life-size displays of the ingeniously cruel torture devices used on prisoners in the Siam of yore.
- **Thai Premier League**; www.thaipremierleague.th. If you're a football fan (the feet-only kind), why not go see a Thai Premier League match? Most of the games take place in or around Bangkok. Be warned: with plenty of booze around they can get a little rowdy, and none of teams are likely to be heading to the Champions League anytime soon. Muangthong United are the team to follow if you like backing a winner.

Finding activity partners and making friends

These websites make it easy to find people with similar interests in Bangkok:

- **www.internations.org;** InterNations is a global expat community site with a large presence in Bangkok. The site holds regular social events and features activity groups and a forum on which you can arrange meetups or ask other expats questions about life in the city.

- **www.meetup.com;** MeetUp enables you to make contact with other people in your city and arrange events based on shared interests. There are plenty of Bangkokians on there, organising everything from running, to volunteering, to wine and cheese evenings, to Christian singles nights.

LEARNING THE LANGUAGE

'LEARNING THE CURVES of that variant of Sanskrit, but never really learning it properly, was a healing exercise in a sort of futility, for deep down I suspect I wanted to remain in day-to-day incomprehension relative to the language, which I never learned to speak well. It was like a soft wall enclosing me at all times, and I preferred for many reasons not to penetrate it too adroitly.'

So writes Lawrence Osborne in his lyrical memoir of the city, *Bangkok Days*. Many exiles choose to revel in the sheer incomprehensibility of the Thai capital, making little effort to learn the language and feeling no shame in the handicap. After all, there's a certain freedom in being blind to the messages the city wants you to see. There is, too, a degree of licence: he who understands nothing can hardly be blamed for his transgressions. But in the end, blissful ignorance is not for everyone. Does a foreigner in this city need to learn Thai?

It isn't easy. The Foreign Service Institute, which trains US diplomats, rates languages according to how hard they are to learn for English speakers. As with hurricanes, there are five categories. Category I includes breezes like French, Spanish and Afrikaans. In Category V are howling befuddlers like Japanese, Korean, Arabic, Mandarin and Cantonese. Thai is in Category IV, which means it has 'significant linguistic and/or cultural differences from English'. This is diplomatic speak for: 'it's pretty bloody hard'. Learning the language is not the impossibility some like to claim it is, but unless you're some sort of linguistic savant, it will take work.

The will to learn Thai will also need to triumph over another opposing force: the lack of real necessity to bother in the first place. A foreigner who finds herself living in a village in Chaiyaphum, say, has little choice but to learn to communicate. Thirty years ago, perhaps you could say the same thing about Bangkok. But today, in this international tourism destination and regional business hub, most Thais an expat is likely to meet will at least speak rudimentary English. Many, of course, will speak it fluently. And a few – the boarding school-educated elite – will speak it even better than you do.

As a result, you can comfortably get away with a Thai repertoire that goes no further than *sawatdi khrap* ('hello'), *khop khun khrap* ('thank you') and – if your constitution demands it – *mai phet khrap* ('not spicy'). Some intrepid souls don't even manage that. The expat who has lived here 10 years, married a Thai woman and can't speak a word of the language is a cruel stereotype – but there are more than a few living, breathing examples at large in the city.

Of course, some expats – those posted here with international organisations, in particular – will wilfully confine themselves to a rarefied bubble, socialising exclusively with other exiles or well-educated Thais. Their employers will often take care of their day-to-day affairs and they will have little practical reason to learn Thai.

A common sentiment is: 'I don't plan to stay in Thailand much longer and Thai is useless outside of Thailand. Why should I bother?' But Thailand has a funny habit of holding people in its grasp a lot longer than they originally planned. I have friends who have been threatening to leave the country for years and never, as a result, bothered learning the language. If they'd started studying from day one, they'd be able to threaten to leave in Thai by now.

Of course, many readers will need no encouragement to learn the language. Perhaps you've already fallen in love with Thailand – or with a Thai person – and are anxious to devour as much of the culture as possible. Perhaps you're an

Where you go?

If a Thai person asks you 'Where you go?', don't assume they're being rude – or even that they actually care where you're going. In Thai, asking a person, *'Pai nai?'* ('Where are you going?') – as well as *'Kin khao rue yang?'* ('Have you eaten yet') – has long been a standard greeting. It wasn't until 1943 that the modernising dictator Phibunsongkhram made *sawatdi khrap* the 'official' greeting in the Thai language.

incorrigible language nerd. But for many others, it seems quite rational to dismiss the challenge with a brusque *'mai pen rai'* ('never mind').

As someone who's gone through the frustrations, tedium and, at times, embarrassment of learning the language, I feel the need to persuade you to do the same (and not entirely out of spite). Perhaps these are obvious points, but I'll make them anyway: learning Thai will transform your understanding of Thailand. It will earn you friendships and insight into people who would otherwise be closed books to you. It will be your ticket to independence. And, as Thai language blogger Catherine Wentworth told me, it 'takes you out of your comfy expat zone'. And if you're to get the most out of living in Thailand, you need to do that.

Fortunately, almost in compensation for the difficulty of the language, you can expect a lot of encouragement from Thai people along the way. Thais love it when foreigners attempt to speak their language. This, combined with their tendency to flattery, means that even your most modest efforts will frequently be rewarded with a *'phut Thai keng'* ('you speak Thai well'). This can reach embarrassing extremes ('But all I said was hello!').

Even if you can't undertake a serious study of Thai, it's worth mastering a few basic phrases. Your Thai friends will appreciate your efforts. As Thais put it, crudely but memorably: *kam khi di kwa kam tot* ('a handful of shit beats a handful of fart').

CHARACTERISTICS OF THAI

Thai is a member of the Tai-Kadai family of languages, which are spoken by almost 100 million people around the world. The languages are believed to have originated in Southern China, with speakers migrating into Southeast

Asia around 1,000 years ago. Other members of the family include Lao and Shan. There are still native speakers of Tai-Kadai languages all over Southern China and even in parts of Assam in India.

Like all living, breathing languages, Thai is awash with foreign influence. Much of the vocabulary derives from the ancient Indian languages of Sanskrit and Pali, which were brought to Southeast Asia by the merchants and monks who spread Buddhism to the region. You might think that *sawatdi* sounds like no English word you ever heard of. It actually derives from the Sanskrit word '*svasti*', meaning 'well-being' – which happens to be where the English 'swastika' comes from, too. So in a sense, you've already been saying 'hello' in Thai for years.

These Indian influences entered Thai via Old Khmer during the medieval era, and Thai and Khmer continue to share much vocabulary in common, particularly words related to the monarchy. (That's ironic, given the low status afforded to Cambodians by many Thais today.) And, of course, successive waves of Chinese immigrants have furnished the lexicon with their words – not to mention the street with their *mi* and *kuaitiao* (two words for noodles that derive from, you guessed it, Chinese).

Inevitably, today's lingua franca has had a great influence on modern Thai. Plenty of English words are firmly established in the language, albeit Thai-ified out of all recognition. The word for a menu is simply *menu*, but the word for a menu item is also *menu*. ('This menu looks great!' 'Which menu?') Your girlfriend or boyfriend is your *faen*, actually just the English word 'fan', with a vowel closer to the US pronunciation than the British. If someone behaves outrageously or gets a little too excited about something, a Thai might describe their behaviour as '*wer*'. This might not sound much like English, but it's actually a shortened version of 'over'. Thai – particularly the slang – is packed with words like this.

Indeed, as in many other parts of Asia, many Thais pepper their speech with English, even when it's not strictly necessary; it's an easy way to give yourself an air of sophisticated internationalism. Thaksin Shinawatra, for example, was famous for it. He'd use far more English words in his speech than the Eton- and Oxford-educated Abhisit Vejjajiva, who had less to prove in this department than Thaksin, the provincial upstart from Chiang Mai.

Ironically, nothing can confuse an expat trying to understand Thai more than an English word inserted where a Thai one would do. I was once talking with some Thai friends about the weather, or something equally banal, and one of them said the word '*summoe*', pronouncing the second syllable in the Thai falling tone. I had the poor guy repeat himself four times before realising he was just using the English word for the hot season.

Mind your tone

Thai divides opinions over its phonetic beauty. On some, its nasality and glottal stops grate. For others, it has a pleasantly lilting, sing-song quality. I guess it depends on who's doing the talking. Thai is a 'tonal' language, which means changing the pitch of a word alters its meaning. In English, we use tones, but in a very different way. Most obviously, raising the pitch at the end of a sentence turns a statement into a question: 'Your favourite dish is *phad THAI*?'

There are five tones in Thai: middle, high, low, rising and falling. For example, the single syllable '*ma*', when spoken in the middle tone, means 'to come'. In the rising tone, it means 'dog'. In the high tone, it becomes 'horse'. To fresh Western ears, alas, all three words are likely to sound almost identical. You might be able to discern a difference, though it will initially be hard to put your finger – or more pertinently, your ears and tongue – on exactly *how* it's different.

To Thais, of course, these words sound as different as 'chalk' and 'cheese'. This does nothing to help the hapless expat who's not getting his tones right. If the person you're talking to is used to the sound of foreigners attempting to speak Thai, she may be able to guess what you're trying to say from the context. But many Thais will be unable to do this. After several attempts, if you do finally get the tone right and are understood, you may wonder if the correct version was really so different from your failed efforts. *Jai yen yen*!

There's a classic sentence thrown out to intimidate Thai-language novices which, given my cantankerous nature, I can't resist throwing at you, too: *mai mai mai mai mai*. This, believe it or not, means 'new wood doesn't burn, does it?' If you can say this to the approval of a Thai friend, you'll know you're well on the way to mastering Thai. (Though good luck finding a real-life situation in which to actually put the phrase into practice.)

I'm afraid there's more bad news. You'll also have to contend with sounds you won't be used to making in English. There's the letter ง ('ng'), for example. This sound exists in English, of course, but only at a syllable's end – or, more appropriately, ending. In Thai, a syllable can start with '*ng*'. If you want to say words like '*ngoen*' ('silver', 'money') and '*nguea*' ('sweat') – both eminently useful in this balmy commercial capital – you'll need to get your tongue round ง.

Oh, and there are unvoiced unaspirated stop consonants, a linguist's way of referring to letters like บ. This letter sounds like a cross between 'b' and 'p' and is represented as the latter in the Royal Thai General System of Transcription. The aspirated version – meaning it is pronounced with a puff of air – is represented in the RTGS as 'ph', though it's actually identical to our letter 'p'. This is the reason that 'h' finds its way into the name of the island of Phuket, cueing a lot of rather tiresome puns.

All this can make speaking and understanding Thai a real challenge. Some might use the word 'nightmare'. Until your ears are fully tuned to the language, you'll find confusion is the rule. Did she just say '*chan buat chi*' ('I ordain as a nun')? Or was it '*chan puat chi*' ('I need a wee')? Concentrate, *farang*, concentrate!

Finding the right words

As we've discussed, Thai society is supremely hierarchical. As with the culture, so with the language. Mastering Thai means not only memorising words and how to put them together, but also being able to assess someone's social status and employ vocabulary appropriate to their station in life. Thais do this instinctively, but it's extremely tough for a foreigner to pick up. This connection between the Thai language and the social sphere is conversely what makes learning the language almost essential to understanding the culture.

Let's take pronouns. In English we have, for the second person singular pronoun, the sturdy, all-purpose 'you'. In French, as in many Romance languages, there are two yous: *tu* and *vous* (English used to have the familiar *thou*, now archaic in all but a few British dialects). In Thai, you have, to name but a few: *khun*, *than*, *kae*, *thoe*, *tua eng* and *mueng*, all meaning 'you'. And there are other yous to employ when talking to monks: *luang phi*, *luang pho* and *luang pu*, depending on the clergyman's status. And still more yous for nuns. And for royalty. Yikes.

It's not just pronouns that display this characteristic. In Thai, there are at least six words meaning 'eat'. From the most vulgar to the most respectful, they are *daek*, *kin*, *than*, *rap prathan* and *savoei*, used for royalty. (The word *daek* is considered rude and should only be used among friends).

Of course, as a *farang* you'll be forgiven for your endless mistakes. And make them you will. But mastering this aspect of Thai will give you real insight into Thai society. You'll see – no, you'll *feel* – how having to use different vocabulary with different people forces you to think of those people differently. In a Thai government office, the person referred to with the respectful 'you', '*than*' – the

Swearing in Thai

They say you can tell a lot about a culture by the words it considers rude. For the prudish Anglo-Saxons, swear words are all about sex and body parts. In Quebec, dominated until relatively recently by the Catholic Church, the curses of choice are seemingly innocuous terms – to English ears – like '*baptême*' and '*tabarnac*'. So what about Thai?

Before we get onto that, a warning: don't swear in Thai. I've included this section because, well, swear words are the first things many people – at least those as childish as me – want to know in a new language. And secondly, while you shouldn't use these words yourself, you'll certainly want to recognise when they're being used at you.

In Thai, swear words usually involve animals. The worst things you can call someone are '*ai sat*' ('you animal'), '*ai hia*' ('you monitor lizard') and '*ai khwai*' ('you buffalo'). In a Buddhist culture in which all beings are ranked according to merit, you insult a man by comparing him to a beast – a low, unenlightened thing.

boss – is almost another species, and should be spoken and thought of as such.

THE FARANG SPEAKS THAI!

Should you get good at Thai, you are likely to engender other, more confusing reactions. Some people will resolutely refuse to speak Thai with you, answering everything you say in English. This will generally be because they are determined to use their hard-won English skills, and to take the opportunity of meeting you to practise. Do not take this the wrong way.

Funniest of all, though rather frustrating, you'll get people who understand what you say, but don't become conscious of the fact that you're using the Thai language. Overcome by cognitive dissonance, some Thai people will be so surprised to hear Thai coming from the mouth of a person with a face like yours that they will refuse to believe it is happening at all. Often, they will struggle to reply in English to you, neglecting to 'do the math' and realise that if you can speak Thai, you can surely understand it too.

You'll even hear some Thais express discomfort that you can speak Thai. A friend once told me: '*Farang phut Thai nid noi na rak, farang phut thai keng na klua*' – 'A *farang* speaking a little Thai is cute; a *farang* speaking a lot of Thai is scary'. A common complaint – made in jest, of course – will be that they can no longer gossip about you: '*nintha mai dai laew*'. (They will still gossip about you, of course – just not to your face.) If you're a man, you may encounter women who are quite genuinely uncomfortable with you speaking Thai too well. Remember: anyone who has a strong interest in you being ignorant is probably not to be trusted.

TO WRITE OR NOT TO WRITE

If I were to offer one piece of advice on the subject of learning Thai, it would be this: study the alphabet from the start. The alternative – reliance on the Roman alphabet to represent Thai words – hardly bears thinking about. But let's force ourselves. You'd be forgiven for expecting to find a standardised and accurate system for representing Thai in Roman letters. If you're learning Mandarin Chinese, for example, there is the Pinyin system. It's universally agreed upon, simple and accurate. If you see a word written in Pinyin, you know exactly how to pronounce it.

In Thai, the closest thing to an official transcription system is something called the Royal Thai General System of Transcription (RTGS). The system was first designed by the now-defunct Ministry of Public Instruction in 1932 and has since been updated by the Royal Institute of Thailand several times. Unfortunately, the RTGS is a little too general for its own good, since it fails to give you enough information about Thai words to allow you to pronounce them properly.

Let's start with the worst of the RTGS's sins: somewhat incredibly, it doesn't record tones. Anyone who has attempted to speak Thai without tones will know how far this gets you: not very. It's like trying to speak English using only half the vowels. It's a travesty and, more importantly, it doesn't work.

Neither does the RTGS differentiate between long and short vowels. As far as it's concerned, both แพ ('raft') and แพะ ('goat') are rendered as '*phae*'. (I wouldn't want to cross the Mekong River on a goat.) Even more inexplicably, the system doesn't differentiate between 'ch' sounds and 'j' sounds, both of which exist in Thai. Despite the existence of the perfectly serviceable English letter 'j', words that have that sound in Thai are transcribed as 'ch'.

The result of the RTGS's inadequacies is the dog's dinner of transcription systems in use today. Every Thai person seems to represent the same word differently. Every *textbook* seems to represent the same word differently. At a street stall serving *ahan tam sang* (Thai fast food) close to my office, there's a sign offering a dish called '*tom yum rwm mitr*'. You'll probably recognise the first two words as the name of the famous Thai hot and sour soup. But try saying the third and fourth syllables; what comes out of your mouth is as likely to sound like Russian as Thai.

What's going on here? On the excellent New Mandala blog, a user by the name of 'Seh Fah' posted a comment that explains the mess so well I'm going to paraphrase it here. There are actually three types of transcription system in Thailand, Seh Fah explained:

1. The Precise System of Transcription (PST), a literal system of one English letter for each Thai letter, which gives us spellings such as 'Singha' beer and 'Suvarnabhumi' Airport.

2. The General System of Transcription (GST), a phonetic system of one English letter for each Thai *sound*, which would give us spellings such as 'Sing' beer and 'Suwanaphum' Airport.

3. The Idiosyncratic System of Transcription (IST), whereby the individual is free to randomly select elements of the PST and GST, add a little of his own personal preference, and then vary it at will. This explains the different spellings of Soi Phiphat/Pipat/ Phiphath that one encounters on the street signs while strolling down the *soi*.

The frequent – if not universal – employment of the dreaded IST means you're far better off learning the Thai alphabet. It will make your life a lot easier.

HOW TO LEARN THAI

Some expats choose to teach themselves the language. There are plenty of books out there, not to mention websites that will help you along the way. Some, the very gifted, can pick up the language purely by listening to those around them (though the alphabet is likely a different matter). For most of us, a school is the best way to go. Thai people are very polite and as such are unlikely to feel comfortable correcting you when you make mistakes. So long as they understand, they'll let you chat away in your slightly eccentric *farang*-style Thai. But if you want to learn the language properly, you'll need a teacher whose job it is to point out your mistakes – and explain why you're wrong.

Chulalongkorn University, Thailand's oldest university and among its most prestigious, offers intensive courses lasting six weeks each. Expect a high standard of teaching and a lot of hard work. Perhaps even better known – in the Thai language sphere – is the American University Alumni

Tips on learning Thai

- **Start with ABCs:** Learn the Thai alphabet from the start of your Thai studies. The language will make a lot more sense and you won't need to worry about idiosyncratic transcription systems.

- **Don't be shy:** This applies to all languages, of course, but it's worth repeating here. The only way you will get good at Thai is by speaking it a lot. Sure, you'll make mistakes, but that's to be expected. Thais will expect you to make mistakes and take that into account, so don't worry too much about saying the wrong thing. Throw yourself in there!

- **Make a good impression:** It goes without saying that to speak Thai well, you have to *sound* like a Thai. If you speak Thai words in your normal accent, you won't be understood. When you speak Thai, imagine you're doing an impression of a Thai person. Perhaps you can even imitate a particular friend or person you hear speaking a lot. (Don't worry, they're unlikely to realise what you're doing. Unless you're very, very good.)

- **Say it like a man:** This may seem obvious, but if you're a man, make sure you pay attention to how Thai men speak. It's common for foreigners to spend much of their time with Thai women and to copy their speech patterns. By doing this you can end up sounding camp – which might not be the persona you're going for.

- **Try before you buy:** Always ask for a trial lesson before signing up with a language teacher. The skills of the city's Thai-teaching corps varies enormously, yet a good teacher can make all the difference to your studies. A trial should ideally be free, though some schools will make you pay the standard rate.

Association (AUA). The AUA uses an unusual style of teaching called the Automatic Language Growth (ALG), in which students spend hours watching two teachers talk in simple Thai, but remain silent themselves. Only after hundreds of hours of listening are learners encouraged to begin using the language themselves. The method, which is supposed to mimic the way a small child acquires language, has many fans.

But while the AUA method might suit a student with plenty of free time – a retiree or someone on an extended vacation, for example – it is probably less suitable for the gainfully employed, the short of time. In that case, I'd recommend choosing a school that uses more conventional methods. There are far too many language schools in the city to list here, but it goes without saying that some are far better than others.

You'll want to take into account a lot of factors like price and ease of access. But most important of all will be the competence of your teacher, which can vary greatly even within a single school. And, of course, different teaching styles will suit different students. The main piece of advice I can offer is to make sure you take a trial lesson before signing up to a course. And – gentlemen – it's very nice to be taught by a pretty young lady, but not all pretty young ladies are good teachers.

Useful websites

The following websites are useful or interesting resources for people learning the Thai language:

- **www.womenlearnthai.com** Expat Catherine Wentworth launched her blog 'Women Learning Thai' as an alternative to the mostly male-oriented Thai-language resources she found online when she took her first steps on the road to learning language. Now boasting several regular contributors – including men – 'Women Learning Thai' is as much about the process of learning Thai as directly helping you to learn the language itself. Thai language school reviews by Tod Daniels should come in handy for

---

Habits of successful Thai learners

Catherine Wentworth, who runs the popular 'Women Learning Thai' blog, ran a series of 50 interviews with foreigners who have successfully learned the Thai language: diplomats, local celebrities, teachers, writers and many more. She looked for patterns of behaviour to try and figure out what these accomplished Thai speakers had in common. Of those 50:

- 34 lived in Thailand full-time
- 34 listed living in Thailand as their main reason for learning the language
- 28 were proficient in another language, not counting their own
- 36 were not learning another language apart from Thai
- 32 kept to their studies until they were proficient, taking no long breaks
- 29 stuck to a steady study schedule.
- 34 learned to read and write from the very beginning
- 34 said reading and writing weren't difficult to learn
- 26 speak professional (polite) Thai and 14 speak street Thai
- 22 listed difficulty with tones and pronunciation as the biggest misconception

---

learners looking for a place to study the language, and Catherine's 'ginormous' list of iOS Thai-learning apps is as ginormous as advertised.

- **www.longdo.com** This meta-dictionary searches several other dictionaries to provide you with a variety of definitions for any given word. It's the place to go if searches in your regular dictionaries turn up a blank.
- **www.thai2english.com** This online Thai dictionary has a simple interface that allows you to look up several words at the same time, making it the perfect aid to reading Thai online.
- **www.thai-language.com** This excellent online dictionary site has a host of useful features, including bulk lookup. You can also play audio files of many of the words in

the dictionary to find out how they are supposed to be pronounced, as well as look up Thai words based on their transliteration, which is perfect for those early-days moments when you hear a word but have no idea how it might be spelled. The experts who inhabit the site's forum are more than happy to answer any questions you might have about the Thai language.

- **www.learnthaiwithmod.com** This site is packed with videos of Thai-language lessons by the delightful Mod, an experienced Thai teacher who aims to teach her students 'realistic Thai'.

- **lexitron.nectec.or.th** This online dictionary, developed by Thailand's National Electronics and Computer Technology Centre, is probably the most comprehensive one out there. It powers a variety of other online dictionaries, including longdo.com, as MyLex, an iPhone Thai-English dictionary app. The Lexitron dictionary can also be downloaded onto your computer for use offline.

THAI WORKING CULTURE

To try to understand Thai working culture, let's first consider the Thai word for 'work': '*ngan*'. The word '*ngan*' also happens to mean 'party', a fact which may seem to strange to the foreigner. Can there be two more different human activities than working and partying, you might wonder?

Welcome to Thailand. Until very recently in its history, this country was primarily an agricultural society. To a significant degree, it still is. Most people used to make their living by farming rice. The work of harvesting rice, or harvesting any other produce, was usually too much for one family to do, so other members of the community would pitch in with the work, forming a 'party'. After the work was done, it would be time for *sanuk*: singing, dancing, sharing jokes and a chance for the community to bond.

Thus work, to traditional Thai thinking, is associated with the coming together of the community, with cooperation, and with fun. And, to an extent, it remains that way. Thais like work to be *sanuk*, and they want to feel a sense of community, almost of family, with their colleagues.

The Thai desire to avoid conflict is also a feature of Thai workplaces. Just as conflict could disrupt the important *ngan* of an agricultural community, it can disrupt the work of a modern office. Criticism is something to be avoided, since it's seen as a harbinger of conflict.

Between superiors and inferiors, who are considered to be in a kind of patron-client relationship, this works both ways. An inferior who criticises her boss, even indirectly, might find she is no longer welcome in the team. Likewise, a boss who criticises a staff under his supervision too directly could be seen to be neglecting his duties as patron. This doesn't mean to say that criticism doesn't happen in Thai workplaces, of course. It does, but it will take the form of gossip, which can easily serve to undermine a boss's authority. Gossip, indeed, is rife.

Naturally, the hierarchy within an office is crucial to its function. The opinion and decisions of senior staff members must be respected and should not be openly questioned. The behaviour of junior staff in front of seniors will be governed by feelings of *kreng jai*: of consideration for that person's status and feelings. This can lead to situations that *farang* managers would consider dysfunctional: young staff keeping quiet in the face of bad decisions by the management which they happen to know are wrong.

There's a tolerance for ambiguity in Thai life that can frustrate the *farang*. This is truer than anywhere in an office. When a *farang* manager seeks a definite answer, as *farang* are wont to do, they receive only 'maybes' and equivocation. It's the kind of thing that frustrates both parties.

Having said all this, it's also important to remember that Bangkok has a hybrid Sino-Thai culture, and this permeates the business world as much, if not more, than any other sphere. If you work for an international organisation or company, expect many of your staff to be of Sino-Thai origin. They may be more influenced by Confucian values: filial piety (meaning respect for one's elders and ancestors), diligence and thriftiness.

One commonality between Thai and Chinese culture is a focus on personal relationships, as opposed to formal ones. No matter where in the world you are, success in business is always a function of networks and relationships, but in Bangkok this is particularly true. Having connections with the right people can ensure your business gets favourable treatment. Thais are less keen to do business with those they don't know, and so a certain amount of 'getting to know you' is considered important before deals can be done.

Nepotism is very common. It's seen as perfectly normal that you would want to favour your kin when it comes to deciding who to employ or promote. After all, it's seen as natural to want to spend time with your family, rather than live in the company of strangers. Remember, living and working as a family unit was the norm for the vast majority of Thais until very recently in the country's history. To avoid using your position in work to help your friends and family is to betray your obligations to those people. A *farang* manager, then, needs to bear this in mind, and to avoid being too judgemental in the face of this kind of behaviour.

Thais can often behave in ways that may seem 'corrupt' to the *farang*, but which they consider ethically sound. For example, imagine a company is hiring a new member of staff. One of the company's current employees tells a prospective candidate about it, who ends up getting the job. Sometimes the person who gets the job will pay the employee an under-the-table 'finder's fee' for helping them get the position. The employee may even expect to receive a portion of his or her salary each month.

This is the kind of custom that can cause problems in *farang*-run companies. For most foreign managers, it would be thought beyond the pale. It will be up to you to deal with the issue as you see fit, but your reaction should take into account that such arrangements are considered normal by many Thais. It may even surprise them to learn that you disapprove.

MANAGING THAI STAFF

Should you find yourself managing Thai staff, your job will be to bridge the gap between their working culture and your own. If you're able to do this successfully, you'll forge a hybrid working culture: one that your Thai staff feel comfortable with, but that encourages them to operate in a way more in line with your own principles.

The balance between Thai ways of doing things and your own culture's methods will depend on the kind of organisation you find yourself in. International organisations and firms, which tend to employ highly-educated Thais with experience abroad, will likely have a culture more akin to that found in the West and corporate settings the world over. If you are starting a local business – a restaurant, for example – you'll find that your working culture will need to conform much more to Thai expectations.

One cast-iron rule: avoid direct criticism of staff members. If someone makes a mistake, don't chew them out publicly, don't get angry and don't be too direct when dissecting what went wrong. If need be, choose an appropriate moment to talk to the staff member, and explain how they should do things next time. Instead of criticism, the manager should rely on positive encouragement. Praise what staff do well and try to keep a fun and positive atmosphere. Providing incentives for staff if they meet targets works much better than generating a climate of fear.

Bear in mind that Thais expect work to be fun, and if a somewhat lively atmosphere develops, understand that that doesn't necessarily mean your staff aren't taking work seriously. You, too, should contribute to generating *sanuk*. That doesn't mean playing the clown. However, organising regular away days will help to create the right kind of environment. The environment, while we're at it, will always include food. A manager who bans food in a Thai workplace is a deeply unpopular one.

As a manager in a position of seniority, you are in a patron-client relationship with your staff. They owe you their loyalty, and so long as you treat them with respect and avoid some of the mistakes above, they will give it to you. You, in turn,

Women in business

Although the old-fashioned idea that men should provide for their families while women should look after the home is yet to die out, women do relatively well in Thai workplaces. In 2013, a survey by professional services firm Grant Thornton showed that Thailand led the world in terms of its proportion of female CEOs. Forty-nine per cent of the country's CEOs are women, the highest rate in the world. In terms of senior management positions, globally 24 per cent of positions are held by women. In Thailand the figure is 36 per cent. By contrast, in the UK just 19 per cent of senior managers are female, while in Japan the figure is 7 per cent.

have a responsibility to them: to support them, to treat them respectfully and, sometimes, to treat them to a night out.

One issue you're likely to face as a manager is lateness. Although many Thais are well aware of Western expectations with regard to punctuality, they traditionally place less importance on sticking rigidly to timetables. It's a mentality that derives from the agricultural past, in which the position of the sun was more important than the exact time.

The Bangkok traffic tends to supply an ideal excuse for being late. If you simply cannot abide lateness, you need to make your expectations for punctuality clear. However, bear in mind that to reprimand someone – publicly or otherwise – for lateness is unlikely to go down well, particularly because they will probably have an excuse, and to reprimand them regardless would be to imply they are lying.

If you're having trouble motivating staff, you might try explaining to them that your own boss has certain expectations of you, and that if you don't deliver, you will get in trouble. This may motivate them to do what you hope, though it only works if they like you. So it's very important to ensure that they do.

It's also possible to use certain Thai cultural traits to your benefit. For example, one constant in Thai workplaces is that staff should respect ('*hai kiat*') their seniors. If you don't want someone to be late, you might make it clear that you consider being punctual a way of showing respect to you. You might also make the same argument with respect to *kreng jai*, by telling your staff that if they *kreng jai* you, they will arrive at work on time.

FINDING AND WORKING WITH A THAI BUSINESS PARTNER

Finding a trustworthy, competent and well-connected Thai partner can be crucial to making your business a success. This book has been quite open about how difficult it is for foreigners to truly understand Thai ways of doing things. That's one of the areas in which a Thai partner can help. Any sort of problems you might encounter during interactions with the government, other businesses or

merely understanding regulations, can be solved much more easily with a Thai partner.

At the same time, relationships are crucial to doing business here. If you're trying to run a business without support from people with status and clout in Thai society, you are vulnerable. There are plenty of horror stories out there about foreign-owned businesses being extorted by the police or targeted for harassment by government officials at the instigation of business rivals with good connections. In order to guard against such problems, having someone of stature on your side can be very useful.

CORRUPTION

Corruption and the paying of bribes remain integral features of Thai society. Transparency International, which evaluates countries according to how corrupt they are, ranked Thailand 88th of the 176 countries it rated in its 2012 Corruption Perceptions Index. Although corruption is

The land of the deal

By now, 'the land of smiles' is a well-worn cliché. So I'd like to propose a new moniker for Thailand: 'the land of the deal'. Thais are inveterate dealmakers, a trait that permeates every facet of the society. From the ad-hoc street sale, to the flesh trade, right up to the grand bargains struck by the country's ruling *phu yai*, dealmaking greases the wheels of society, the economy, and prevents conflict.

Most long-term residents of Thailand will know that it's never difficult to shift second-hand goods in the country. For instance, if you were selling a gold necklace, you could quite happily stand on the street, approach passersby, and find a buyer. Everything has its price, and if there's profit to be made, many Thais will jump at the chance, regardless of the formality of the setting.

The practice of haggling and barter is another obvious manifestation of this. While fixed prices do apply in many situations, such as formal, 'branded' stores, there are often chances to haggle where you might not expect. Hotel prices, car rentals, and sometimes even electronics goods can be bargained for.

But on another level, what I'm really getting at is that Thais are believers in compromise. Conflict is to be avoided where possible, and compromise is often the means through which this is accomplished. After a car accident, those involved may argue about whose fault it was, but where it's clear, the next order of business is always to haggle over how much the offending party must pay the victim.

Political conflict may present itself in the form of masses of protesters occupying the streets, but it is often solved behind the scenes with grand bargains between the principal players. At the time of writing, Thailand appears to have achieved a kind of political stability, likely through a back-room deal between the current government and the army, as well as other factions. In the land of the deal, every problem has its solution – if the price is right.

often difficult to spot, it's highly pervasive and remains an issue that anyone doing business in Thailand will need to contend with.

The practice of paying corrupt officials for public services has a long historical vintage in Thailand, dating back to the era of the feudal *sakdina* system (*see page 95*). At that time, officials were appointed to represent the king's government but were not paid by the crown. Instead, they were expected to use their positions to remunerate themselves. If they were collecting taxes, they would retain a portion of the money. If they were providing services, they would charge fees to perform their duties. There were conventional limits on how much such officials were expected to charge for services, and to be 'corrupt' in this context meant not to charge money to perform one's duties, but to charge *too much*.

The idea that public officials should charge some kind of a fee to perform their duties has never quite disappeared. To this day, officials in government bureaucracies continue to exploit their positions for financial gain. It's rare for a public official to refuse to perform their duties at all without a bribe. However, money, when offered, can be used to 'speed things up'.

Corruption is almost built into the system: the salaries of government officials remain very low. Civil servants, from police to pen-pushers to prison guards, are all paid at rates that make it very difficult, if not impossible, to survive without a supplementary income.

While there are many Thais who abhor corruption and understand how it can be a detriment to society, most accept it as part of life. The practice of presenting 'gifts' to public officials as a kind of 'thank you' for performing their duties is well accepted. The paying of kickbacks to officials overseeing auctions for public contracts is also rife.

Some forms of corruption are considered more serious than others, and this is reflected in the Thai language. A gift of good will to a public official expected to perform a duty, known as '*sin nam jai*', is thought least serious. Moving up in terms of severity are '*kha nam ron nam cha*' ('tea money'), '*praphuet mi chop*' ('improper behaviour'), '*sin bon'* and *'rit thai'* ('bribery' and 'extortion') and *'thutjarit to nathi'* (dishonesty in duty). Interestingly, the English word 'corruption' has been adopted in Thai as *'khorrapchan'* to describe what is considered the most socially destructive, criminal behaviour.

A 1993 survey of thousands of Thais by academics Pasuk Phongphaichit and Sungsidh Piriyarangsan in *Corruption and Democracy in Thailand* (*see page 326*) suggested that very few Thais thought that paying a bribe to a police officer to avoid having to go to the station to process a traffic violation constituted 'corruption'. Respondents thought that so long as the amount was small and the police officer did not ask for the money, the act was not corrupt, merely 'buying' convenience.

Anyone doing business in Bangkok will need to face up to the issue of corruption. This might take many forms: requests of bribery from the police; being asked to pay to ensure goods go through a port without delay; being told that without providing a committee with some 'encouragement', your firm will not win a vital auction.

When a junior official informs you that a bribe will be required in order to make a certain process happen, you have almost no way of knowing if he is telling the truth. For this reason, most of the money won't be paid until after the thing has happened, though even then, you won't know if it would have happened anyway.

Some expat businessmen take a firm line against corruption. Others pragmatically accept reality, that there are certain costs in doing business in the land of the deal.

FAST FACTS ABOUT BANGKOK

CHAPTER 10

English name
Bangkok

Thai name
Krung Thep Maha Nakhon, or just Krung Thep

Ceremonial name
Krungthepmahanakhon Amonrattanakosin Mahinthar-ayutthaya Mahadilokphop Noppharatratchathaniburirom Udomratchaniwetmahasathan Amonphimanawatansathit Sakkathattiyawitsanukamprasit (translation: City of angels, great city of immortals, magnificent city of the nine gems, seat of the king, city of royal palaces, home of gods incarnate, erected by Visvakarman at Indra's behest)

Founded
1782

Population
8,280,925 (2010)

Population, Bangkok Metropolitan Region
14,565,547

Area
1568.737 km²

Climate
Tropical wet and dry

Coordinates
Latitude 13°44′ North; Longitude 100°30′ East

Timezone
Indochina (ICT), GMT +7 hours

Dialling code
+66

Economic output
US$98.34bn (2010)

Governing body
Bangkok Metropolitan Administration (BMA)

Governor
Sukhumbhand Paribatra (2009–)

Legislative body
Bangkok Metropolitan Council

Districts (*khet*)
50

Subdistricts (*khwaeng*)
169

LOCAL POLITICS AND GOVERNMENT

Bangkok is one of only two special administrative areas in Thailand, the other being Pattaya. The city is governed by the Bangkok Metropolitan Administration (BMA), which comprises two branches: the executive, in the form of the Governor of Bangkok, and the legislative, in the form of the Bangkok Metropolitan Council. The structure and functions of the BMA are defined in the Bangkok Metropolitan Administration Act 1985.

Bangkok is divided into 50 districts (*khet*), in turn divided into 169 subdistricts (*khwaeng*), which are the equivalent of a province's *amphoe* and *tambon*, respectively. Each district elects one or more councillor, which together form the Bangkok Metropolitan Council. The BMC is the city's legislative body, which issues local ordinances and scrutinises the governor's performance.

Unlike the governors of the other 76 provinces in Thailand, the Governor of Bangkok is directly elected for a four-year term. The current incumbent is MR Sukhumbhand Paribatra of the Democrat Party, a great-grandson of King Chulalongkorn who was first elected in January 2009. In March 2013 he was re-elected, beating Pongsapat Pongcharoen of the ruling Pheu Thai Party in a close poll.

The powers of the governor are not clearly defined. Together with four appointed deputies, he (I use 'he' because the incumbent is a 'he') implements policies concerning the management of Bangkok. His areas of responsibility include transport, waste management, planning, housing, roads, security, education and the environment.

These responsibilities are shared with departments of Thailand's national government, which makes the governing of Bangkok a messy process. A clause in the BMA Act states that the governor is supposed to carry out the orders of the cabinet, the prime minister and the ministry of interior. In reality, the governor can come into conflict with the premier, especially when the two posts are held by politicians from opposing parties. Turf wars and NIMBYism between city and state are common.

This was never more clear than during the devastating

floods that hit half the country's provinces in 2011. In November, when parts of Central Thailand were under up to three metres of water and Bangkok was threatened with inundation by approaching floodwaters, Governor Sukhumbhand and the Yingluck Shinawatra administration came into conflict. The governor was determined to keep his city dry at all costs. This put him at odds with the government, which wanted to relieve flooded provinces to the north by opening sluice gates and allowing water to flow through the city's drainage canals. In the event, the centre of the city stayed dry. In fairness, a flooded capital in a country as centralised as Thailand wouldn't have helped anyone.

FAMOUS BANGKOKIANS

Pridi Banomyong

Pridi Banomyong is remembered as the 'Father of Thai Democracy'. He began his political career as an idealistic young radical, having received a government scholarship to study law at the Sorbonne in Paris. He was one of the seven so-called 'Promoters' who met in 1927 to plot an end to absolute monarchy, and eventually did so in 1932.

In 1934 Pridi founded Thammasat University – along with Chulalongkorn University, one of Thailand's top two institutions. Pridi's finest hour came during the Second World War. In 1942, when Phibunsongkhram issued a declaration of war against Britain and the United States, then-Finance Minister Pridi refused to sign it. He was demoted to regent for the young King Ananda. While playing this role, he set about organising the Free Thai resistance against Japanese rule.

But it was the shooting of King Ananda on June 9, 1946 that was to ruin Pridi, who was prime minister at the time. His political enemies in the Democrat Party spread rumours that he was involved in the plot to kill the king and had wanted to establish a republic. Public opinion turned against Pridi and in August he was forced to resign and leave the country. King Bhumibol was later to tell his biographer William Stephenson that he did not believe Pridi was involved in the death of Ananda.

Pridi was to return to Bangkok briefly, but in November 1947 another coup made it unsafe for him to stay in the country. Pridi went into hiding before being spirited away from Thailand in a Shell oil tanker, helped by the British and Americans, who hadn't forgotten his leadership of the Free Thai during WWII. Pridi is remembered today as one of Thailand's greatest statesmen ever. His birthday, May 11, is celebrated as Pridi Phanomyong day, and Bangkok has four roads named after him.

'A' Supachai Sriwichit

Rarely pictured without a huge grin on his face, A Supachai, as he tends to be known, is understandably pleased with himself. He's one of the most powerful agents in Thai showbusiness. Think Entourage's Ari Gold, but much, much gayer.

Famous for his huge collection of Hermes Birkin bags (which retail at anything up to US$37,000 each), this flamboyant Southerner has an enormous stable of young talent in the Thai entertainment industry. As well as the ubiquitous *luk khrueng* superstar Nadech Kugimiya, he looks after Am Phatcharaporn Chaichuea, Mario Maurer, Mark Prin, May Fuenagarom and Po Nattawut Sakotjai. These names may well mean nothing to you, but trust me, they're pretty big.

A Supachai, who grew up on a Nakhon Sri Thammarat rubber farm, spends much of his time touring Thailand looking for the nascent stars of the future. When he sees someone he likes the look of, he introduces himself. It's said he looks at them through his phone. Only if they look good on the screen does he take things further.

Once he has the raw material, he sets about building a 'star'. They're invited to stay at his THB50 million home in Bangkok, which hosts his star-training centre. There, the young wannabes practise 'personality', singing, dancing and acting. He observes them carefully and figures out what occupation they're best suited to. Then he invests: if that includes paying for their teeth to be fixed, or sending them off to Korea for surgery, so be it.

Ananda Everingham

Ananda Everingham is one of Thailand's biggest movie stars. Half Australian, half Laotian, his parents' love story is legendary. His father, John Everingham, was working as a journalist in Laos after the country was taken over by the communists in 1975. He fell in love with Ananda's Laotian mother-to-be, Keo Sirisomphone.

In 1977, government agents arrested John and threw him out of the country. The chief of the Laotian secret police started blackmailing Keo, saying he would send her to a re-education camp unless she became his mistress.

Over in Thailand, John got wind of the plan and plotted to rescue Keo. Three attempts failed, but in May 1978, he slipped under the muddy waters of the Mekong and swam a mile to the Laotian side in scuba gear. On the opposite bank, Keo, who had been told of the plan by a friendly diplomat, was waiting for him, pretending to be an angler.

After reaching the shore, he gave her a spare scuba mouthpiece and the couple dipped back under the water. The crossing was terrifying for Keo, who couldn't swim. After 20 minutes, they were picked up by a Thai patrol boat and were finally free to marry and begin a new life together in Thailand.

Ananda was born four years later in 1982. At 14 years old, while working in his parents' Bangkok restaurant, he was discovered by an agent from Thailand's largest entertainment company, GMM Grammy. He has since become a huge movie star. His most famous role was the lead in the 2004 Thai horror hit 'Shutter'. In June 2008 he released his own movie, 'Sabaidee Luang Prabang', the first Laotian commercial film shot since the communists took power in 1975.

Chuwit Kamolvisit

Chuwit Kamolvisit used to be a brothel tycoon. Today, he's a moral crusader, fighting against the corruption of the very same Bangkok police he used to pay off while running his empire of vast Vegas-style massage parlours. At least, that's his story. Call him what you like – 'colourful', 'controversial', 'hypocritical' – he's a bona fide Bangkok character.

Chuwit was born in 1961 to a Chinese father and Thai mother. Having grown up in Chinatown, he studied at Thammasat University before starting – but never finishing – an MBA at university in San Diego. Then he returned to Bangkok, ready to put his studies to the test. After overhearing two men talking about a massage parlour licence that was up for sale, he bought it, opened Victoria's Secret and never looked back.

Through his company, the Davis Group – he has been known to use the name 'Davis Kamol' – Chuwit opened a string of huge 'massage parlours' on Ratchadiphsek Road. These *ap op nuat* ('bathe, sauna, massage') behemoths, with names like Copacabana and Emmanuelle, made him an extremely wealthy man.

Then everything fell apart. In January 2003, he hired a gang of 600 men to raze several bars and businesses on a plot of land on Sukhumvit Road that he'd bought weeks earlier for half a billion baht. He'd planned to use the land to build a Holiday Inn. The tenants, whom he hadn't bothered to alert about the demolition, thought they had valid leases and cried foul. The police arrested the tycoon and he spent a night in a cell before making bail.

Soon afterwards, furious at the police he'd paid so much cash to over the years, Chuwit appeared on national television and dished the dirt on the cops' bribe-taking. He claimed to have a list of 1,000 officers and 10 generals who'd taken cash from him. Chuwit was no saint, but for someone important to call out police corruption like this was an almost revolutionary act. He became a celebrity overnight.

Chuwit entered politics, promising to 'clean up' the city and crack down on police corruption. In September 2003 he formed his own party before running for Bangkok governor in August the next year. He ran a memorable campaign with posters featuring him holding up a sledgehammer, his face convulsed with anger. '*Prap khon kong*' went his slogan – 'suppress the corrupt'. He placed third, winning the votes of 300,000 Bangkokians, or about 16 per cent of the vote.

In the 2005 general election, he joined the Chat Thai Party and was elected an MP on its party list. In January 2006, the

Constitution Court disqualified Chuwit, ruling that he had not joined Chat Thai for at least 90 days before the election. In 2008 he launched another failed bid for the Bangkok governorship, again coming third. In May 2011, he formed a new party, Rak Prathet Thai ('Love Thailand'), and his angry visage again became a feature of the Bangkok streets. In the election of July that year, he won 4 seats and landed himself back in parliament. Since then he has continued his 'anti-corruption' campaign, publicising the existence of illegal casinos run under the supposed knowledge of the police.

Chuwit never built his Holiday Inn. Instead, he turned the plot into Chuwit Park – a rare oasis of calm on the seedy end of Sukhumvit Road. 'I have no future in politics,' he told *Manager* newspaper in 2005 'One day I will be killed and my body will be laid down in the street. Do you know why? Because this is the way things work in Thailand.' At the time of writing, Chuwit remained alive and well.

Pornthip Rojanasunand

Dr Pornthip Rojanasunand is Thailand's most famous forensic pathologist (surely every country has one). With her 'punk rock' hairdo, all highlights and hairspray, the doctor is instantly recognisable. Many expats know her simply as 'that woman with the hair'.

Dr Pornthip, who was born in 1955, first came to prominence in 2003, while working as deputy director of Thailand's Central Institute of Forensic Science (CIFS). As the death toll mounted during former premier Thaksin Shinawatra's 'war on drugs' (*see page 39*), she claimed the evidence suggested the police were carrying out extra-judicial murders of drug dealers.

Over the ensuing years she continued to face off against the cops, challenging their often dubious versions of events in murder investigations. In the aftermath of the 2004 tsunami, she led a team working to identify bodies of the victims in the Andaman region.

Devastatingly for her credibility, Dr Pornthip has been a vocal supporter of the GT200, a 'dowsing rod' that can supposedly detect drugs and explosives. Despite the device having been proved bogus, and its maker imprisoned in the UK, Pornthip has stubbornly stuck with her claim that it 'works'. This may have been because she was director of the CIFS when it bought some of the devices for large sums of money. It may also point to the fact that the army, which has protected her against threats from the police, has continued to use the device itself.

In May 2013 Yingluck Shinawatra's Council of Ministers decided not to extend her term as CIFS chief. Always outspoken, Dr Pornthip suggested her removal had been at the instigation of politicians who were 'upset with her work'.

Sumet Jumsai Na Ayudhya

The imagination of architect Sumet Jumsai Na Ayudhya has supplied Bangkok with some of its most memorable buildings. His most famous work is undoubtedly Sathorn's Bank of Asia Building, better known as the 'Robot Building', for reasons that are obvious to anyone who's seen it. The structure, built in 1986, was chosen by the Los Angeles Museum of Contemporary Art as one of the 50 seminal buildings of the 20th century.

Born in 1939, Sumet – who, as his surname indicates, is of royal descent – was educated in Europe, studying at Cambridge University and later joining its Department of Architecture as a member of the faculty. Like Rangsan Torsuwan (*see page 61*), his most famous work coincided with Thailand's boom years in the 1980s and 1990s.

In a similar vein to the Robot Building is the Elephant Building from 1997, a structure comprising three skyscrapers joined at the top, complete with an eye and two tusks. Some love the building, others are always sure to vote for it in polls for the world's ugliest edifices. Sumet was also responsible for the cubist Nation Building, home of *The Nation* newspaper.

Not everyone is a fan of Sumet's whimsical approach to architecture. In 2010, the satirical news website 'Not The Nation' ran a story claiming: 'Famous Thai architect Sumet Jumsai announced this week that designs for a new building in the shape of his own penis had been approved… The Cambridge-educated architect's previous efforts, the Elephant

Building and Robot Building, were also based on juvenile infatuations,' the site said.

Sumet has worked to preserve Thailand's architectural heritage. He is also a painter and outspoken social and political commentator. He has notably spoken out against Thailand's lèse-majesté law, claiming it is damaging the reputation of the institution it is meant to protect. In 2012, he was one of eight people of royal lineage to sign a letter to Prime Minister Yingluck Shinawatra asking for it to be changed.

Sulak Sivaraksa

Sulak Sivaraksa is one of Thailand's best-known intellectuals and social critics. Despite being an avowed monarchist, Sulak believes the institution should be subject to criticism in order to ensure it can 'review itself from time to time'. He entitled his 1998 autobiography *Loyalty Demands Dissent*. As a result of his outspokenness Sulak has been charged with lèse-majesté on several occasions. He has always beaten the charges, sometimes, he claims, following the intervention of the king himself. Today he enjoys an almost unique reputation as a man who can say the kind of things no one else dares.

Born into an affluent Sino-Thai family in Bangkok in 1933, Sulak was educated in Wales and passed the Bar in London in 1961. On returning to Thailand, he founded *Social Science Review*, which became the country's foremost intellectual magazine.

But it was an encounter with a progressive Thai prince, Prince Sitthiporn, that changed the direction of his life. The prince compared Sulak's work as an editor to 'intellectual masturbation' and told him he knew nothing of the suffering of Thailand's poor. The meeting led Sulak to spend time in the country's rural hinterland to understand how poor farmers really lived. He then embarked on a lifetime of activism.

In the 1970s he was forced into exile for two years following the bloody events of 1976 and the re-imposition of military rule. When he returned, he launched dozens of NGOs and activist organisations. He has challenged environmentally destructive developments on many occasions. He is also a strong critic of former premier Thaksin Shinawatra, famously accusing him of a 'notorious sexual life' and fathering illegitimate children. In February 2006 he took to a PAD stage to denounce Thaksin as a 'pitiful dog'.

Sulak believes in Buddhism as a force for social change, reinterpreting the Buddhist precepts as demands for social and economic justice. Nevertheless, in 2007 he spoke out against making Buddhism Thailand's official religion, believing it would only serve to make the conflict in the Deep South worse. He has served as an international ambassador for Buddhism and forged links between Buddhists around the world, including founding the International Network of Engaged Buddhists with the Dalai Lama, who he counts as a friend. He has twice been nominated for the Nobel Peace Prize.

Nattawut Saikua

Together with Jatuporn Prompan and Veera Musikapong, Nattawut Saikua was one of the three core leaders of the United Front for Democracy Against Dictatorship. Having led red-shirt protests in 2009 and 2010, he was imprisoned for nine months following the end of the 2010 protests for a period. Today, he is a government minister in the cabinet of Yingluck Shinwatra.

Born in 1975, Nattawut grew up in Nakhon Sri Thammarat province in the South. A highly talented orator, he became a school debating champion before later working as a speech trainer. He subsequently became a TV star as a comedian on 'Sapa Joke' ('Joke Parliament'), a programme that lampooned Thai politics.

He joined Thaksin's Thai Rak Thai Party in 2005 and formed a faction with Jatuporn and Veera. In 2008, he became a spokesman for Samak Sundaravej's government and subsequently a spokesman for Somchai Wongsawat.

After Abhisit Vejjajiva came to power in late 2008, Nattawut, Veera and Jatuporn led the red-shirt movement against his government, whipping up the crowds with fiery oratory. In one speech, Nattawut told the crowds they should burn Bangkok down if the army staged another coup against an elected government. After the bloody and fiery end of the 2010 protest on May 19, Nattawut and the rest of the UDD leaders surrendered themselves to the authorities. They were bailed in February 2011.

In the July 2011 general election, Nattawut was elected MP for the Pheu Thai Party. In January 2012, he became deputy minister of agriculture and cooperations. He lives in Bangkok with his wife Sirisakul and their two children.

S.P. Somtow

S.P. Somtow is Thailand's most famous composer, as well as an award-winning writer. He has composed five symphonies, a ballet and several operas.

Born in Bangkok of vaguely royal extraction in 1952, Somtow Papinian Sucharitkul was educated at Eton College and St Cathcrine's College, Cambridge. His reputation as a composer burgeoned in the 1970s, though he grew tired of life in Southeast Asia and emigrated to the United States, where he started a new career as a novelist and gained citizenship.

He has written 53 books in several genres, including horror, fantasy and science fiction. In 2002 he won the World Fantasy Award for his novella *The Bird Catcher*. He has won various other awards for his writing and was president of the Horror Writers Association.

In 2001, he became a Buddhist monk for a period and decided to return to Thailand to resume his career as a musician. He founded Bangkok's first international opera company, Opera Siam, and the Siam Philharmonic Orchestra, and has produced several operas, many of which centre around Thai themes and legends.

Somtow has been a vocal critic of Thaksin Shinawatra. In 2006, Nigerian Nobel Prize laureate Wole Soyinka withdrew as keynote speaker at the SEA Write Awards Ceremony to protest the ousting of Thaksin in a coup. S.P. Somtow replaced him, berating Soyinka for pulling out and telling the audience he had 'never felt more free'. He continues to work in Bangkok as a prolific composer and conductor.

CULTURE QUIZ

SITUATION 1

You are on your way to a meeting and decide to take a motorcycle taxi to get there. You walk to your local *win* and indicate you want a *motosai*. A driver steps, or rather, staggers forward. His eyes are bulging and he is red in the face. He smells of *lao khao*. He gets on his bike and starts kick-starting it. What do you do?

Ⓐ Get on the back and tell him where you want to go.

Ⓑ Tell the group you want a different driver.

Ⓒ Ask him for a swig of whatever it is he's been drinking.

Ⓓ Ask him if he is drunk and take his word for it when he says no.

Ⓔ Make an excuse and walk off to find another *win*.

Discussion

Obviously Ⓐ isn't a sensible course of action, unless you have a death-wish. Option Ⓑ is problematic. It's certainly not the done thing to try to choose your *motosai* driver and by publicly asking for a change, you're causing the first guy to lose face. His drunkenness only makes him more likely to take offence. If you chose option Ⓒ, you probably don't need my advice. Party on, you crazy sonofabitch! Option Ⓓ isn't sensible as the driver is likely to lie in this situation. Option Ⓔ is the best course of action. You stay safe and avoid conflict.

SITUATION 2

You are driving in your car on Sukhumvit Road. Suddenly, you are cut up aggressively by a brand new Mercedes Benz. What do you do?

Ⓐ Change lanes, speed up, pull up alongside the car and stick your finger up at the occupants.

Ⓑ Beep your car horn several times.

Ⓒ Breathe deeply and say '*mai pen rai*'.

Ⓓ Speed up and stay right behind the car to make it clear that it's in your way.

Discussion

Confrontation isn't a good idea on any of the world's roads, but it's particularly foolish in Thailand. You have no idea who is in the car, and since it's an expensive vehicle, it could be someone you don't want to mess with. Options **A**, **B** and **D** are all bad ideas, as you probably guessed. You'd probably get away with **B** unscathed, but you never know. Option **C** is the only sensible course of action, as it is in many situations in Thailand.

SITUATION 3

You have set up a burger restaurant in Bangkok. One of your staff members, Nok, mishears an order for the 'prawn burger' as the 'pork burger'. The customer complains and refuses to pay for his meal. No other waiters are aware of the mistake. How do you react?

A At the next waiting staff meeting, describe what Nok did and tell your wait staff that they need to take care not to confuse 'prawn' with 'pork'.

B Wait a little while, then take Nok aside and tactfully explain to her the difference between 'prawn' and 'pork'.

C Put up a sign in the back of the restaurant with a picture of a prawn and a picture of a pork chop, labelled 'This is a prawn' and 'This is some pork', respectively.

D At the next waiting staff meeting, tell your wait staff that they need to take care not to confuse 'prawn' with 'pork', without drawing attention to the mistake.

E Loudly reprimand her in front of her colleagues to make sure she doesn't do it again.

Discussion

The main issues here are loss of face and the need to avoid criticism in the work place. By publicly dressing down Nok or drawing attention to the issue, as in **Ⓐ**, **Ⓑ**, **Ⓓ** and **Ⓔ** you are humiliating her in front of her colleagues. **Ⓓ** is the worst option by far, since it entails a very public loss of face for Nok. It will not endear you to her colleagues either. **Ⓒ** is condescending. The best thing to do is to talk to her privately, as in **Ⓑ**. If this is the only time this has happened, you probably don't need to tell all the staff about it. If other staff are making the same mistake, addressing the issue globally is the right idea, though you should avoid mentioning any names.

SITUATION 4

You are in Thonglor and want to go and see your friend in Bang Na. You stop a taxi, open the passenger door and ask the driver to take you. He responds to your request by asking for a THB300 flat fee for the journey. Do you:

Ⓐ Agree. At least you've found someone to take you to your friend's place.

Ⓑ Tell him to go screw himself.

Ⓒ Laugh, shake your head and say 'meter', and if he refuses, walk off.

Ⓓ Slam his door and walk off.

Discussion

It's getting harder and harder to find taxis who'll take you where you want to go these days (*see page 184–186*). If you agree to pay THB300 as in **A**, you're being ripped off. You might not consider it a large price to pay, but you also encourage the taxi driver to continue to demand exorbitant sums and refuse to use his meter. Options **B** and **D** are very tempting but are confrontational and could lead to an angry reaction. Option **C** is the only sensible course of action. He'll almost certainly refuse the meter, of course, but it's worth a try.

SITUATION 5

You are a man on a long car journey with some Thai friends. Some of you need to pee so you stop the car by the side of the road in front of a patch of jungle. Do you:

A Pee on a tree.
B *Wai*, then pee on a tree.
C Pee on some grass.

Discussion

Option **A** is to be avoided. Many Thais believe that trees are inhabited by a spirit, and thus shouldn't be peed on. Nevertheless, some say that option **B** is acceptable: a *wai* is enough to placate the ghost. But option **C** is the safe option. Grass isn't significant enough to serve as a spirit's place of residence.

DO'S AND DON'TS

DO'S
- Stand up for the Royal Anthem when it's played before films in the cinema.
- Stand still when the Thai national anthem is played in public places (every day at 8am and 6pm).
- Say '*kha*' (if you're a woman) or '*khrap*' (if you're a man) at the end of the first few sentences when you talk to a new person in Thai.
- Return a *wai*, unless it's from service staff.
- Take your shoes off before entering someone's home.
- Bear in mind the potential for losses of face in social interactions.
- Beckon people by keeping your palm down and waving your fingers back and forth.
- Agree the fare with tuk-tuk drivers before you get in.
- Ask for a helmet before getting on a *motosai*.
- Haggle for prices in markets.
- Buy a copy of this book for friends visiting Bangkok.
- Smile, even if you're pissed off. Scowling doesn't get you far in Thailand.
- Make an effort to learn Thai. Things will make a lot more sense once you do.
- Learn the Thai alphabet from the start. Transliteration's a drag.

DON'TS
- Point at people.
- Point at things or people with your feet.
- Use your feet to move things (unless you're playing football).
- Touch people on the head.
- Mock the royal family or Buddhism.
- Leave sacred objects (such as amulets) and semi-sacred objects (such as books) on the floor.
- Stamp on dropped coins or banknotes, or anything with the king's image on it.

- Hang portraits of commoners higher than those of the king.
- Lose your temper in public or shout at a Thai person.
- *Wai* service staff or children.
- Walk around bare-chested in the city (women and men).
- Get angry when you try and fail to stay dry at Songkran.
- Try to shake someone's left hand.
- Cause a Thai person to lose face, by publicly humiliating them.
- Try to haggle in restaurants.
- Get the Chang logo tattooed on any part of your body (for reasons of taste).
- Buy a suit or gems from a shop a tuk-tuk driver brings you to.
- Ask to change *motosai* driver. If your driver looks drunk, find another *win*.

WORDS AND PHRASES

Thai	Meaning
ahan	food
arai	what
aroi	tasty, delicious
a-me-ri-kan	America
ang-krit	Britain, England
bia	beer
buri	cigarette
di-chan, chan	I, me (for a woman)
farang	foreign, foreigner
fa-rang-set	France, French
fon	rain
keng	clever
kyat	he, she, they
khon	person
khon thai	a Thai person
khun	you
krung thep	Bangkok
metoe	meter (as in taxi meter)
motosai	motorcycle, motorcycle taxi
muang thai	Thailand
nao	cold
ngoen	money
ottrelia	Australia
phaeng	expensive
phet	spicy
phiset	special (used to order a larger portion at a street stall)
phom	I, me (for a man)
praisani	post office

prathet thai	Thailand
ran ahan	restaurant
rao	we, us
ron	hot
rong phayaban	hospital
rong raem	hotel
rong rian	school
rot bat	bus
sataem	stamp
soi	a road or street leading off a larger one
suai	beautiful
tang	money, change
thaksi	taxi
than	you (more formal)
thanon	road, street
win motosai	motorcycle taxi group
yoeraman	Germany

Numbers

Thai	Meaning
sun	zero
nueng	one
song	two
sam	three
si	four
ha	five
hok	six
jet	seven
paet	eight
kao	nine
sip	ten

sip-et	eleven
sip-song	twelve
sip-sam	thirteen
yi-sip	twenty
yi-sip-et	twenty-one
sam-sip	thirty
si-sip	forty
ha-sip	fifty
hok-sip	sixty
jet-sip	seventy
paet-sip	eighty
kao-sip	ninety
nueng roi	one hundred
song roi	two hundred
nueng phan	one thousand
nueng muen	ten thousand
nueng saen	one hundred thousand
nueng lan	one million

Useful phrases

For politeness, you should add '*kha*' (if you're female) or '*khrap*' (if you're male) to the end of the following phrases.

Thai	Meaning
Chuai duai!	Help!
Kep tang duai.	Can I pay please?
Chek bin.	Can I have the bill please?
Mai phet na.	Not spicy, please.
Phet phet na.	Spicy, please.
Aroi mai?	Is it tasty?
Aroi mak.	It's very tasty.
Kin/than khao rue yang?	Have you eaten yet? (A common greeting)

Pai nai?	Where are you going? (A common greeting)
Khop khun khrap/kha.	Thank you.
Phut ang-krit dai mai?	Can you speak English?
Phut thai dai mai?	Can you speak Thai?
Phut thai dai.	I can speak Thai.
Phut thai mai dai.	I can't speak Thai.
Phut thai dai nit noi.	I can speak Thai a little bit.
Phut cha cha noi.	Please speak slowly.
... yu thi nai?	Where is...?
Mai pen rai.	Never mind, it doesn't matter.
Pen khon thi nai?	Which place/country do you come from?
Pen khon...	I am from...
Mai mi tang.	I have no money.
Thao rai?	How much?

RESOURCE GUIDE

DIALLING THAILAND
+66 + number without the zero

EMERGENCIES AND HEALTH
The emergency services can be called by dialling 191. The operator will probably not speak English, so ask a Thai speaker to do it for you. Alternatively, call the English-speaking Tourist Police on 1155. In case of fire, dial 199.

You may also wish to find out what your nearest hospital is and save its emergency contact number in your phone.

In case of a snake bite, keep the victim still and the bite area below heart level. Wash the bite with soap and water. Call your nearest hospital for an ambulance. If possible, bring the snake, dead or alive, with you. The Chulalongkorn Hospital Emergency Department has a comprehensive supply of antidotes. They can be called on 0-2256-4214.

HOSPITALS
The following hospitals are accredited by the Joint Commission International, the international arm of the United States' main accreditation body.

Bangkok Hospital
0-2310-3000
www.bangkokhospital.com
2 Soi Soonvijai 7
New Phetchaburi Road
Bangkapi, Huai Khwang
Bangkok 10310

Bamrungrad Hospital
0-2667-1000
www.bangrungrad.com
33 Sukhumvit 3, Wattana
Bangkok 10110

Praram 9 Hospital
0-2202-9900
www.praram9.com
99 Soi Praram 9 Hospital
Huai Khwang
Bangkok 10320

BNH Hospital
0-2686-2700
www.bnhhospital.com
9/1 Convent Road, Silom
Bangkok 10500

Samitivej Hospital
0-2711-8181
www.samitivejhospitals.com
133 Sukhumvit 49
Klongtan Nua, Wattana
Bangkok 10110

INTERNATIONAL SCHOOLS

British
The following schools are all accredited by the Council of International Schools.

Bangkok Patana School
0-2785-2200
www.patana.ac.th
643 La Salle Road (Sukhumvit 105), Bangna
Bangkok 10260

British School of Bangkok
0-2656-9961
www.bsbangkok.ac
36/36-1 Sukhumvit Soi 4, Khlong Toei
Bangkok 10110

Rasami British International School
0-2644-5291
www.rbis.ac.th

48/2 Soi Rajavithi 2
Rajavithi Road
Sam Sen Nai, Phayathai
Bangkok 10400

The Regent's School
0-2957-5777
www.regents.ac.th
601/99 Pracha-Uthit Road, Wang Tong Lang
Bangkok 10310

Shrewsbury International School
0-2675-1888
www.shrewsbury.ac.th
1922 Charoen Krung Road
Wat Praya Krai, Bang Kholame
Bangkok 10120

St Andrews International School
0-2393-3883
www.standrews-schools.com
7 Sukhumvit Road Soi 107, Bang Na
Bangkok 10260

American
The following schools are accredited by United States school associations.

American School of Bangkok
0-2620-8600
www.asb.ac.th
59-59/1 Sukhumvit Road Soi 49/3, Wattana
Bangkok 10110

Berkeley International School
0-2747-4788
www.berkeley.ac.uk
123 Bangna-Trat Road, Bangna
Bangkok 10260

Trinity International School
0-2661-3993
www.trinity.ac.th
30 Sukhumvit Soi 36 Lane 2
Khlong Tan, Khlong Toei
Bangkok 10110

Wells International School
0-2730-3366
www.wells-school.com
2209 Sukhumvit Road
Bangchak, Phra Khanong
Bangkok 10260

Other

Australian International School of Bangkok
0-2260-4575
www.australian-isb.com
162/2 Sukhumvit Soi 20, Khlong Toei
Bangkok 10110

Global Indian International School
0-2977-3739
www.globalindianschool.org
39/39 Moo 1, Soi Watchinwararam
Pathum Thani-Sainai Road
Pathum Thani 12000

International School of Bangkok
0-2963-5800
www.isb.ac.th
39/7 Soi Nichada Thani
Samakee Road, Pakkret
Nonthaburi 11120

Lycee Francais International de Bangkok
0-2934-8008
www.lfib.ac.th
498 Ramkhamhaeng Soi 39, Wang Thong Lang
Bangkok 10310

Thai-Japanese Association School
0-2251-5852
www.thai-japanasso.or.th
161 Nantawan Building 16th Fl
Rajadamri Road
Lumphini, Patumwan
Bangkok 10330

LANGUAGE SCHOOLS

AAA Thai Language School
0-2655-5629
www.aaathai.com
29 Vanissa Building, 6th Floor
Chidlom Road, Pathumwan
Bangkok 10330

AUA
0-2657-6414
www.auathai.com
AUA Thai Program
Chamchuri Square Office Tower, 21st Floor
Phayathai Road
Bangkok 10330

Chulalongkorn University Intensive Thai Program.
0-2218-4886
www.arts.chula.ac.th
Maha Chakri Sirindhorn Building
Faculty of Arts Chulalongkorn University
Phayathai Road, Pathumwan
Bangkok 10330

Everyday Thai Language School
0-2676-2030
www.everyday-thai.com
Prima Sathorn Building, 2nd Floor - Unit 8202
31/1 Narathiwat Road
Yannawa, Sathorn
Bangkok 10500

My Thai Language School
0-2642-3525
www.mythailanguage.com
121/62 18th Floor RS Tower
Ratchadaphisek Road
Din Daeng
Bangkok 10400

Pro Language
0-2250-0072
www.prolanguage.co.th
10-10A 10th Floor Times Square
246 Sukhumvit Road
Bangkok 10110

Thai Smile
0-2267-5080
www.thaismilelanguage.com
942/137.4 Rama 4 Road
Surawong
Bangrak
Bangkok 10500

Thai Solutions
0-2612-9411
www.thaisolutions1502.com
128/206 Phaya Thai Plaza Building
19th Floor, Room E
Phayathai Road
Ratchathewi
Bangkok 10110

Walen
0-2253-9371
www.thaiwalen.com
246 Times Square Building, 3rd Floor
Sukhumvit Road
Khlong Toei
Bangkok 10110

SOCIAL CLUBS

American Women's Club of Bangkok
(open to all nationalities)
0-2712-3380
72/1 Sukhumvit 38
Bangkok 10110

The Bangkok Club
0-2679-5550
www.thebangkokclub.com
Sathorn City Tower, 28th-31st Floor
175 South Sathorn Tower
Sathorn
Bangkok 10120

The British Club
0-2234-0247
www.britishclubbangkok.org
189 Suriwongse Road, Bangrak
Bangkok 10500

The International Women's Club of Thailand
0-2258--5336
www.iwcthailand.org
Clubhouse, Unit 3
16 Sukhumvit Soi 34
Bangkok 10110

The Lions Club of Bangkok
0-2969-9500
25/69 Rattanatibeth Road
Bangkasor, Muang
Nonthaburi 11000

The Rotary Club of Bangkok
0-2656-1634
www.rotaryclubofbangkok.org
975 President Place, Room 1711
Phloenchit Road, Lumphini
Bangkok 10330

PLACES OF WORSHIP

Buddhist
Needless to say, if you're a Buddhist you've come to the right place. There are at least 400 temples in Bangkok. Many of them provide courses on Buddhism in English.

Christian
Most Christian denominations are represented in Bangkok. The services in most churches are in Thai, although there are some that conduct English-language services. Among the most popular are Assumption Cathedral, the city's main Catholic church; the International Church of Bangkok, a non-denominational church that holds services in a rotating selection of venues; and Christ Church Bangkok, a small Protestant church on Convent Road in Silom.

Islam
Bangkok has a large Muslim community and there are several mosques in the city. Some of the best known include the Haroon Mosque on Charoen Krung 36, the Islamic Centre of Thailand Mosque on Ramkhamhaeng Soi 2 and the Darulmuttageen Mosque on the bank of the Saen Saep Canal on Khu Khwo Road.

Hindu
Bangkok's most popular and famous Hindu temple is Mahamariamman Temple, better known as Wat Khaek. This beautiful building is found on the corner of Silom and Pan Roads.

Sikh
Bangkok has a large and well-organised Sikh community. Bangkok's main gurdwara is the Sri Gurusingh Sabha Temple on Chakraphet Road in Chinatown. For more information, go to www.thaisikh.org.

Judaism
There are three synagogues in Bangkok, Beth Elisheva Synagogue on Sukhumvit Soi 22, Even Chen Syngagogue in the Silom area and the Chabad House near Khao San Road. For more information see www.jewishthailand.com.

MALAHIDE LIBRARY
PH: 8704430

FURTHER READING

People and culture

Inside Thai Society. Niels Mulder. Silkworm Books.
- Dutch anthropologist Niels Mulder's classic on Thai society is one of the most insightful looks at Thai religion and beliefs available in English.

CultureShock! Thailand. Robert Cooper. Marshall Cavendish.
- The companion to this book is an entertaining guide to Thai society written by former British anthropologist and diplomat, Robert Cooper

Very Thai. Philip Cornwel-Smith. River Books.
- The result of an incredible feat of research by British writer Philip Cornwel-Smith. Entertaining and full of fantastic colour photographs of everyday Thai pop culture.

Reading Bangkok. Ross King. NUS Press Singapore.
- Professor Ross King provides an erudite tour of Bangkok, spanning eras and the geography of the city. A fascinating look at the city's built environment and the processes that led to it becoming what it is today.

Sacred Tattoos of Thailand. Joe Cummings. Marshall Cavendish.
- Well-known scholar of Buddhism and Asian art Joe Cummings explores *sak yan*, Thailand's sacred tattoo tradition, illustrated by the beautiful photography of the late Dan White.

Corruption and Democracy in Thailand. Pasuk Phongphaichit and Sungsidh Piriyarangsan. Silkworm Books.
- The result of a thorough study of attitudes and the practice of corruption in Thailand, this book explains the workings of corruption in the kingdom and why it persists. A little old now but still highly relevant.

Thai Food. David Thompson. Ten Speed Press.
- David Thompson, an Australian chef who probably knows more about Thai cuisine than any other foreigner, explains the origins of Thai cuisine and provides a thorough survey of dishes, ingredients, techniques and regional styles.

History and politics

Thailand: A Short History. David K Wyatt. Silkworm Books.
- The classic work on Thai history by Cornell University history professor David K Wyatt is a sober and concise introduction to the history of Bangkok and Thailand.

Thaksin. Pasuk Phongpaichit & Chris Baker. Silkworm Books.
- Husband and wife team Pasuk Phongpaichit and Chris Baker's look at the life and political career of Thaksin Shinwatra is essential reading for those trying to understand the country's recent political crisis.

Siam Mapped. Thongchai Winichakul. Silkworm Books.
- Siam Mapped is a seminal look at the birth of the Thai nation through a focus on the mapping of Siam and its relations with the European empires.

Legitimacy Crisis in Thailand. Silkworm Books.
- This collection of academic essays edited by Mark Askew makes essential reading for anyone trying to further their understanding of Thailand's political crisis.

The Politics of Despotic Paternalism. Thak Chaloemtiarana. Cornell Southeast Asia Program.
- The essential work on the era of Sarit Thanarat, which had a huge influence on the politics of Thailand and helped define the role played by the monarchy today.

Fiction and memoir

Bangkok Days. Lawrence Osborne. North Point Press.
- British novelist Lawrence Osborne came to Bangkok

for the cheap dentistry. Then he stayed. In this lyrical memoir Osborne casts a perceptive eye on the city and the foreigners who make it their home.

Bangkok Found. Alex Kerr. River Books.
▪ Writer and Asia scholar Alex Kerr's memoir of his life as an expat in Bangkok is an interesting and smart read. Kerr's long experience as an Asia scholar enables him to make insightful comparisons with the customs and beliefs of Japan and China.

Four Reigns. Kukrit Pramoj. Silkworm Books.
▪ Kukrit Pramoj, former prime minister of Thailand, was an accomplished writer, producing *Four Reigns* in 1953. This saga of the lives of the Thai aristocracy explores how the society's values changed over the first half of the 20th century, and how its people adapted to a changing world.

Sightseeing. Rattawut Lapcharoensap. Grove Press.
▪ Thai-American writer Rattawut Lapcharoensap's short stories in his collection *Sightseeing* received great critical acclaim. His tales explore the relationship between Thais and foreigners, casting a wry and compassionate look at the way the country 'sells' itself to the world.

Bangkok 8. John Burdett. Vintage.
▪ British crime writer John Burdett's *Bangkok 8* is regarded by many as the finest novel in the 'Bangkok Noir' genre. With his protagonist, *luk khrueng* detective Sonchai Jitpleecheep, Burdett has the ideal vehicle to explore the city's underbelly and cast an unflinching eye on Thai culture.

Language

Thai for Beginners. Benjawan Poomsan Becker. Paiboon Publishing.
▪ This book and its follow-ups, *Thai for Intermediate Learners* and *Thai for Advanced Readers*, are popular and well thought-out manuals to the Thai language suitable for self-study.

Easy Thai: An Introduction to the Thai Language. Gordon H. Allison. Tuttle Publishing.
- This old-fashioned book won't teach you many useful phrases, but it will teach you to read and write the Thai alphabet 'with little time wasted', as the cover claims. It worked for me, anyway.

Oxford River Books English-Thai Dictionary. OUP Oxford.
- You probably won't want to carry this tome around with you, and online dictionaries are starting to make it obsolete. But fans of real, hard-copy books will appreciate this extensive dictionary.

Thai Reference Grammar. James Higbie and Snea Thinsan. Orchid Press.
- This huge green slab of a book can be considered the bible for the serious Thai learner. Very thorough with clear examples throughout.

Heart Talk. Christopher G. Moore. Heaven Lake Press.
- In Thai, feelings and emotions tend to expressed using compounds that include the word '*jai*', meaning 'heart'. Crime novelist Christopher G. Moore's useful and insightful book is a thorough run-down of the Thai language's 'heart words'.

Doing business

Bridging the Gap. Kriengsak Niratpattanasai. Phongwarin Printing.
- This compilation of material from Kriengsak Niratpattanasai's *Bangkok Post* column is a good introduction to working with Thais for the expat manager.

Thais Mean Business. Robert Cooper. Marshall Cavendish.
- Robert Cooper, author of *CultureShock! Thailand*, applies his skills as an anthropologist of Thai culture to the business world.

ABOUT THE AUTHOR

Dan Waites landed an unremarkable middle-class childhood in the cathedral city of Durham, England. After graduating in mathematics and doing a master's degree in computer science at the University of Manchester, he went to work as an IT consultant in the City of London. But spending his life writing code wasn't for him.

Craving excitement – and wanting to get as far away from the City as humanly possible – he moved to Bangkok for the first time in 2004. As he eked out a living in that most typical of expat occupations – teaching English – the chaotic, endlessly fascinating Thai capital got a hold on him.

In 2008, now back in the UK writing letters for the Mayor of London, he decided to make another dash for it. This time that meant moving to Phuket to work as a reporter/sub-editor at the island's most august news journal, the *Phuket Gazette*. After a colourful couple of years interviewing subjects from popstars to paedophiles – and learning to decode some fiendishly heavy Thaiglish – Dan left to work with Burmese refugees in the Thai-Burmese border town of Mae Sot.

After covering 2010's historic general elections in Burma for the Democratic Voice of Burma, Dan got drawn back to Bangkok to work as a sub-editor for *The Nation*, spending the rest of his time doing freelance journalism. He covered business and politics in Burma and Thailand for publications including *Forbes Asia*, *Business Report Thailand*, *Asia Times*, *World Politics Review* and *Asian Correspondent*.

Having immersed himself in Thai culture for years, Dan had managed to pick up the Thai language and in late 2011 took a job in Bangkok as an interpreter for an international humanitarian organisation. His job – visiting prisoners and assessing humanitarian conditions in jails – means he's seen the insides of a lot more Thai prisons than the average law-abiding citizen.

He spends the rest of his time enjoying Bangkok and writing about his biggest passion – food. As restaurant critic for local news and reviews website Coconuts Bangkok, as well as Tatler's Thailand's Best Restaurants guide, his stomach is well taken care of. He has no plans to leave Bangkok anytime soon.

INDEX

accommodation 67–68, 77, 79, 170–173
amulets 126–127

backpackers 65–67
Banglamphu 65, 171, 248–249, 259
banking 179–180
births 200–201
boats 192–193
BRT (Bus Rapid Transit) 192
BTS Skytrain 68, 71, 77, 79, 171, 189–191
Buddhism 65, 88, 102, 111, 113–124, 259, 325
buses 184, 192
business culture 286–294

canals (*khlong*) 19, 62, 68, 71, 75–76, 85, 86, 193, 267
car ownership 193–194
Chao Phraya 11, 19, 61, 62, 65, 192, 259
Charoen Krung 69–70
Chatuchak 80, 256
Chinatown 68–69, 87
Chinese community and culture 9, 19, 68, 86–88, 99, 260, 273, 287
churches 325
cinemas 72, 254–255
class-consciousness 147–148
compliments 144
cooking 196
corruption 41, 291–294
cuisines of Thailand 205–206
cycling 256, 257

domestic help 175–176
dress 133–134, 155, 166
drinking 103, 117–118, 212–213, 242–243, 249–250, 252
driving licences 194
Dusit 24, 63, 65

Ekkamai 77–78, 91, 97, 171, 245–246, 248
Erawan 2, 58, 123

family values 92–93
farang viii, 77, 130–131, 136, 137–138, 277–278, 287–288
farang-Thai relationships 148–154
festivals and holidays 258–263
flooding 49, 172, 298–299
food 5, 196, 204, 239
    foreign cuisines 77, 171, 234–239
    street food 60, 77, 79, 80, 171, 223–233, 234
friendships 146–147

gambling 112
gay and lesbian 161–163, 247
gender 149, 152–154, 161–163
gift-giving 145

health 195, 318
hierarchy 4, 64, 93–96, 131–132, 135, 147–148, 275–276, 287
Hinduism 88, 325
hi-so 96–98, 241
history 11–56
honorifics 98–99
hospitals 195, 200–201, 318–319

Indian community 88–89
indie subculture 253–254
internet 177
Isarn *see* Northeast Thailand

Japanese community 92
journalism 198–199

Kanchanaburi 265
Khao San Road 65–67, 76, 248–249, 258
Khlong Toei 78, 83, 196
kik 156–158
Korean community 92

ladyboys viii, 163
language schools 280–284, 322–323
language viii, 94, 98, 137, 140–142, 147, 149, 175, 270–284, 314
law and the judicial system 100
literary scene 266–267, 268
local government 298
Loi Krathong 88, 259–260
Lumphini Park 73, 256, 259–260

marriage 150, 153, 156, 201
medical 195, 318
Middle-Eastern community 76, 77, 92
minorities in Bangkok 85, 90
monarchy 7, 20, 24, 29–30, 142–143
money and banking 178–180
monks 114–115, 118–121
mosques 325
motorcycle taxis (*motosai*) 172, 187–189, 308
motorcycles 193
MRT 77, 191–192
music 242, 251–253
Muslims 85–86, 325

names 98–99
Nana 88, 89, 92, 243
newspapers 196–199
nightlife 241–250
Northeast Thailand 82–83, 141, 160

parks and gardens 256–257
Pathum Wan 71–74
Patpong 71, 96, 246–247
Pattaya 264
Phahonyothin 79
Phloenchit 91, 171
Phra Pradaeng 257
Phrom Phong 77
Phuket 264
politics 54–56
population 82–92, 121, 296
Pratunam 74, 171

Ratchatewi 74–75
Rattanakosin 24, 62–65, 69
RCA 247–248
'red shirts' (United Front for Democracy Against Dictatorship) 42–54, 55–56, 96
relationships 148–152
religion 114
restaurants 215–219, 220–223
river taxis 86, 193
rocket festivals 261–262

sakdina 45, 95–96, 293
Sampheng 68, 87
Sanam Luang 64
sanuk 107–108, 109–111, 286, 289

Sathorn 171
schools 199–200, 319–323
sex industry 4, 89, 92, 96, 158–161, 246, 247
shopping 71, 74, 196
Sikhs 325
Silom 70, 71, 171, 246–247, 258
skin colour 108–109
slums 78, 83
social clubs 324
Soi Cowboy 244
Songkran 88, 110, 258–259
spirits (supernatural) 122–128
sports 256, 268
Sukhumvit 75–78, 88, 91, 243–246
supermarkets 196
synagogues 326

table manners 204, 207–214
tattoos (*sak yan*) 127–128
taxis 58, 184–189, 192–193, 310
telephone 176–177, 297
television 177–178
Thonburi 67–68, 267
Thonglor 77, 97, 171, 245–246, 248
tipping 214, 215
toilets 180–182
transport 182–194
transsexuals viii, 163
tuk-tuks 187

universities 64, 65, 72
utilities 172, 173–175

VAT 180
vegan/vegetarian 239
Vietnamese community 85
visas 167–169
visiting Thai homes 145–146

wai 3, 94, 131, 134–137
walking 183–184
water, potable 174–175
weather 57–58, 108, 166, 172, 242
weekend getaways 263–265
work permits 169–170
working culture 94, 286–294, 309

Yaowarat 68–69, 70
'yellow shirts' (People's Alliance for Democracy) 40–54, 55–56, 74, 96, 256

Titles in the **CultureShock!** series:

Argentina	Finland	Philippines
Australia	France	Portugal
Austria	Germany	Russia
Bahrain	Great Britain	San Francisco
Bangkok	Hawaii	Saudi Arabia
Beijing	Hong Kong	Scotland
Belgium	India	Shanghai
Berlin	Ireland	Singapore
Bolivia	Italy	South Africa
Borneo	Jakarta	Spain
Brazil	Japan	Sri Lanka
Bulgaria	Korea	Sweden
Cambodia	Laos	Switzerland
Canada	London	Syria
Chicago	Malaysia	Taiwan
Chile	Mauritius	Thailand
China	Morocco	Tokyo
Costa Rica	Munich	Travel Safe
Cuba	Myanmar	Turkey
Czech Republic	Netherlands	United Arab Emirates
Denmark	New Zealand	USA
Ecuador	Pakistan	Vancouver
Egypt	Paris	Venezuela

For more information about these titles, please contact any of our Marshall Cavendish offices around the world (listed on page ii) or visit our website at:

www.marshallcavendish.com/genref